Deadly
Goals

Deadly Goals

The True Story of an All-American Football Hero Who Stalked and Murdered

by Wilt Browning 1937-

Down Home Press, Asheboro, N.C.

© 1996 by Wilt Browning
First printing, April, 1996

1 2 3 4 5 6 7 8 9

ISBN 1-878086-55-3

Library of Congress Catalog Card No. 96-083029

Printed in the United States of America

Book design by Beth Glover
Cover design by Tim Rickard

Down Home Press
P.O. Box 4126
Asheboro, N.C. 27204

Dedicated to
all those who loved
Jeannie Butkowski,
none more than
Carrie and Ben Prickett,
her mother and father.

Contents

Acknowledgments

This is going to be difficult," Carrie Prickett had said that day three weeks before Christmas, 1993, the fifth Christmas since Jeannie Butkowski, her daughter, had died. "It's going to be difficult because Jeannie was Christmas. But I'll try."

And for two days, Carrie and Ben Prickett opened their home and their hearts and their emotions to me, a stranger. Without their memories and their pain, this book would have been incomplete because it was essential that we understand that Jeannie Butkowski lived and loved and laughed.

And died.

With the certainty that I could not have been as gracious as they, I thank the Pricketts most of all.

Amelia County Sheriff Jimmy Weaver, a big man with a big smile, a firm handshake and a coffee pot always kept hot on the burner, knew before I did that the story of the death of Jeannie Butkowski would become a book. And I thank him for his encouragement and for his help in gathering essential information. And I thank, too, Chief Deputy Sheriff Wes Terry, the lead investigative officer on the case, for his assistance and for suggesting to me late in my own research into this project that there were other stones to be turned, other sources to be mined. This story is more complete because of him.

For encouraging me to take a close look at the Pernell Jefferson story when to discourage me would have been personally less painful, Dr. Herb Appenzeller, retired athletic director at Guilford College, will always have my deepest appreciation. But my debts of gratitude to this dear friend were adding up long before I began this project. For almost as long as I have known this special Quaker, he has encouraged me in my daily writings for the *News & Record* of Greensboro and has urged me on in my avocation as an author.

Like the Pricketts, Susan Demos* knew virtually nothing of me when her mother called to tell her I was nosing around in a past that still is a painful memory for Susan. Yet her candor was astonishing and her contributions to my understanding of what transpired in her life and that of Pernell Jefferson, once someone she loved, were crucial to this effort. I wish her happiness as she continues her career in sports administration.

The insights and memories of so many others were essential, not the least of which were Sam Prickett, Jeannie's brother, and the former Denise Bratten who had shared a Chesapeake, Virginia, address with Jeannie through those final, terrifying months of Jeannie's life. I wish them peace.

Pernell Jefferson. He was one of the most talented small college football players I ever saw, a man who once so impressed me that I called a friend with the Cleveland Browns to report upon his ability to return punts and kickoffs. And when I visited Pernell at the Augusta Correctional Center at Craigsville, Virginia, he did as he said in a letter that he would do — he greeted me as an old friend. We talked candidly and for long hours about good times and bad. From the beginning, he made it clear that this is a story he wanted to share, and in that way this is his story.

I appreciate his trusting it to me.

His former coach, Tommy Saunders, the first person to warn me that Pernell's was a complicated story in which the truth can seem to wear many shades of gray, was immeasurably important to the gathering of much of the information contained in this book. It was, I am sure, an unhappy experience for Tommy and his family, because Pernell was and still is like a son, still is loved in the Saunders home. I pray that their children, Tommy Jr. and Bikki, will someday understand.

Pernell's brother, Willie Jefferson, helped me understand that the older brother he idolized was little different from young people we all have known. Except as an athlete. Willie remains deeply loyal to his sibling, and I appreciate that.

Much of what appears in these pages will perhaps always be a riddle. Buddy Collins, a lawyer, neighbor and friend, helped keep me focused upon the elusive line between truth and fiction, and helped me in my effort to understand the legal aspects of this story. "The best lie," he told me more than once, "is the one closest to the truth." And in truth, I still seek the best lie.

My visits to the prison where Pernell is an inmate were made easy by the facility's assistant warden, Stewart Taylor, and his associate, Carolyn Byram, who coordinated those hours of interviews. They have my regards.

My good friend, Gary McCann, served as my sounding board throughout this project, patiently listening as I talked about various twists and turns to this story as I was researching and writing the major project about Pernell that was carried in the *News & Record* on Sunday, March 20, 1994, and later as I launched the more detailed version that this book represents.

And just when I thought I would never write another book, Jerry Bledsoe was there once again to encourage and coach me in this effort as he had done on other occasions for other books. Because stories such as this are his forte as one of America's most successful true crime authors, his recommendations were invaluable.

Finally, I owe my continuing love and appreciation to my wife, Joyce, who lost her nightly Yahtzee partner during the months of this work in progress.

To the Reader:

All of the people who have a part in this story are real. These things happened and these are their memories and their recollections. This is not fiction. However, some of the names have been changed in the interest of privacy. They are marked with an asterisk upon first use.

Introduction

My name is Pernell Jefferson, Virginia State Prisoner No. 188173. On Aug. 6, 1991, I was sentenced to life in prison in the death of Jeannie Butkowski. By law, I must serve at least 25 years. With good time, that could be reduced by as much as five years. I will not be eligible for parole until sometime during the year 2,011 at the earliest. In 2,011, my son will be 29 years old. I will be 48. I will probably be a grandfather. I will have nephews, nieces and cousins I have never seen.

By the time I win my freedom, I no longer will know how to cope with the future space-age technology as far as the personal skills I developed in the 20th century. Twenty-five years is so long that, logically speaking, some of the people hurt most by my imprisonment probably won't still be alive to help me celebrate my freedom.

I once had another, shorter number — 22. I was a football player. A very good football player. No more. Still in the early years of my imprisonment, I am beyond those seasons even if freedom came tomorrow. But that no longer is important.

I am a college graduate. None of the people with whom I now share my confinement is impressed. Degrees mean little here.

What you are about to read is an account of how I came to be in this place, looking down the years at some distant, uncertain first moment of freedom that may not come until I am a very old man, or that may come only with death itself.

The book you are about to read will no doubt show you two different characters of myself. A bright and a dark side. Dr. Jekyll and Mr. Hyde. I am not proud of that. I have been advised by other inmates of the Virginia prison system to keep all this to myself. And maybe that would be the wise route. But the truth as I see it is that I once was a decent person, and hope to be again. What the last ten years — my dark decade — have taught me is that bad things can happen to decent people and that, and only that, is the reason I have cooperated and participated in the development of *Deadly Goals*.

Some things you will read will be disturbing and horrifying. My role in the research for this book has not been to glorify or make excuses for my attitude but to offer an understanding of what I was going through. Violence, sleepless nights, obsessiveness, paranoia, euphoria, power struggles, circulation problems, and tragically hasty personal decisions.

For eight years, a time in which even the medical profession did not fully understand the monster, I was a victim of the mental conditions and serious physical problems caused by steroid use. Sometimes called "steroid rage," this condition, which physicians first began to understand as a result of studies begun during the '80's, is now known as "steroid psychosis," a mental disorder.

This disorder led me to many criminal acts which were never a part of my adolescent and teen-age years. Many of the acts were perpetrated upon people who cared for me and loved me. And through the pain and hurt I caused them, they still wanted to protect me because they had seen the good — the warmth and the caring — in me.

The hurt and pain that I caused, I now understand, was horrendous and became the driving force, I am told, in the victim's mother's successful lobbying effort with the Virginia General Assembly to pass anti-stalking laws. I must tell you that only recently have I understood that stalking was seen as part of the terror people knew at my hands, and if these new laws can prevent even one tragedy, an important move toward more sanity will have been taken.

I now am conviced that had I not been using steroids, my personality would not have been that of obsessiveness and paranoia in my relationships with former girlfriends. My problems did not only start with my female friends but with guys in bars and night clubs. But the great tragedies were, in most cases, to the women who cared about me.

I have opened up my personal life to show my problems associated with anabolic steroids. A friend once told me, "one man with courage makes a majority." And it is in that spirit that I have found the strength to speak from my world behind bars and beyond the fences stacked with razor-sharp barriers. My hope is that this book will serve as a warning.

No matter what anyone says, there is no such thing as a "good" drug other than those used with care by licensed physicians. Please understand what I'm saying, because I'm living proof of how drugs can destroy you and those you love. Only after four years of studying and associating myself with experts from Harvard University, the University of Illinois at Chicago, and Penn State University have I come to understand what was going on in my mind and body. Until recently, I never knew the extent of the pain I caused. I couldn't appreciate or understand what I was doing and therefore had no way of comprehending the damage I was causing. As I write to you today, I'm aware — and I am eager — for young people to understand the nature of the monster anabolic steroids became in my life.

If after you read this you still are contemplating using the "roid" then please contact me personally: Pernell Jefferson, P.O. Box 1000. Craigsville, Va., 24430-1000. We need to talk.

Pernell Jefferson
Inmate No. 188173
Department of Corrections
Commonwealth of Virginia

1

The Homecoming

The winter day had turned dark and Carrie Prickett waited for the telephone to ring, wondering what she would say, how she would feel.

Neither Carrie nor Ben, her husband of 36 years, spoke. So much already had been said that no words came now. Only the steady ticking of an antique mantle clock, Ben's prized possession, intruded upon the silence.

They waited.

Then the phone was ringing. Though the call had been expected, the ragged ringing jarred the Pricketts from their thoughts the way an alarm clock does when morning comes too soon.

"Hello," Carrie said softly.

She listened to the voice on the other end of the line, then said only "Okay. Thank you," before gently placing the phone back into its cradle.

"They're on their way," she said.

Ben, a retired Navy man, only nodded. And he and his wife were silent again, each lost once more in thought. This, they knew, would be one of the most bittersweet moments of their lives.

Three miles away, two men dressed in the conservative dark suits of their profession began the short trip to the Pricketts' neat, middle-class home in Virginia Beach. Quickly, they became part of the last of the Wednesday afternoon rush-hour traffic speeding along Providence Road. The traffic had lightened by the time they turned left onto Timberlake Road and into a neighborhood of unpretentious homes set among tall hardwoods and pines. Both men searched for the sign marking Steeplechase Drive.

"There it is," one said.

Carrie and Ben had turned on the front porch light just as they had done hundreds of times when any of their three children, Carrie, Sam and Jeannie, was going to be late. They stood alone at the window of their living room watching, waiting for the headlights.

"The house on the corner of Dunhill, where the porch lights are on," the man in the passenger seat said.

"Right," the driver acknowledged.

He slowed and turned off his headlights, coming to a stop just beyond the Pricketts' mailbox. Still, with nothing more than the lights of the neighborhood to push back the night, the Pricketts could see the coffin, polished and gleaming, in the back of the hearse.

Carrie opened the front door and stepped onto the small front porch, followed by her husband. Neither spoke. Together they held open the screen door in a gesture important only to them. "Welcome home, Jeannie," Carrie wanted to say, but her voice was stilled by her sobbing. A tear tumbled down Ben's strong face and he drew his wife to him in a firm hug.

For five minutes, which later seemed both an eternity and an instant, the couple stood together, never leaving the small porch, never walking across the 25 feet of dormant winter lawn that separated them from the funeral car and the coffin that contained the tiny, delicate bones of their beloved Jeannie.

Jeannie, their baby, had been murdered. Murdered, soaked in gasoline, burned and left for months in a dry creek bed a long way from home. Now, the only thing the Pricketts had to take to the cemetery were those fragile bones that, scattered by the elements and by forest creatures, had been harvested from the dark Virginia soil.

But at least they had the bones.

For more than eight months they had searched for her, driving across lonely rural roads they had never seen before, sending out flyers bearing Jeannie's picture, sleeping little, enduring much, all that time waiting for the knock on the door or the telephone call that would bring her back to them. The call finally had come with the new year.

And now Jeannie was home one last time.

The two funeral home employes sat motionless, staring straight ahead, saying not a word.

A neighbor drew back a corner of the drapes a sliver and peeked out upon the scene, quickly letting the drapes fall back into place so as not to intrude.

Even on the porch, Ben could hear the forlorn ticking of the old mantle clock in the distant den as he held his wife, unable to still her shaking.

Out on the street, the driver reached for the ignition, and the engine of the big Cadillac stirred again. The headlights flashed on and the hearse drew slowly away from the curb. It turned right onto Dunhill as the Pricketts watched it go, holding each other, consumed by their grief.

"I wanted her to come home, Ben," Carrie said, looking into her husband's face after the hearse had disappeared from sight. "I wanted to open the door to Jeannie just one more time."

"I know," he said. "I know."

*   *   *

Carrie Prickett could remember little about the summer of 1989 that had come and gone since Jeannie had disappeared. Neither could she recall much of the autumn that had followed, nor of the Thanksgiving that had offered so little for which to be grateful. Gifts had been opened at Christmas, but this time there had been none of the joy of other holiday seasons when Jeannie had taped tiny golden bells to the top of the mirror in the foyer and had decorated the tree, pretending to be annoyed, as usual, at her mother's procrastinations.

Four times, Carrie and Jeannie had spoken on the phone, arranging their Saturday ritual that Friday all those months ago when May flowers had begun to bloom. They had planned to meet at noon at the hair dresser's before going to lunch and beginning an afternoon shopping spree.

That Friday had been payday, and most of Jeannie's wages as a secretary in the office of the clerk of court in Norfolk would have to go to pay first-of-the-month bills, she told her mother. But she'd keep $30 in cash, she added with a laugh, just in case she needed it during their visit to the mall.

"I said 'Goodbye, Jeannie,' and hung up the phone the fourth time we talked that day," Carrie recalled years later. "I didn't know I was saying goodbye forever."

But now relatives from Georgia began gathering at the L-shaped ranch home on Steeplechase Drive to console Jeannie's parents, her sister Carrie, and Sam, her brother. Neighbors brought food. And on February 24, 1990, friends and family as well as the curious filled the Holloman-Brown Funeral Home chapel. Tony Butkowski, who once had been married to Jeannie and whose name she had kept, sat in silence with his mother and brothers and sisters. "Precious Memories" played softly on the organ as they gathered.

For more than eight months, Carrie, Jeannie's sister, had been the strong one. If she had wept for her sister, she had done so in privacy. Like her father, she had held out hope that Jeannie would be found alive. Now Carrie approached the coffin in the pretty little chapel. She stopped as though she did not want to draw near, then she moved close, running her fingers along the edge of the smooth closed lid. Finally, Carrie looked at the picture of her sister that had been placed among the flowers that formed the coffin's funeral blanket. She began to sob, deep painful sobs, and she suddenly felt dizzy. Then she collapsed under the weight of the emotion she had repressed since Jeannie had disappeared nearly a year earlier. Relatives moved close, Sam and Ben and uncles from Georgia, seeking to bolster Jeannie's sister against her grief.

"Let not your hearts be troubled," Jeannie's pastor, the Rev. Paul D.

Moore of Indian River Baptist Church, read from The Book of John a short time later. "Ye believe in God, believe also in me. In my Father's house are many mansions. If it were not so, I would have told you.

"I go to prepare a place for you. And if I go and prepare a place for you, I will come again, and receive you unto myself, that where I am, there ye may be also...."

Moore took the text for his sermon from the parable of the Good Samaritan. "The culprit in this case," he said, "is in need of compassion toward him. Jeannie's family has replaced vengeance and hatred with compassion and has requested that First Corinthians, Chapter 13, be read, as an expression of the family, toward the life taken on earth."

Moore's voice was strong as he read the passage about charity. Finishing, he looked up. There was silence in the room. "Jeannie loved all, regardless of origin, nationality," he said, "and thus was friends with all."

After the service, a procession that stretched for three miles made its way to Rosewood Memorial Park. There, in the shade of an old evergreen tree in a section known as Singing Towers, the family gathered one last time beside the casket covered with a blanket of peach-colored baby roses from friends at the courthouse where Jeannie worked. They listened as Moore read the familiar Twenty-Third Psalm.

"There will be no separation in Heaven," the minister told those gathered when he had finished the reading. "No mysteries. No violence. No murder. No darkness."

The crowd remained silent as David White, a policeman, stepped forward to read from a poem he had written.

> *To a friend much loved.*
> *To a friend who will always be remembered.*
> *The loving smile that warmed our hearts and made our day.*
> *Your life was not in vain.*
> *Your life filled ours with warmth and joy.*
> *We will miss you, Jeannie, and you will always be in our lives and*
hearts.
> *A part of us passed away with you.*
> *Your life brightened ours like a falling star, lighting the sky.*
> *Yes, Jeannie, your life touched us all.*
> *You will never be forgotten.*

Later the Pricketts placed a bronze plaque at this spot:

Regina Marie "Jeannie" Prickett Butkowski
Beloved Daughter

August 5, 1959
May 6, 1989

"I named her Regina Marie," her father said later. "She never really liked the name, so she wanted to be called Jeannie."

2

Ten Fingers, Ten Toes

In the year in which his daughter had died, Ben Prickett still wore a crew cut, a holdover from his career as a Navy enlisted man. But the first time Carrie Carlyle saw him late in 1953, he had long hair, a style popularized by a new young singer named Elvis Presley. Ben was sitting with his girlfriend a few pews from Carrie and her boyfriend in Avondale Baptist Church in Avondale Estates, Georgia, one of Atlanta's eastern suburbs.

Less than a year later, Carrie, whose boyfriend had gone into the military and had been sent to Korea, was teamed with Ben to take part in the church's annual door-to-door neighborhood survey. From that day, they never dated anyone else, and in July 1954, they were married.

For a time, Carrie kept her job as a telephone operator, and Ben reported to work each day at the Federal Reserve Bank in downtown Atlanta where he counted stacks of overworn currency. He spent a weekend a month in the Navy reserves.

Before the couple would spend their first Christmas together, Carrie became pregnant and on Valentine's Day, 1955, Ben quit his job counting money and signed on for active duty in the Navy. He was assigned to the amphibious base near Norfolk, Virginia. Carrie remained behind in Atlanta, where their first child, Sam, was born June 16, 1955. Before the summer had broken, mother and infant had joined Ben in a tiny apartment in the Oceanview neighborhood not far from the Navy base.

Ben's and Carrie's first daughter, who would be given her mother's name, was born less than two years later, arriving at Portsmouth Navy Hospital on April 5, 1957. Like Sam, Carrie was born with fiery red hair.

Soon, the growing family would move with Ben to his new assignment at Roosevelt Roads in Puerto Rico, and there at 7:30 a.m. on August 5, 1959, Carrie would again be admitted to a maternity ward.

As Carrie was wheeled into the delivery room of the U.S. Army hospital near San Juan a little more than 12 hours later, she noticed that two low platforms, one slightly higher than the other, as though they were bleachers for a sports event, were in place on one side of the room.

"Mrs. Prickett," said the Army doctor who greeted her, "we have a few young doctors here who would like to study our procedures. Do you mind having them watch the delivery?"

"Not if you'll let me watch, too," she answered. The doctor smiled. "That can be arranged," he responded and ordered a mirror be rolled into place and positioned so that Carrie, like the young doctors, could watch the miracle.

At 8:20 p.m., the doctor placed a tiny baby girl on Carrie's stomach. She looked at the little one. "Hi, baby," she said softly.

"I remember that she had hair as red as a copper penny, lots of it," Carrie recalled years later. "And I remember I checked her fingers and toes the way all mothers do, just to make sure everything was working. She had ten of each. And everything was working perfectly."

For nearly a week, Carrie remained in the hospital while her third child grew strong. And when several times each day the newborn babies were rolled out of the nursery and delivered to their mothers, Carrie's young daughter each time was handed to the woman who shared Carrie's room. Each time, Carrie would remind the nurses, "That's my baby."

It was an understandable mistake. The woman in the next bed had hair as red as Carrie's infant daughter's.

Back in their small apartment, Carrie worked hard to make sure her two older children, Sam and Carrie, adjusted to the infant. Confirmation that Carrie, then only 30 months old, had accepted her baby sister came in an unusual way. One day while her mother was busy, Carrie stood outside the Pricketts' apartment trying to stop cars driving through the neighborhood.

"Please come in and see our baby," she pleaded with strangers until a woman knocked on the apartment door and announced that she had been invited by a proud sister to see the infant.

Following his tour of duty at Roosevelt Roads, Ben moved his family once again to Virginia's Tidewater area, where he continued to serve as a Navy administration specialist. Later, Carrie got a job with the Army Corps of Engineers and began to make a career as a computer specialist.

Their lives were typical of families of Navy enlisted men. They moved to a small house at 1301 Towanda Court in a subdivision called Indian River Estates, then a part of the county known as Norfolk Nineteen, later to become a part of the city of Chesapeake. It was a street of young families, most of them tied to the Navy, and within the seven households lived 17 children. Among the Pricketts' closest friends were the neighboring Brattens — parents Brad and Arlene and daughters Tina and Denise. Denise was a year younger than Jeannie, but the two little girls quickly became friends. Tina became close to the two older Prickett children. All soon were as brother and sisters.

Also sharing Towanda Court were the Whalens, whose daughter, Kim, developed a friendship with Jeannie that would last a lifetime. In 1965, Jeannie and Kim entered first grade together at Sparrow Road Elementary School less than two blocks from their homes. Denise followed a year later.

Years afterward, Denise would have many warm remembrances of growing up on Towanda Court and her early friendship with Jeannie, memories of Barbie dolls and shared secrets, among them that Jeannie some day hoped to marry Davy Jones of the singing group, The Monkees.

"That's good," Denise had replied at hearing the news, "'cause I love one of the Monkees, too, Mike Naismith. And after we're married the four of us will always be buddies."

Though Denise developed a strong sports interest that Jeannie and Kim did not share, their friendships flourished. "Once Denise started playing softball a lot, and Jeannie discovered makeup, they no longer shared the same interests," Jeannie's mother later remembered. "But they remained close friends and Jeannie's friendship with Kim also grew stronger."

All three eventually became students at Indian River High School. One of Denise's classmates was Tony Butkowski, a tall, lanky high school football player with black, curly hair and blue eyes. Jeannie, too, had known Tony since elementary school. His father had died in a car crash in 1967, and her parents were friends of his mother and stepfather. Still, Jeannie didn't become friends with Tony until they reached high school. She was only 15 when their friendship blossomed into young love. Prohibited from dating until she was 16, Jeannie didn't have her first date with Tony until her 16th birthday. From that happy day until her graduation in June 1977, she dated no one but Tony. At the same time, Denise was dating one of Jeannie's classmates, Perry Edwards Jr.

Shortly after Jeannie's graduation, Tony's stepfather, Bill Hoffman, also a Navy man, received orders to report to a new assignment near Albuquerque, New Mexico. Tony still had one more year of high school, and with Jeannie's encouragement, he lobbied for permission to stay behind and finish at Indian River High, where he was an outstanding student in addition to being a member of the football team. He failed to prevail, however, and his departure with his family was a time of great sadness for Jeannie, who had taken a full-time job with Stewart Sandwich Co. and had enrolled in night classes at Tidewater Community College.

In the first weeks after Tony had settled into his new high school in New Mexico, he and Jeannie talked regularly by telephone, often for hours at a time. And although the calls became less frequent as time wore on, Jeannie remained deeply in love. As Tony's graduation neared, she bought an airline ticket to Albuquerque to attend his commencement. But a week before she was to leave, a letter arrived bearing an Albuquerque postmark but addressed in a hand Jeannie did not recognize. It was from Tony's new girlfriend and it suggested that Jeannie's presence at his graduation might be awkward, since she and Tony were making marriage plans. In shock, Jeannie phoned Tony, who not only admitted that he was in love with somebody else but that it was he who had suggested that his new girlfriend write the letter.

Hurt and angry, Jeannie changed her plans and flew instead to California, where her older sister, Carrie, had just given birth. "She said she'd use the airline fare to go take some pictures for me," said her mother, who thought that Jeannie displayed uncommon resilience in the face of her disappointment.

Still, in the coming months, Jeannie and her parents received letters occasionally from the Hoffmans. Brief updates of Tony's wedding plans usually were included. In time, he did marry his sweetheart from Albuquerque, but first he enrolled at the University of New Mexico to study business.

By that time, Jeannie's father had retired from the Navy and taken a Civil Service job in Norfolk. He and Carrie sold their home of 18 years in Indian River Estates and moved a little more than four miles away into a new house on Steeplechase Drive. Jeannie continued to live with them, and while she stayed busy with her job and night classes, she seemed disinterested in romance. "I guess for about six months there, she must have gone out with several boys," her mother remembered years later. "But I'm not even sure they were dates. It was more like she was going to go somewhere with a friend, and that friend just happened to be a boy."

With time, Jeannie moved out of the Pricketts' home for the first time to share an apartment with two other young women, one of whom was dating a sailor who arrived one evening in the company of a handsome Colombian Navy enlistee named Tito. Jeannie liked Tito immediately and they soon were dating.

When it became clear that Jeannie's feelings for Tito were becoming serious, both Carrie and Ben voiced some private reservations, Ben more pointedly than his wife. They didn't like this overbearing young man who had suddenly come into their daughter's life. When it became apparent that marriage might be a possibility, they worried that Jeannie could end up living in a strange land, far from them. But they kept these thoughts from their daughter.

"I learned that you can't pick out who your children will marry," Carrie said later, "and I learned that if you go against their wishes you run the risk of losing your children forever."

Before Jeannie's relationship with Tito had run a year, the Pricketts' fears seemed to be coming true. He presented Jeannie with a half-carat diamond engagement ring, and the wedding was set for early May, 1981.

Despite their misgivings, the Pricketts began planning for the wedding. They rented the clubhouse at Kempsville Golf Club for the reception and placed an expensive order with a local florist. Long-time family friend Nora Casey agreed to prepare all the food for the reception, and the Pricketts paid for Jeannie's $600 wedding dress. The wedding party was chosen, tuxedos ordered, bridesmaids' dresses created, the music and the musicians chosen and scheduled, a photographer hired. A minister had agreed to perform the ceremony. Tito got a marriage license. Dozens of wedding presents began piling up in the Pricketts' living room as the day drew near.

Two weeks before the wedding, Jeannie, now a thin five-feet-two with dark eyes, auburn-colored hair and with the body of a model, looked more beautiful than ever as she tried on her her long, white wedding dress so that adjustments could be made.

A week later, Tito's sister arrived from Colombia to represent her family at the wedding, a house guest of the Pricketts, as was her brother.

But in the days before the wedding, things began to go awry. Jeannie discovered that Tito had continued to write to the woman he had left behind in Colombia, and a noisy argument ensued. Then on Thursday before the Sunday wedding, Tito was arrested in Norfolk for speeding and driving under the influence of alcohol. He told authorities he was worried about his impending wedding, and he called Jeannie to bail him out.

On the day before the wedding, Tito and Jeannie got into yet another loud argument in the Pricketts' home. "He was mouthing off at her," Carrie said. "That's the way Tito was, very verbally abusive to Jeannie. It was all Ben could do to keep quiet when that happened."

This time, though, it was Carrie who couldn't remain silent. She came to Jeannie's defense.

"Tito," she said, bristling, "if you don't want to be married to Jeannie, you tell us right now."

Tito did not respond.

"Are you telling me you want the wedding cancelled?" she pressed. "You don't want to get married?"

An awkward pause ensued before Tito finally answered. "That's right," he said. "I don't want to get married."

The house fell silent. Tito walked out, got into his car and drove away.

Stunned, Jeannie ran to her room crying, and after attempting to comfort her, Carrie began canceling all the wedding plans. She called the minister, notified the photographer and the musicians. Most of the food already had been prepared, she learned when she called her friend Nora, and would have to be frozen for later use. The flowers were ready, too, and since Sunday would be Mother's Day, Carrie had them sent to nursing homes to be given to mothers who might not otherwise get any attention. Finally, depressed and exhausted, she sank into her couch beside her husband. Ben, who had spent nearly $5,000 on his daughter's wedding, was getting drunk.

After a few hours, Tito returned. He and Jeannie talked quietly, then left the house together for a dinner they had planned with friends. Tito and his sister remained with the Pricketts three more days until Tito left for a new assignment in Florida.

Jeannie went on as if nothing had happened, seeing the cancelled wedding as just a delay. She and Tito talked frequently by telephone and wrote regularly. Late that summer, Jeannie packed many of her belongings, including a prized stereo, into her car and drove to Florida. Although she didn't say so to her parents, they thought that she was leaving with intentions to be married. She stayed only a week, however, and returned without her stereo and some of her other things, but she never told her family what happened, and they didn't ask about it. They were just relieved that she never wanted to see Tito again. Eventually, they learned, he returned to Colombia and married the woman he had left behind.

By the summer of 1982, Jeannie's first love, Tony, had completed his junior year at the University of New Mexico, and his marriage was ending. His stepfather completed his career in the Navy and decided to make the Virginia Tidewater area his retirement home. Tony agreed to help his family move back to the area where he had grown up. He had heard about Jeannie's planned wedding from his mother, Mary Ann, who had continued her friendship with Carrie. He even had telephoned his regrets to Jeannie when he heard about the last-minute cancellation. Now, with his own marriage at an end, Tony called again to tell Jeannie that he would be returning briefly with his parents and would like to see her. She accepted excitedly.

"Her reaction wasn't surprising," her mother said years later. "Tony was always the love of her life. We all loved Tony. If Tony came back today to see me, he'd still call me Mom."

The visit went well, allowing Tony and Jeannie to renew their relationship, and after Tony returned to his classes at the University of New Mexico, he kept in touch. Their romance blossomed anew over the long-distance line. Jeannie even resigned from her job with the sandwich company and went to work for a temporary service so that she would have more flexibility when Tony came to visit during breaks from his studies.

Being rejected at the last minute by Tito now seemed nothing more than a bad memory. Jeannie's romance with Tony was more intense than ever. As Tony began his final year of studies, Jeannie quit her job in Virginia Beach with with the temporary service and joined him in New Mexico. She found a job as a hostess in the same Albuquerque restaurant in which Tony worked as a waiter in the evenings.

And once again Jeannie began to plan her wedding. She and Tony designed and ordered the engagement ring she would wear. The one-of-a-kind ring contained three small round diamonds and one large oval diamond that was its focal point. The large diamond was the brilliant solitaire from the ring Tito had given her.

Jeannie and Tony were married on a visit back to Virginia on January 3, 1983, at Indian River Baptist Church where Jeannie was a member. Jeannie wore the $600 dress her parents had bought for the aborted wedding two years earlier with Tito. Soon after the simple ceremony, which was attended only by family and close friends, the newlyweds returned to New Mexico, but they planned to stay only the five months Tony needed to finish his degree. That done, they returned to Virginia Beach and moved in with Jeannie's parents. Jeannie soon went to work in the office of the clerk of court in Norfolk, where her childhood friend, Kim, who had recommended her for the job, was employed. There she also became close friends with another court employee, Christine White, the wife of a Norfolk police officer. Tony found work in the accounting department of a bank, moved on to another bank, and later entered management training that led to a position with Lowe's, a giant builders supply company. He spent most of his leisure time sharpening his bowling skills, hoping to fullfill a long-time dream of becoming a professional.

Jeannie had continued her friendship with Denise, who in 1979 had married her high-school sweetheart, Perry Edwards Jr., and settled into a career as a photo lab color technician. Now Jeannie and Tony became mixed doubles bowling partners with Denise and Perry.

Jeannie and Tony remained in her parents' home for three years, and as time went on, the Pricketts noticed that Tony was not showing the interest in Jeannie that he had at the beginning. Jeannie felt shunned at first, then became suspicious, but instead of confronting her husband, she tried harder to please him, carefully watching her weight, trying to remain the slim, trim beauty he had married, but that didn't prove to be enough.

"Tony, you're a wonderful person," Carrie said to her son-in-law on a quiet evening in 1985. "But you want people to always be perfect. In all the history of the world, there has been only one perfect person, and they crucified Him."

In an effort to save her marriage, Jeannie and Tony considered moving out of her parents' home and into a townhouse they hoped to purchase, but the move never came. Tony got a new job with Nabisco that frequently took him away from home for a week at a time. In the fall of 1985, he was transferred to Pennsylvania and he went without Jeannie. Within weeks, he filed for divorce.

26

Jeannie was devastated. She still loved Tony and didn't want the marriage to end, but she didn't contest the divorce. She even remained close with Tony's family, who continued to be friends with her parents. To keep her equilibrium, she began seeing a psychiatrist and spent many hours talking with her friend Denise, whose marriage she envied. Denise was now a mother. Her first child, Dawn, was born in November, 1985, and the baby was a delight to both. Jeannie began spending more and more of her evenings with Denise and her family. In the summer of 1986, Denise and Perry moved into a rented four-bedroom house at the corner of McCosh and Hibben in Chesapeake. Two days later, Perry left. This time, it was Denise who was devastated. The divorce proceedings would drag on for two years.

Now it was Jeannie's turn to console Denise.

"Jeannie was still getting over the divorce from Tony," Denise remembered years later. "And when it happened to me, she tried to help. She'd go to visit her psychiatrist and she'd tell me what the doctor had said and what had seemed to help her. We spent a lot of time crying on each other's shoulders."

Denise was having a difficult time financially as well as personally, and she asked Jeannie, who still lived with her parents, to move in with her.

"I needed a roommate to help me share expenses," she recalled. "What better roommate could I have had than Jeannie? She loved my daughter and Dawn already was calling her Aunt Jeannie. Everybody thought we were sisters anyway. It made sense to me."

But Jeannie decided it would be better to remain with her parents, although she and Denise continued to be like sisters. Gradually, both began to pull their lives back together. Jeannie attempted to give herself a flashier look early in 1988 by buying a sports car, a mint-condition 1985 Nissan 300 ZX, for which she purchased a personalized license plate, TIGRE Z. She tried to keep busy, joining a bowling league (she averaged 165), a softball league, and learning to master the billiard table. Although she was a non-smoker, she was one of 17 young women chosen by a tobacco company to entertain at nightclubs with skits, audience-participation events and giveaways in the spring of 1988. She had inherited her mother's outgoing personality but not her shyness, and she was a natural on stage.

That summer, Jeannie took her vacation to serve as a traveling hostess at ports of call on a yacht race from Florida to Newport News, and she hoped to do it again the following year.

Although, she picked up a little extra money with her outside activities, there was little extravagance in her budget. "Jeannie was always the kind who was very careful with money," Denise said. "She never wanted to get into a situation where she'd be over-extended."

Denise faced similar challenges. Still, the two old friends were able to set aside enough money to have fun. They reserved Friday nights for going to clubs, and these outings were carefully figured into their weekly plans $10 at a time. On one Friday night, Jeannie would get to spend the $10 on mixed drinks, which would have to last through the long evening, while Denise sipped soft drinks. The next weekend, Denise would get the $10 and Jeannie would be the driver.

Occasionally, they would meet guys who appealed to them, but Jeannie devoted most of her attentions to Mike Reardon, a handsome Norfolk policeman. Reardon had seen Jeannie on visits to the courthouse on police business. He knew Jeannie's friend and co-worker Christine White and her husband David, who also was a police officer. Through the Whites, he had learned that Jeannie was divorced. He had stopped by her desk several times for what Jeannie thought was idle conversation before he had asked her out the first time. For Jeannie, it was a relationship that had seemed to click from the beginning. Denise could tell that Mike was important to Jeannie, because she paid even more attention than usual to her hair, makeup and clothes when she knew that she would be seeing Mike.

"Jeannie was so particular that if I went to the street to get the mail from my mailbox with rollers in my hair, she would lecture me about how I looked. And she would practically order me not to go out of the house again looking like that," Denise remembered.

Mike seemed perfect for Jeannie. He was tall, broad-shouldered, well-built with a deep tan and dark hair. Denise thought that he looked enough like Tony to be his brother. At 26, Mike was a former football player at Guilford College in North Carolina, and he still looked the part. He was dedicated to physical training, and he talked Jeannie into joining him in his regular work-out sessions at a health spa in Norfolk, which Jeannie took as a sign that he might be developing a serious interest in her.

Jeannie took to weightlifting immediately and wanted to learn more about it. Although Mike tried to advise her, he realized that his knowledge and training were limited. But he had a friend who worked at the spa who knew all about weightlifting. They'd once played football together at Guilford College, he said, and he was sure that his friend would be able to help her.

A gold chain glistened on Pernell Jefferson's powerful chest as Mike introduced him a short time later.

"Pleased to meet you, ma'am," Pernell said, smiling and offering his hand.

3

The Crossroads

The town of Benson lies in the heart of North Carolina at the western edge of the state's coastal plain, just north of the southeastern United States sand belt that extends from nearby Fayetteville southwest through South Carolina and into Georgia.

U.S. Highway 301 still makes its way through the heart of town, but it no longer carries the heavy burden of north-south traffic that it once did. In its place, Interstate 95, the major traffic artery linking East Coast cities with the warmth of the Florida sun, carries motorists east of Benson's downtown area and few ever stop. Just north of town, the final segment of transcontinental Interstate 40 has become the favored route for North Carolinians bound for their favorite beaches between the Outer Banks and South Carolina's Grand Strand, but most of those bypass Benson, too.

Long ago, passenger trains regularly made stops in the town, but now Amtrak limiteds barely slow as they rumble through the heart of Benson on daily runs north and south between Miami and New York.

Though light industry has in the last 20 years become an important part of Benson's economy, Johnston County remains mostly devoted to agriculture. Indeed, it is a town known in North Carolina for its Mule Days, a summer celebration of parades and other attractions that brings in visitors not only from surrounding counties but from neighboring states as well.

Like most Southern towns its size, Benson is a blue-collar town with a taste for blue-collar religion. Its preference is mostly Protestant and primarily Baptist and it is in Benson that one of the nation's oldest and biggest gospel singing conventions is still held each year.

It was to Benson, her hometown, that Joann Richardson Jefferson returned from Stuart, Florida, with her two sons after her marriage fell apart in 1966. Her elder child, Pernell, was just three years old, her younger, Willie, only 11 months.

For a time, they moved in with her parents, William and Priscilla

Richardson, but Joann soon found a place of her own, a small, white, wood-frame home a short walk from a Missionary Baptist church and only a few blocks from Benson's old, affluent neighborhood. There, Pernell and Willie would grow up, and it was to that house that they would return again and again throughout their lives.

Finding work to support her two sons was difficult for Joann. From late spring through the oppressively hot summer months, she often labored in the vast fields near Benson, helping harvest crops of vegetables and sweet potatoes. Occasionally, she worked in a downtown candy kitchen, but in hard times, she had to resort to welfare to feed her growing sons.

No support came from her children's father, Willie Thomas Jefferson, a construction worker who once had scratched his nickname, Hook, in the wet cement he had helped pour for a railroad bridge near Benson. The boys almost never heard from him and for most of their young lives had no memories of him.

Life became less difficult for Joann and her boys when she finally was hired as a custodian at Benson Elementary School, where her sons were students. Still, she had to continue to work nights caring for bed-ridden people in Benson to make ends meet.

Pernell and Willie regularly attended Sunday school and preaching at the Missionary Baptist church less than a block from their house. For a time, both sang in the choir in which most of the members were relatives. They sang so sweetly that churches throughout the county sought them for special programs.

"There were Sundays we'd be in church almost all day," Willie recalled. "We'd sing in our church on Sunday morning, another church would want us to come sing in the afternoon, and maybe we'd go to another one Sunday night.

"But Mom always had Sunday dinner waiting for us. Fried chicken. Green beans. Homemade biscuits."

For Willie, these were happy times. Years later, Pernell also would find contentment in remembering them.

"I came from a good family," he said. "People in my family made something of themselves. We didn't have a lot of money, but we had a lot of care and love. And the strong people in our family were the women — my mother and my aunt."

If anything, Joann Jefferson was a disciplinarian. When she got word on one occasion that Willie had been disrespectful to a teacher, she marched into the classroom, asked the teacher to excuse her for a moment and spanked her son while 32 startled fellow students watched.

In the absence of their father, Pernell and Willie found other men to fill some of that void. For a time, William Richardson, an older cousin who

30

worked at the Jesse Jones Sausage Company, took the boys under his wing. Later, they would find companionship from W.C. Swain, a construction worker who had become Joann's friend.

"For a time, he was like a stepfather to us," Willie recalled.

Other relatives, too, took an interest in Joann's sons. "My Aunt Katie and Uncle Smitty took us to the beach every summer until I was in senior high school," Pernell later remembered. "They were like a second set of parents to us.

"And Aunt Mable and Uncle Willie. We stayed in their house a lot in the summertime. And Willie and I would go fishing with Uncle Leslie and his two daughters, Linda and Shirley. Their mother made the best homemade biscuits in Benson."

Almost from the time he entered first grade, it was clear that Pernell was exceptional. Though he was a capable student, his mother thought Pernell's future lay in his athletic ability. He played all sports, but he especially loved baseball, football and basketball and played them with an ease and intensity that held out the promise of a bright future. As soon as classes ended each school day, Pernell headed straight for the gym or the playing field, and he usually stayed until supper was on the table at home. But one night at supper, when he was only eight, he made a surprise announcement. He wanted to quit sports. He was tired of it, he said, and other kids had better shoes than his.

"You must not quit," his mother told him sternly. "My sons aren't quitters."

Shortly afterward, she paid $30 for a new pair of athletic shoes, an act her son would still recall fondly many years later.

"Me and my kid brother, we grew up poor," Pernell said, "but whatever we needed we got. If we needed something, Mother would go lacking herself until next month to get it for us."

"Mother didn't have thirty dollars to spare," Willie later recalled. "Thirty dollars was an awful lot of money to us back then. My mother was willing to sacrifice for Pernell.

"Mom knew Pernell was a very good athlete. And she knew he was a very good student. Pernell'd do his homework in thirty minutes and it'd take me two hours. When Pernell helped me, I always made A's and B's.

"Mom understood this. She knew that athletics and education might make a great difference in Pernell's life some day. And she was right."

Sports also kept Pernell out of the trouble in which so many of the other boys from his section of town often found themselves.

"Actually, I was scared of trouble," he remembered. "I was scared to fight. I can only remember two fights when I was growing up. We just didn't grow up with that in our house and in our family."

Once, though, Pernell got a taste of what could happen to him. It

31

came shortly after one of his youth league baseball games had ended near 10:30 on a summer night when he was 13.

The lights at the cozy playing field still illuminated the surrounding neighborhood as Pernell began walking the six blocks home along Church Street. The money his mother had given him to buy a soft drink still jingled in his pocket.

Just as he approached the convenience store directly behind the Benson Police Department, the store's outside lights suddenly were switched off. Assuming the store was closing, Pernell continued on toward home. Within an hour, Benson police officers knocked at his door and asked Pernell to accompany them to the police station for questioning about a robbery at the convenience store.

"We know you were there," an officer told Pernell after he was escorted into the police station. "Somebody saw you."

"Yes, sir," Pernell said, "but I was just walking home from the baseball game. I was going to stop at the store and buy a soda. That's what I always do after a game. But they turned the lights off and I thought they were closing."

Pernell was frightened and he began crying as the officer continued his questioning. Soon, his mother and his aunt, Kate Smith, arrived and phoned Pernell's uncle, Norman (Phil) Richardson, a magistrate in nearby Smithfield.

Twenty minutes later, Richardson was at the Benson police station and pulled his nephew aside for a private talk.

"Okay, Sonny Boy," he said, using the only name by which he ever addressed Pernell. "Tell me about it."

"Uncle Phil, I didn't do it. I thought the store was closing, so I didn't even stop like I usually do."

"You'd better be telling me the truth, Sonny Boy," his uncle said.

"I am telling you the truth." And the tears came again.

Moments later, an officer asked to speak to Richardson. He told him that Pernell was being released, that another suspect had been arrested. Within minutes, Pernell was passing the new suspect in a narrow hallway. He was startled. He felt as though he were looking at his double.

"The guy's still around town," Willie said years later, "and if he walked in here right now, you'd do a double-take because he still looks just like Pernell."

By the time Pernell entered South Johnston High School, sports had become the foundation upon which he would build his popularity. With a close, older friend named Tol Avery to idolize, Pernell became a three-sport star at South Johnston. During his sophomore year, he was the running back on the football team, for which Avery was the quarterback. Pernell continued to carry the ball through his junior season and then was shifted to quarterback for his final season (his friend Tol had gone on to college). He also was a star on the school's track team, but his first love was another spring sport, baseball.

Once, Pernell appeared in two simultaneous sporting events at South Johnston. In the spring of his senior year, between innings of a baseball game, he several times rushed to the nearby track to perform, at one point anchoring the winning relay team still wearing his baseball uniform.

In the classroom, Pernell was not nearly as spectacular a performer, however, though he managed to maintain a low "B" average.

At the beginning of his junior year, Pernell had begun dating a classmate, Sarah Wheeler,* from the community of Four Oaks, leading to an on-again, off-again relationship would last through his remaining time at South Johnston. Sarah was a petite, attractive freshman when Pernell met her in study hall on the second day of school.

"I thought Pernell was very handsome," she remembered years later. "I didn't even know he played sports. I had no idea."

Sarah was just 14, and Pernell became her first romance. "He was a very lovable person," she recalled. "Everybody loved Pernell. Especially the teachers. He was so polite. You know, 'Yes, ma'am,' and 'No, ma'am.'"

Before the year was out, Sarah was known throughout the school as "Pernell's woman," and he had become very possessive of her. As time went on, she began to feel smothered by his attentions and expectations, and at the beginning of her sophomore year, she decided to do something about it.

"Pernell," she said as the two of them walked along an upstairs hall at South Johnston early that autumn, "we need to talk."

"What about?" said Pernell, who was beginning his final year of high school as the star of the football team.

"Us," she said.

"Okay," he responded warily, stopping to look at her.

"Pernell, I like you a lot," she said. "You're a nice guy and I enjoy being around you. But I want to back off a little bit. Do you understand?"

"No, I don't understand," he said, his voice rising.

"Pernell, I'm just fifteen years old. This is your last year at South Johnston and we don't know what's going to happen after that. We can be friends, but let's ease off a little."

Sarah turned and hurried off to her next class. She looked back and saw Pernell still standing in the same spot, watching her go.

A few minutes later, a commotion developed at the bottom of a flight of stairs not far from where Pernell and Sarah had stopped to talk. Pernell lay motionless and apparently unconscious at the base of the stairway. A group of students quickly gathered, and some ran for help.

One of Pernell's football coaches, Ronald Avery, was in his classroom not far away, and when he heard that his star quarterback had fallen and was hurt, he pushed his way through the crowd but could get no response from him. "Somebody call the rescue squad," he called.

"I thought he was dying," Avery said years later.

Pernell still had not moved when medical attendants arrived and checked for vital signs. Avery thought he saw a worried expression on the face of one of the medics. Pernell was placed on a stretcher and rushed to the hospital.

Avery hurried to his classroom, gave his students quick assignments and left for the hospital, where the medics told him that Pernell appeared to have suffered cardiac arrest during the trip. Deeply worried, Avery waited uneasily for word from the doctors. But when a doctor finally emerged, he told him that Pernell would be okay.

"Just let him lie there for a while and then take him back to school," the doctor said.

Avery was confused. "The medics said he might have had a cardiac arrest in the ambulance," he said.

The doctor smiled.

"Well, he convinced the rescue people of that. In the excitement and the urgency of the moment, that can happen if somebody wants you to think he's dying. But he was faking it."

"Faking?" Avery was incredulous.

"There's nothing wrong with him except that he must have wanted to get somebody's attention," the doctor said.

But word already had spread quickly through South Johnston High that the school's star athlete was seriously injured, and Sarah was distraught when she heard it.

"I still don't know what really happened," she said years later. "I just heard that Pernell had been rushed to the hospital and I know I had a hard time waiting until I got home on the school bus. I planned to ask my Dad to take me to the hospital. I was really worried."

But when she got home, she was startled to find Pernell on her front porch.

"What happened to you?" she asked, as he smiled broadly.

"Oh, I just fell on the stairs," he said. "Guess I knocked myself out."

"What did the doctors say?"

"They said I just got a little knock on the head and that I'll be all right."

Relieved, Sarah rushed to his arms. Their relationship continued as before, and Sarah came to realize that backing away from her involvement with Pernell would not be easy.

34

Before the year was out, she would try several more times to ease away, but never with success.

"Pernell would get demanding," Sarah recalled. "Too bossy. He always wanted things his way. It got to where it was like I was married to him. He'd get angry and yell at me. It always happened when I wanted to back off. My biggest problem with Pernell was the breaking up. He didn't like that. It was like it hurt him so much, he couldn't handle breaking up."

During Pernell's closing days of high school, in the spring of 1980, Sarah tried once again to break off from him. This time, he became angrier than she'd ever seen him.

The blow from Pernell's strong right hand caught her by surprise, and she ran away, confused and angry, her ears ringing. When she got home that day, she unexpectedly encountered her father, Walter Wheeler,* who had arrived home from work early. He immediately saw that she was upset.

"Sarah, what's wrong?" he asked.

"Nothing," she said.

"What's wrong?" he repeated sternly.

"Pernell," she said softly.

"Pernell what?" her father pressed.

"Oh, dad..."

She hesitated.

"What about Pernell?"

"He got a little mad."

Silence followed while her father waited for her to elaborate.

"He scared me," she said.

"Did he hit you?"

"Just once."

Angry, her father turned to leave.

"Where are you going, Daddy?" Sarah asked anxiously.

"I'm going to find Mr. Jefferson," he said.

Shortly, Walter Wheeler was knocking on Pernell's front door. Pernell's mother answered.

"Mrs. Richardson," Wheeler said, "I'm sorry to bother you, but I need to talk to you about Pernell."

Inside, out of sight, Pernell was listening intently.

"He hit Sarah today and I won't allow that to happen," Wheeler said.

"Oh, my," Joann responded. "I'm so sorry."

"If it ever happens again, I'll have to do something about it," Wheeler said. "Tell him that."

"It won't happen again," Joann said, her embarrassment obvious. "I promise you that."

After being lectured by his mother, Pernell apologized to Sarah, who forgave him and went back with him.

"He never beat me again," Sarah said years later. "To tell you the truth, I think he was afraid of what my father would do to him. He didn't want Dad coming looking for him again."

Although Pernell weighed only 150 pounds, far too light to be thought a likely prospect by most college football coaches, he had been getting the attention of a handful of college recruiters, among them those from North Carolina State, where his close friend, Tol Avery, was the starting quarterback.

Avery encouraged him to join the Wolfpack, as the State team was known to its fans, and Pernell was tempted, but he knew that the chances of an undersized quarterback or defensive back getting more than token playing time with such a team were remote. Instead, he turned his attention to smaller colleges within the state, where he believed he could become a star. His first choice was Elon College, near Burlington, which had just won the National Association of Intercollegiate Athletics championship. But when he visited the campus, the coaches concluded that Pernell was too slow. He drove home under the crush of disappointment.

After this rebuff, Pernell decided to try for a scholarship in either track or baseball. But as his senior year drew toward a close, a man emerged from the stands at one of his last baseball games and introduced himself as Steve Davis, a football coach at Guilford College.

Pernell knew little of the Quaker school in Greensboro, but he was impressed when Davis told him that M.L. Carr of the Boston Celtics and World B Free of the Philadelphia 76ers had played basketball at Guilford.

He accepted an invitation to visit the campus on the first weekend in May, 1981. His brother Willie, his cousin Donnell Smith, and his uncle Andy Smith made the trip with him, and before the four started back to Benson on Sunday, Pernell knew where he would be spending the next four years. He became the last player to sign with the Quakers that spring.

As soon as he got home, Pernell hurried to Sarah's house to tell her the news. That night, they celebrated by making love.

4

Where Winning Isn't Everything

From the beginning, Pernell and Guilford College were an unlikely pairing. In a fundamental way, the institutional notion of athletics and Pernell's view of sports were at counterpoints almost from the moment he stepped onto the campus dominated by ancient oak trees. Guilford College had been established in 1837 by the Society of Friends and for more than 100 years the peaceful Quakers had had an uneasy association with football, principally because of its violent nature. For generations, faculty pressure had periodically arisen to discontinue the sport.

Consequently, not only had Guilford never been a reservoir of talent for the National Football League, it could claim many mileposts in the sport that were unique.

The legendary University of Alabama coach, Paul "Bear" Bryant, then a rookie head coach at the University of Maryland just five days out of pre-flight school near the end of World War II, got the first of his all-time record 323 victories against the Quakers in 1945. The score was Maryland 60, Guilford 6.

A Guilford graduate named Charles "Block" Smith once coached the team for six years, even though he won just three games, lost 41 and tied three. During the same period, Smith coached the basketball team as well, with no better results, his teams winning just three games while losing 68.

Like every coach Guilford College ever had, no matter the sport, Smith finally resigned of his own accord. No coach in the school's history ever was fired or pressured to resign for not winning games.

In the early 1970s, Guilford's football team was so inept that it came within one game of tying a national record for consecutive defeats by losing 32 in a row. When that opportunity for dubious national recognition was shattered by an unexpected 36-31 victory over Randolph-Macon, some on campus, mostly long-suffering faculty, were crestfallen for weeks that their team had been denied even that moment of questionable glory. But the students tore

37

the goalposts down.

No individual player ever symbolized Guilford's dismal football fortunes more than Don Cupit. He spend his first two collegiate seasons, 1969 and 1970, at Virginia Military Institute, where the football team won only one game. Hoping for better fortunes, Cupit transferred to Guilford College for his junior and senior seasons. He arrived right in the middle of the Quakers' long losing streak, and his new team lost 19 more games without winning any, giving Cupit a four-year college career of 1-39.

When Herb Appenzeller was hired from Chowan Junior College in 1956 to coach the football team, he was called to the office of Guilford's president, Dr. Clyde Milner, to talk about the approaching season. What he got was a lecture on the importance of good sportsmanship and the lofty ideals of sports as part of the college experience. After Milner had finished, Appenzeller sat for a moment contemplating what he had just heard.

"Doctor Milner," he finally said. "I want to understand you correctly. Are you telling me that if we can beat the devil out of them, don't do it?"

"Why, yes, my dear man," Milner responded. "That's exactly what I'm saying."

"I guess he thought we were going to be good," said Appenzeller after recalling the story. Appenzeller's first team at Guilford failed to beat the devil out of anyone, winning just one of eight games.

Still, Guilford had high expectations from time to time. When John Stewart was hired prior to the 1963 season as the replacement for Appenzeller, who had earned a doctorate and was becoming the school's athletic director, Stewart confidently predicted that his first Quaker team would finish the season undefeated. It finished without a victory in ten games.

Still, there was no grassroots movement to replace Stewart, no hangings in effigy. Indeed, Stewart could not discern that ten straight defeats had had any appreciable effect on the small campus.

Occasionally, there were coaches at Guilford who became troubled by the pacifist nature of the Quakers and tried to make the school more competitive. One was the football coach who felt that a new team logo that reflected the aggressive nature of the sport might help. A talented Western Guilford High School student, Duke Hilliard, designed three possible logos, among them a fierce, angry Quaker that the coach preferred.

School administrators were rapid and unanimous in their dissent and ordered that a more fitting logo be designed. Within days it was unveiled: a silhouette of the oldest spreading oak tree on campus. That became the school's official emblem. It still appears on all school correspondence and publications, but it never has been applied to the football team's helmets.

At Guilford, the finer points of football were never fully appreciated. In 1959, during Appenzeller's tenure as head coach, the Quakers once rescheduled a late summer practice session to the early morning hours so that the Green Bay Packers, then one of the National Football League's marquee teams, could use Guilford's facilities for an afternoon drill in preparation for a pre-season game in the area.

Appenzeller, still wearing his coaching attire, had rushed from his sessions with his own players to stand along the sidelines while the legendary Vince Lombardi and his staff put the Packers of Paul Hornung, Bart Starr, Jim Taylor and Max McGee, all in their famous golden helmets with the "G" on the sides, through their paces. Appenzeller had stood there spellbound, his arms folded in front of him, and for a time was not aware that Dr. Milner, the school's president, had joined him without speaking.

"Oh, my good man," Milner finally said to Appenzeller with enthusiasm, "I believe we're going to have a pretty good ball club this year." Milner turned and walked away before Appenzeller could explain that the "G" on the players' helmets stood for Green Bay, not Guilford.

It was into such football innocence that Pernell Jefferson arrived in the late summer of 1981, bent upon achieving fame.

As a potential defensive back, Pernell was assigned to Tommy Saunders, an assistant coach. For years, Saunders had seen undersized defensive backs come and go, and the information he was given about Pernell prior to the beginning of practice didn't indicate that he would be any different.

"I just knew he was a quick kid," Saunders remembered years later. "Small, 145 to 150 pounds. I knew he had been a quarterback down there at South Johnston. And I knew he could get into school. That's it."

Pernell was a step ahead of Saunders, though. He understood that he was likely to be nothing more than a face in the crowd, so he made sure his face would be remembered.

He showed up at practice wearing a Mohawk haircut. It worked. "This guy must want to play," Saunders told a fellow coach as he watched his players go through their first afternoon of conditioning.

Pernell was working hard to impress Saunders, but while he was making a quick turn on an agility drill during that first practice session, he felt pain shoot through his left ankle. He tried to keep his footing but suddenly found himself lying on the field with Saunders rushing to his side.

Soon, Pernell was being helped away, a bulging bag of ice lashed to the outside of his left ankle. He was taken to a Greensboro hospital where X-rays showed a broken ankle.

The injury was a devastating blow to Pernell. Even before he could get to know his new teammates, he was an outsider looking in, a sports invalid leaning on crutches along the sidelines, watching practice. Depression gripped him and he wondered if he would ever play again. It took days, but he finally pushed the doubts and depression aside and began working toward his goal once more.

Even as his ankle was healing, he continued the strict weight training program required for all members of the football team, and it was beginning to make a difference. Though his weight still fluctuated between 150 and 155 pounds, he felt stronger. And by the time he was able to return to the lineup as a reserve defensive back halfway through the season, he was beginning to develop something close to an addiction for weightlifting. Not only did he take regular turns in the Guilford College weight room, he also began to frequent several Greensboro health clubs, where he met competitive weightlifters who were willing to share their training secrets. When Pernell began to hear from them about non-prescription drugs that could accomplish miracles, he listened with interest and filed the information away in his memory. He was determined to make himself strong enough so that neither injuries nor anything else could keep him from his goal of becoming a football star.

Although Pernell was nearly three hours away at Guilford, some things had not changed for his girlfriend back in Johnston County. After school started that fall, Sarah stopped between classes to chat with a male student she didn't know. A football player soon approached them.

"Hey, man," he said to the male student whose name Sarah had not yet learned. "Better move on and find somebody else to talk to. That's Pernell Jefferson's woman."

Sarah was furious.

"It was as though I wasn't permitted to have friends of my own," she said years later.

By that time, Sarah already knew that she was pregnant, and she didn't plan to let Pernell know about it. They had broken up during the summer, although he had talked about getting back together before he left for Guilford. Since he'd gone, though, she hadn't heard from him at all.

"I was going to have the baby and if he never came around, he'd just never know anything about it," she said later, recalling her feelings at the time.

But word soon got around the school that she was carrying Pernell's child, and a South Johnston football player who visited Pernell at Guilford one weekend told him about it. When Pernell returned to Benson for the Thanksgiving break, he went to see Sarah.

"Is it mine?" he asked.

"It's yours," she said, warily, uncertain of his response.

"He was thrilled," she remembered years later.

Sarah gave birth to a son at Smithfield-Johnston Memorial Hospital on March 1, 1982. She asked a friend to notify Pernell.

"They told me that when he was told, Pernell went dancing around the room celebrating," Sarah said. "They said he got up on a table and was dancing and yelling."

For three days, the child remained unnamed. "I didn't know what I wanted to name him," Sarah recalled. "A friend wanted me to name him Patrick. Patrick Wheeler. It sounded okay, but it wasn't exactly right. The people in the hospital just knew him as 'Boy Wheeler.' Then I told them to put 'Pernell' down for his name. Pernell Maurice Wheeler.*"

Two weeks after his son was born, Pernell came home for spring break.

"I'll never forget him coming to our house," Sarah said. "When he came in, I was just sitting there, holding the baby. Pernell smiled the biggest, prettiest smile...."

He reached out tentatively and touched the baby, then lifted him from her arms and clutched him to his chest.

"Pernell," he said. "Pernell Junior."

When he returned the baby to Sarah, he hugged her and kissed her on the cheek.

"Thank you," he said.

5

The Turning Point

In his freshman year on the Guilford football team, Pernell had managed to get onto the field only for a few kickoffs and punt returns late in the season. But long before practice had begun in the summer before his sophomore year, he had become confident that this year he would be a starter on defense.

Although, he barely had survived his first year of college academically, he was stronger than he ever had been, virtually addicted to muscle building.

Before classes began, Pernell learned that he had been assigned to share a dormitory room with a freshman candidate for the football team, Lamar Boykin. Still growing, Lamar was taller than Pernell, rangier and faster, and he was the closest thing to a natural defensive back that Pernell had ever seen.

Although they were competing for the same spots on the team, Pernell and Lamar hit it off from the beginning, and by the time of the season's first game, both not only were starters, they were close friends and confidants.

Always the optimist, Pernell seemed almost carefree to Lamar, a man at peace with the world and in love with his own existence. And when Pernell returned the opening kickoff 100 yards for a touchdown in one of the season's early games, he was suddenly the college football star he'd been determined to become. Lamar sensed that his new friend even walked with an attitude bordering on arrogance after that.

But if Pernell felt self-assured about his ability, his position coach, Tommy Saunders, no longer was certain.

Although, Pernell's explosiveness as a kick returner was paying big dividends, the elusiveness and individual style that made him good at it were becoming problems on defense. Saunders, a disciplinarian, pushed for strict attention to assigned plays and assigned zones, but Pernell resisted.

Even when Saunders began sending in another player, Keith Milner, Pernell still did not respond. After all, Milner wasn't doing noticeably better.

"It was like neither one of them wanted to hit anybody," Saunders recalled. "And neither wanted to stay where he was supposed to be. They'd get out of position and we'd get killed."

The problem quickly became acute. In desperation, Saunders pleaded with head coach Charlie Forbes to move John Hoots, also a sophomore, from his running back slot to the strong safety position Pernell had been playing. The switch was made on Wednesday prior to the game against Mars Hill. Hoots spent most of that practice learning the position and by the end of practice on Friday he seemed at home there.

Still, Hoots remained on the bench through the first half of the Mars Hill game. But the game wasn't going well for the Quakers, and at halftime, Saunders huddled briefly with Forbes.

"I don't have much choice," he said to Forbes. "I'm putting Hoots in at strong safety in the second half."

Told of the lineup change in the dressing room at halftime, Pernell argued vehemently with Saunders, but to no avail. He sat sullenly on the bench during the second half.

A day later, after the coaches had studied the game films, Forbes sought out Pernell.

"You're not going to start any more until further notice," Forbes told him, then quickly departed, leaving no quarter for discussion.

"That was a killer," Pernell later recalled. "I was crushed."

He retreated to his dormitory room, fell heavily onto his bed and for a long time lay staring at the ceiling.

He had endured the long rehabilitation for his broken ankle, had worked hard to come back, only to find rejection. Injuries happen, he reasoned, but this latest blow, this demotion, was because another player was bigger and stronger.

And this, he knew, was no temporary setback. He and Hoots both were sophomores. Unless he got big enough and strong enough to compete with Hoots, the best he could hope for was an occasional punt or kickoff return. But he knew there was a way that he could do that. His weightlifting friends at the health clubs had been telling him about it.

The following day, Pernell acquired a vial of Winstrol V from a teammate who had boasted from time to time that he was using steroids. In the privacy of his dorm room, he pushed the needle into the fatty part of his right hip and drained the steroid into his system.

In the coming days, on the recommendation of an acquaintance at a health club, Pernell added a Winstrol tablet called Stanozdol to his injections of Winstrol V. The combination became what was regarded as a modest stack of steroids in weightlifting terms. Pernell had launched his first steroid cycle. Others would come in quick succession as his workouts became more intense.

He doubled his dosage, then tripled it. He began eating twice as much. Steadily, his lifts increased. So did his weight. And as he grew bigger and stronger, as if by magic, he gained more and more confidence. He also won the attention of his coaches, who saw his new regimen as red-blooded resolve to win back his starting position. They admired him for it, and at mid-season, they rewarded him, giving him a new starting position on the boundary side of the secondary, where he immediately proved himself.

"Maybe it took me a while, but I finally realized I had to get Pernell onto the field," Saunders said. "I made it easy for him. I put him on the boundary side of the field because I wanted him to do just two things — go up or go back."

There would be other changes in a defensive secondary that was looking for consistency. Lamar was shifted into Pernell's old position on the wide side of the field, normally called the strong side in most defensive schemes. Lamar, who possessed good size and the speed to compete against fast wide receivers sent deep into the zone, became the key to the new defensive secondary.

On the first day of practice under the new alignment, Saunders knew he had finally hit upon the right combination.

Back in the starting lineup again, Pernell once more was happy. By the time of the homecoming game late in the season, Pernell had received accolades for his dramatic kickoff and punt returns. Gone now were the personal doubts and uncertainties that had plagued him only a couple of months earlier. In a Wednesday practice session, he capped off the day's special teams work by returning a kickoff for a touchdown with a dazzling run.

As he trotted past Forbes at the end of practice, Pernell made a promise.

"Gonna give you one of those Saturday, Coach," he said cockily.

On Saturday, just prior to the game, athletic director Herb Appenzeller walked along the sidelines, stopping beside Pernell, who was doing his stretching exercises.

"Think you can run one back today?" Appenzeller asked.

"Just watch me, Dr. A," Jefferson answered with a grin.

Remembering that he had left some game tickets on his desk in the field house 200 yards away, Appenzeller hurried off to get them. He was delayed in getting back, and just as he stepped out of the fieldhouse, a roar arose from the crowd in the distance.

Pernell had returned the opening kickoff more than 80 yards for a touchdown. Lamar rushed to hug his roommate. Drowned by the roar of the crowd were the cheers of another of Pernell's new friends, Susan Demos.

6

Equality in Black and White

When Susan Demos had entered Guilford College in the autumn of 1980, she had been following a family tradition. Her mother, her grandfather and her great-grandmother all had graduated from Guilford. Her mother's father had been a professor there.

Soon after her own arrival at Guilford, a school so liberal that it had been among the first in the South to admit black students and had boldly recruited Japanese students during the Japan-hating years of World War II, Susan had begun gathering about her a new set of friends without regard to race or any other prejudices. The daughter of a Quaker mother and an orthodox Greek father, Susan had from childhood been taught about the brotherhood of man by both parents. But it had not been until her sophomore year that she had met Pernell, a freshman who, like Susan, reported to the dining room in Founders Hall every day to bus tables. Pernell smiled freely and conversation over clanking dishes had come easily. Susan found him charming and liked him immediately.

"We were just friends for a while," she recalled.

But by February 1982, more than halfway through his freshman year, Pernell had asked Susan for a date. Having been influenced in her formative years principally by the liberal Quaker beliefs of her mother, Irene*, Susan had no qualms about inter-racial dating. In high school, she had for most of her junior year dated a black classmate. After they had gone to a school dance together, Susan had gone early the next day to pick up the newspaper for her father and at the end the family driveway, she had discovered "Nigger Lover" spray-painted in white on the black asphalt.

Years later, it still bothered her. "How could whoever wrote those words hate me?" she asked. "They didn't even know me."

More importantly, though she didn't know it at the time, nor did she understand it for years, the incident had instantly changed her relationship with her father, George.* As he had rolled a dark sealer over the hateful words, he had remained silent, and he would never speak to Susan about the incident.

"My Dad was a great person," she said years later. "Anybody who knew us would tell you my Dad thought I walked on water. But we never did communicate on deep, important things."

Susan still was struggling with her father's silence when she accepted Pernell's invitation to a Chinese restaurant and a movie.

"Pernell was a lot of fun," she said. "We were always doing things together. We both liked Chinese food. We were always going to different sports events together. For me, it was exciting. There was so much Pernell had not been exposed to."

Susan and Pernell had sports in common — in high school she had competed in track, basketball and volleyball — but socially, their differences were great, and in a sense, Pernell became a challenge for Susan. Pernell was the product of a background vastly different from Susan's and from that of most of the students at Guilford, where for decades the student body had been made up in large measure of sons and daughters of the wealthy. Pernell lacked some of the social graces that were second nature for other students. His grammar was often inconsistent and his clothes were not of the latest fashion nor from expensive shops. Susan had set about changing all that. She had taught Pernell etiquette without insulting his pride. She had bought clothes for him that would make it possible for him to more readily blend in with his trendy classmates.

"He loved new shoes," she remembered. "And he loved to share what he had. I'd buy him a new pair of shoes and a week later they'd be gone. He'd given them to somebody who had liked them. I'd go buy him another pair. I bought him so many shoes I was going broke."

Susan also bought the first set of contact lenses Pernell ever owned. "He was thrilled the day he got them," she said.

A shirt, a pair of shoes at a time, Susan had been gradually becoming Pernell's woman, at first without realizing what was happening. "I don't even remember when that happened," she said later. "I just know that I wanted to make a point and Pernell gave me the chance to do that."

The old Quaker teachings of her childhood, now reinforced by much of what she saw and learned at liberal Guilford College, became once again important in her life. Susan had come to believe that her mother and father stood a world apart from one another in their views about equality and racism.

"I know now that it wasn't so much my Dad as it was the difference in his times and my times," she said years later. "And the two were on a collision course. The point was — and not everybody agreed with me — that I felt that everybody is equal. And I set about making sure Pernell was equal to all the other students at Guilford by buying him the same kinds of clothes everybody else had. I thought that if Pernell looked equal, then he must be

46

equal. I will always believe that everybody is equal. But I will never try to prove it that way again."

Before his first year of college had ended, a trend had developed in Pernell's life. Most of his male friends were black; most of his female friends were white, a curiosity that would not trouble Susan until years later.

"I always thought Pernell looked for white women," she said. "Where he's from, whites and blacks still don't mix like they do in other places. Back around Benson, whites still own the big farms, and blacks work for them on those big farms. I always thought he resented that his mother had had to work on those farms picking vegetables when he was growing up. So, for Pernell, to have a white girl on his arm meant he had arrived. I was a status symbol for Pernell. So were all the other white girls in his life."

By the time Pernell had begun gaining attention as a football star near the end of his sophomore season, Susan had begun seeing changes in his personality. He was becoming more domineering, more possessive. He had begun questioning her about things she felt were insignificant.

Then came the violence. "I don't even remember the first time he hit me, because he wound up hitting me so much," Susan later recalled

Ironically, as his violence toward her increased, Susan became even closer and more dependent on Pernell.

"You always want to go away, but when I did, Pernell would always beg me to come back, or threaten me if I didn't. That worked pretty well. Low self-esteem on my part was a big part of that."

Circumstances also were conspiring to confirm Susan's sinking impression of herself. As her relationship with Pernell grew deeper, she felt all the more alone, estranged even from friends on campus the two once had shared.

"Pernell was the center of attention. He'd tell me nobody cared about me, it was him they were interested in, and when that gets reinforced again and again, you start to believe it's true. After a while, Pernell and I were both sick. I was as much like Pernell as I could possibly be. I wanted to leave, but I felt it was just me in the world and I felt if I left Pernell, I wouldn't have anybody."

Guilford's football team wasn't championship caliber in 1982, finishing the season with five wins and five losses, but it was improving, and there was no doubt that Pernell was becoming one of its stars. He was determined to shine even brighter on next year's team. But as the school year wore on some began to wonder whether he would remain academically qualified to play. Because of the demands of football practice and his weight-lifting regimen, he had taken a light class load in the fall semester, then had doubled up

47

for the next semester by enrolling in two night classes. But his study habits were poor and he began falling behind.

Then when the football team turned out for spring practice, Pernell suffered another painful injury to the ankle he had broken nearly a year and a half earlier. Once again, he was hobbling along the sidelines on crutches. And he feared that he might lose his starting spot on the team. Worried and depressed, he dropped his night classes and failed both subjects, compounding his problems.

Susan became the brunt of his growing anger and frustration. At one point, without provocation, he suddenly grasped one of his crutches near the bottom and, swinging it as if it were a baseball bat, slammed it into the shin of Susan's right leg, knocking her to the ground in excruciating pain. By now she had accepted that that was just the way Pernell was, and she was helpless to do anything about it.

7

At the Sight of Blood

By the beginning of his junior year, things had begun looking up for Pernell. He had stayed on campus through the summer, passing enough classes to keep up his eligibility for the football team. His ankle had healed once more, and he was again playing brilliantly. He believed that he owed it all to steroids, and he had become as dependent on them as Susan had become dependent on him.

While the use of anabolic steroids was being discouraged in college athletics early in the 1980s, neither the National Association of Intercollegiate Athletics, of which Guilford College was then a member, nor the National Collegiate Athletic Association would move to ban them until 1990. Years before that, however, Guilford's football coaches and athletic director wanted drug testing for athletes but were turned down by school administrators who cited privacy and other student rights.

Pernell's coaches suspected that he was using steroids and questioned him about it on several occasions, but he always denied it.

"One of my coaches — I won't tell you who — said to me one time, 'Baby, I know you're juicing,'" Pernell recalled. "He would say in so many words that I needed to stop. But it was kept a secret."

"I asked," said Tommy Saunders, who became close to his players. "But he never told me he did. You almost have to catch them with the damn stuff to stop it. I knew kids who had to be on it because they'd go away one size and come back another."

Saunders had another reason to worry, as well. Playing high school football for his father back in Pennsylvania years earlier, he also had been an under-sized defensive back and at one time had dabbled with steroids himself when they were just becoming popular, but they had made him feel irritable and he had stopped using them for that reason.

"The thing that caught your eye was how big Pernell had gotten," recalled Head Coach Charlie Forbes, who would leave Guilford in 1991 to become the head football coach at Lenoir-Rhyne College in Hickory, N.C. "I never did know he was on steroids. He worked hard. He was in the weight room all the time. You'd have a hard time getting fringe players to spend time in the weight room, but Pernell was always there."

Pernell was not just an expert at lifting weights, he had become equally adept at stacking and cycling steroids. He was on intimate terms with a pharmacy index of performance and muscle enhancers including oral Methandrostendone, called D-balls, and Methylttesterone stacked with such injectables as Testosterone Cypionate, Testosterone Propionate and Deca-Curabolin, which he used in various combinations, all in massive doses.

His steroids of choice, he would boast to confidants, were Dianabol (the popular drug that inspired the weightlifters' credo: Die young, die strong, Dianabol), Anadrol 50 and Testosterone Cypionate. But over time, he also used several steroids designed specifically for the treatment of horses. These he would "stack" with the Dianabol, Anadrol 50 and Testosterone Cypionate.

He became proficient at the art of "cycling," with each cycle running from eight to ten weeks depending upon how much additional strength he thought he needed. Beginning with his injury in spring practice in 1983, Pernell committed himself to one long, dangerous cycle that lasted more than six months. And it gave him exactly what he wanted. He'd never felt stronger, never played better.

As a college football star, he would never again have to worry about losing his place in the starting lineup.

At the same time, though, he was becoming more and more violent, and Susan's life was becoming more and more frightening.

Lamar saw the changes in Pernell's once friendly and easy going personality, and it worried him. Pernell was far more easily annoyed and more aggressive than ever. He sometimes picked fights with teammates, including one during practice against running back Mike Reardon that was quickly broken up by coaches and teammates.

"I remember it well," Reardon said years later. "I ran out on a pass pattern and Pernell tackled me without the ball. He was strong, really strong. And when Pernell hit you, he could hurt you. I didn't even get the pass and he still tackled me and we started pushing and shoving, regular practice field stuff. But I had to run sprints after the game and I'm not sure he did."

Pernell provoked confrontations in nightspots, once starting a fight with the son of college football oddsmaker Jimmy "The Greek" Snyder, also a student at Guilford, merely because Pernell felt that young Snyder acted as though "he was better than everyone else."

Lamar often had to rescue Pernell from such scrapes before he got into trouble, and he tried to reason with his friend about the dangers he saw in his personality changes. But Lamar had no idea exactly how dark and violent

Pernell's moods could be. Only Susan knew that.

"He beat me every week," she recalled. Yet she couldn't bring herself to leave him.

"I really loved Pernell, probably more than anybody I ever dated. Pernell had become a monster. But it wasn't Pernell alone. I had become as crazy as he was."

Indeed, during a visit to his dorm room, Susan once attacked Pernell, leaping on his back, gouging and kicking, but exacting no damage.

"She was nuts," Pernell said. "And that wasn't the only time she did that. She tried to beat me six or seven times, at least."

Later, Susan would not disagree. "I had no life," she said. "By the time I left school, I had no friends. People would avoid me. Pernell had them all."

Though her family lived only 30 miles away, Susan's trips home came less frequently. Finally, months began to pass between visits. It had become more difficult to go home with so many bruises to explain.

"I didn't want Mom to know about the abuse," she said later, "plus I didn't want Dad to know that Pernell was black, and I loved him. I just felt he would lose it if he knew."

Her mother had met Pernell, and had no objections to his race. But she didn't like him and didn't think he was right for Susan. Susan didn't want her to know how deep the relationship had become. She also didn't want her to know that she was spending most of the money her parents sent her on Pernell.

"I knew if I came home, my parents would want to know why I was not dressed very well," Susan said. "I just didn't wish to explain that to them."

Also she now saw her father as a racist, a hypocrite who told her one thing but actually believed another.

"It hurt," she said. "I was aware that I was not what my Dad wanted me to be. I had done what he and my mother had said I ought to do — not judge people by the color of their skin — and he wasn't there to back me up when things didn't turn out well."

Unwilling to talk with her parents, without friends and utterly dependent upon Pernell emotionally, Susan fell deeper and deeper into despair.

"It was like I was in prison," she said. "I know what prisoners of war feel like."

Hers was a classic case of battered mate syndrome, but she didn't recognize it.

"I wound up thinking that Pernell was right, that everybody loved Pernell and nobody loved me and that that was just my lot in life and I couldn't do anything about it. It wasn't what I had planned for my life, but I had come to accept that that's the way it would always be."

She lived according to his wishes and his dictates.

"He was scary," she recalled, trying to explain. "But he was not only scary, he would carry out his threats enough for you to know that he would do what he said he would do."

Guilford's football team didn't live up to its players' hopes during Pernell's junior season, improving only marginally, winning five games, losing four and tying one. But Pernell was named to a district all-star team and his status on campus had grown. He had begun attracting attention from numerous women students, and he began dating a classmate named Ruth,* an exchange student from England.

Susan first learned of Pernell's relationship with Ruth from classmates. She kept quiet about it for weeks, but her suppressed anger bubbled to the surface when she unexpectedly encountered Ruth between classes.

"Pernell's my man," she told Ruth, a bite in her voice.

Ruth exploded. "Who the hell do you think you are? You think you're so special. I've got news for you, dearie. Pernell beats me the same way he beats you."

Ruth turned in a huff and walked away. For a long time, Susan didn't move. She was stunned.

"I always thought I was alone in the world, that I was the only one who had ever been treated that way," she said.

When she confronted Pernell about Ruth, he simply admitted it, and used the relationship to torment her even more, taunting her about it even in front of others. Still, Susan could not bring herself to do anything about her situation. Although she was helpless to understand it, her devotion to Pernell grew even more intense. But she did learn something that would save her some pain.

In one of Pernell's rages, he grasped Susan by the upper arms, jerked her to his face and bit her nose. "It happened so fast," Pernell remembered. "I couldn't believe that it had happened. It took me about thirty seconds to calm down. I was upset, but I didn't know I'd bit her."

Later, he would recall this as perhaps the first time that he had become concerned about the effect steroids were having on him.

As blood trickled from the bridge of her nose, Susan saw Pernell undergoing a transformation that she later described as "from Mr. Hyde to Dr. Jekyll." By the seconds, his mood softened. He became contrite, alarmed that he had hurt her. He seemed close to tears. She would never forget that reaction, nor would she ever want to for as long as she knew Pernell.

"I found out that night that Pernell hates blood," she said. Her survival instincts ignited. "From that day on, for as long as I was with Pernell, the

52

only way I could get him to stop beating me once he started was to bleed. So, I learned to bleed. I'd learn to cut myself when he was beating me, or scratch myself so that there would be blood. At the sight of blood, he'd quit just about every time."

Not long after this, Susan's rival for Pernell's attentions, Ruth, also had a memorable encounter with Pernell. She was driving her small Chevette when she saw him walking on campus and pulled over to chat.

"I didn't see you yesterday," Pernell said belligerently.

She tried to explain that her plans had changed at the last minute and she had been unable to notify him. He refused to accept the explanation and ordered her from the car. Fearfully, Ruth stepped out, but it was not she that he attacked. He turned instead upon her car, pounding the driver's side window until it shattered in a heap onto the seat. He then grasped the top of the closed door and rocked the car until it turned on its side.

It was the end of Ruth's relationship with Pernell. She didn't file charges against him, but she soon sold the car, which wasn't severely damaged, and returned to England.

In a sense, Susan had won. But her graduation in the spring of 1984 was without joy. She did not celebrate with her classmates, most of whom no longer bothered even to say hello. Her future looked dismal, for she could not imagine herself without Pernell.

"Pernell Jefferson made my college years the most miserable time of my life," she said years later. "I hated my experience at Guilford because of him. And I will never forgive him for that."

8

The All-American

As Guilford College's 1984 football team drilled in the oppressive heat of pre-season practice, Head Coach Charlie Forbes became depressed about what he was seeing.

Already, he had lost three outstanding defensive players to injuries in non-contact drills. And new quarterback Doug Kenworthy, who had waited two years for a chance to play, had not made the progress in pre-season practice that Forbes had hoped. Despite injuries to key defensive players, Forbes' young offensive team could make no progress against the patched-together defense. Pernell, Lamar and linebacker Scott O'Kelley, all key players on the defensive unit, had been able to avoid the kinds of injuries that had sidelined teammates and still were performing well.

During the week prior to the opening game against Lenoir-Rhyne, a despondent Forbes met with athletic director Herb Appenzeller. The pre-season meeting was customary, but this one was different.

"Dr. A," Forbes began somberly, "I've never misled you about our chances each year."

"I know, and I appreciate that," Appenzeller said.

"Well, you know we are injured on defense," Forbes continued. "But what you don't know is that our backs are so young and inexperienced that we haven't scored a touchdown against our defense all summer."

Forbes then told Appenzeller that the 1984 Quakers would not win a game and that, in his opinion, it was now time to consider discontinuing the football program, a possibility that had arisen on the campus from time to time for years. He would soon begin looking for a coaching job with another program for the 1985 season, he told Appenzeller.

"Have you said this to your coaches or to anyone else?" a startled Appenzeller asked.

"No, sir."

"Don't tell a soul," he counseled. "Let's keep it between us for now."

As Appenzeller pondered what he'd heard, he decided to wait until later in the season to address Forbes' concerns. Meanwhile, disappointed in his offense, Forbes chose two defensive players as co-captains for the season, breaking his own tradition of naming co-captains game-by-game.

For 1984, the honor would be shared by linebacker Scott O'Kelley of High Point, N.C., and Pernell Jefferson.

In the opening game of the year against Lenoir-Rhyne at Hickory, where quarterback Doug Kenworthy had grown up, one Guilford touchdown pass was wiped from the scoreboard because of an offensive penalty. But Kenworthy, playing better than he had practiced at any point during the late summer, rolled out of the pocket and threw another on the next play, giving the Quakers a surprising 14-7 halftime lead.

Pernell, who was now bigger and stronger than he'd ever been — 205 pounds, much of it in rippling muscles — then broke two tackles on the kickoff that opened the second half and returned the ball 54 yards to the Lenoir-Rhyne 45. Suddenly, for a moment, the season seemed not so dismal to Forbes. Later, when Lamar intercepted a pass, juggled it briefly, and then returned it 39 yards for a touchdown, victory was assured. Guilford won 31-15.

Already the team had won one more game than its coach had predicted.

In the second game against Davidson College, Pernell made three dramatic, important plays. When Davidson punter Jay Poag went back to kick, Pernell sensed a fake play and instead of dropping deep to return the kick, he rushed toward the line of scrimmage and cut Poag down for a three-yard loss, setting up a touchdown that gave Guilford a 17-0 lead at halftime. But Davidson struck for a touchdown on its first possession of the second half and seemed to be on the verge of a comeback until Pernell returned the ensuing kickoff 74 yards, a play followed by a field goal. Once again Davidson came back, however, scoring a touchdown on its first possession of the final period. Trying for two points on the conversion attempt with a pass play, Davidson was hoping to draw to within six points, but Pernell made a sensational diving end-zone catch for an interception. Later in the period, Brent Tart, a junior who also had played at South Johnston High School and who had come to Guilford at Pernell's urging, scored on a 70-yard run in the final period giving the Quakers their second victory in two games, this one 27-12.

Tart and Pernell were the heroes of the game, and their pictures were carried side-by-side in Greensboro's News & Record the next day. Pernell was enrolled in a co-operative German class across town at Bennett College that semester, and when the class met on Monday following the Davidson game, the professor noted that a sports hero was present.

"I saw your picture in the paper, Mister Jefferson," said the professor. "Congratulations on a fine game. But that picture sure doesn't look like you."

"It wasn't," the student said. "The paper got the wrong picture."

In Guilford's third game of the season with Fayetteville State University, Pernell was once again the team's undisputed hero. Twice he intercepted passes as Fayetteville State was threatening to score. And with his team trailing 7-3 at halftime, he returned the second half kickoff 74 yards, making it possible for Johnny Hines to score two plays later, giving Guilford a lead it wouldn't lose.

A week later, Guilford defeated Emory & Henry, 13-0, and the team that was not expected to win a game all season was still undefeated after four weeks. When the weekly NAIA national rankings were published the following Monday, Guilford was listed at No. 8. Neighboring Elon College, with two national championships already tucked in the school's trophy case, was ranked No. 2. Only five days later the two long-time rivals would meet once again.

A decade later, Pernell still could recall the fine details of that day.

"As we came out of the dressing room to warm up, I remember we had to walk right past where Elon's wide receivers were warming up, and their receivers coach (Hornsby Howell Jr.) spoke to Lamar and me. He said, 'Well, Mr. Jefferson and Mr. Boykin, I hope you will take it easy on our little ol' receivers today.'

"That's when I knew they had focused on me and Lamar in practice. I said, 'Coach, I'm afraid your guys are in for a long day.'"

But for a time, it would seem to be a long day for the Quakers instead. Guilford's jittery offense fumbled the ball twice deep in its own territory early in the game, and twice the Quaker defense held Elon to field goals for an early 6-0 lead by Elon.

Later, Guilford coach Charlie Forbes would say, "I never thought we'd be able to sustain a long touchdown drive against them." But in the second quarter, quarterback Doug Kenworthy marched the Quakers 57 yards to a touchdown that would give Guilford a surprising 7-6 lead at the half.

There had been two big plays in the drive. The first was a 30-yard run by tailback Terry Jones that moved the ball deep into Elon territory. There, Elon began to stiffen, pushing the Quakers back on two successive downs so that Guilford faced a crucial third-and-12 at the Elon 18. Kenworthy went for the touchdown. Dropping back to pass, he found receiver Doug Rine all alone in the end zone for the score.

With Pernell and Lamar playing well in the defensive secondary, the game settled into a defensive struggle. But Elon regained the lead late in the third period when fullback Gary Pierce carried several would-be Guilford tacklers with him five yards into the end zone. In a play that would become very important, Elon went for two points on the conversion attempt and failed. The score stood 12-7 in Elon's favor.

For a time, that seemed enough. With less than seven minutes to play and facing a crucial third down, Kenworthy kept the ball on a scramble in an attempt to pick up the needed five yards for a first down. He got only one, and Guilford faced a fourth-and-four situation.

But an Elon player was charged with unsportsmanlike conduct after the play. The 15-yards penalty gave Guilford a first down and hope. A pushing penalty would later cost the Christians five more yards on a third-and-ten situation. And when Kenworthy found flanker Reggie Peace on an 18-yard pass play, Guilford had a first down at the Elon 11 with 5:27 left to play.

Moments later, Kenworthy dramatically kept the ball on a scramble play that left Guilford just a yard short of the Elon end zone on first down.

For three plays in a row, Elon's defense was magnificent, stopping the Quakers for no gain. But on fourth down, Guilford running back Johnny Hines leaped over both lines at right tackle and tumbled into the end zone for the touchdown. Guilford had a 13-12 lead with just three minutes and 11 seconds to play.

Elon had another chance to win in the closing seconds of the game. At the Guilford 31-yard line with eight seconds to play, Elon only needed a 48-yard field goal to win, but Elon head coach Mackey Carden knew that his kicker had never hit one from that far.

He called instead for a short pass to the sideline and a quick step out of bounds to stop the clock. With luck, Elon would pick up eight to ten yards, moving the ball within range for a field goal with two or three seconds left for the attempt.

But it was Guilford that got lucky on the play.

When Elon quarterback Sam Fromhart took the snap and quickly dropped back to pass, he collided with one of his own players. Thrown off balance, Fromhart struggled to regain his footing but suddenly felt the pressure of an on-rushing Quaker lineman. In his attempt to elude the tackler, Fromhart lost control of the ball. Before Fromhart could recover, the eight seconds had ticked away and the game had come to an end.

Guilford had one of the most important victories in the college's history, and roommates Lamar and Pernell had been among the defensive stars. Lamar had intercepted an Elon pass to stop one scoring threat, and Pernell had made seven solo tackles.

In the excitement of the victory, Pernell ripped off his helmet and grabbed Lamar in a bear hug, then he rushed off to hug several other teammates and finally Coach Saunders. Although he'd had no dazzling returns or interceptions, he thought that he had played the best game of his life. While the celebration on the field was dying down, he felt a tug at the sleeve of his jersey and turned to see a silver-haired woman dressed in Elon College colors.

"Mister Jefferson," she said. "I must tell you that watching you play today was certainly worth the price of admission." Then she was gone. But her words lingered. A decade later Pernell still considered them to be one of his greatest compliments as a football player.

Head Coach Charlie Forbes told Greensboro sportswriter Tom Northington that this win had been his best in his 11 years at Guilford. When the national NAIA rankings were announced two days later, Guilford had moved up to No. 4. Elon had dropped to seventh.

A week after the Elon game, Guilford beat Bridgewater College 35-7. The game was so one-sided that Charlie Forbes used four quarterbacks, including three freshmen. The Quakers were suddenly 6-0. Only once in the past ten years had Guilford won as many as six games in a single season. On Monday, the team became No. 3 in the national rankings.

"People yell at me from across campus now, 'Congratulations, coach!'" Charlie Forbes told a reporter that week. "We're beginning to become known, and that has never happened here before."

Pernell, the team's star, was getting even more attention than his coach, enjoying a fame few athletes, including M.L. Carr and Lloyd Free, had ever known at Guilford. He knew that his contributions to the team were far greater than his own remarkable plays. He had encouraged other key members of the team to begin using steroids, and many of them had followed his example with similar gains in strength. Although he had lost precise count, Pernell later estimated that more than 20 of his teammates were stacking steroids.

Pernell and his teammates had become campus heroes. But that was about to end. On an Indian summer Saturday at the end of October, Guilford's offense fumbled the ball six times in a game against Hampden-Sydney College and watched as three of those fumbles turned into scores for their opponents. Hampden-Sydney won 31-17.

Since the victory over Elon, Forbes had been worried about just such a game, and now the coach got tough. He lectured his players about commitments and goals, never telling them that his own expectations had been so low in late summer. And the following Saturday, he stormed through the dressing room ranting and raving at halftime with his team trailing Salisbury State 14-7. His lecture worked. In the final 30 minutes of the game, Guilford scored 31 points and safety Tim Everhart intercepted two passes to post another victory, 38-21. Once again, Guilford's prospects as an NAIA playoff team looked good.

Though Pernell was still playing well, he had not had the dramatic impact that he'd had at the beginning of the season. In the next game against Catawba, he recovered a fumble deep in Guilford territory to stop one threat, but it wasn't enough. Catawba, which had lost five games in a row, upset the

Quakers 19-17, eliminating any possibility that Guilford would be selected for the national playoffs.

The season ended dismally on a chilly Saturday in Athens, West Virginia, where Concord College beat Guilford 21-9. Guilford's only touchdown came on a 90-yard kickoff return by Pernell in the fourth quarter.

Pernell's season had been sterling, even if his team's had not. He was the leading punt returner in the nation, and he soon would be named to the NAIA All-American team for 1984. He even had made a dramatic comeback academically and was carrying a grade point average of just less than 3.0 in his physical education major, though the grades on his other subjects remained low.

Because he had had an outstanding season, Pernell's photograph appeared once more in the *News & Record* and his German professor at Bennett College once again took note of it.

"Well, Mister Jefferson, may I congratulate you on a fine football season," he said after a class in mid-November. "I see, though, that the newspaper once again ran the wrong picture."

"I saw that."

"Sir, whoever you are, I perhaps can accept that the newspaper may have made such a mistake once. But I cannot accept that it would happen twice. I do not believe that you are Pernell Jefferson. Who are you?"

The conversation ended abruptly. The student gathered his books and left. The Bennett College professor reported the incident to the Guilford College administrators.

9

Trouble in Chapel Hill

After her graduation, Susan Demos had moved to Chapel Hill, where she had taken a job with a grocery brokerage company and had moved into an apartment near the campus of the University of North Carolina. She had continued seeing Pernell, although far less frequently, and had attended most of his football games in his final season at Guilford. Although she continued to suffer from his periodic outbursts of violence and verbal abuse, she remained devoted to him, and after he was named All-American, she bought a used, low-mileage Datsun 240, adorned it with a personalized license plate — NAIA A-A — and drove it to Guilford College, where she presented the keys to Pernell.

This was not the only gift he received in the wake of his fine season and subsequent honors. He also was wearing a big, crested gold ring bearing the inscription NAIA All-American. The continuing adulation gave him a swagger and confidence that he'd never known before, so much so that he didn't seem concerned when in December he was notified that he would have to appear before a faculty committee investigating honor code violations involving his German class at Bennett College, charges which could result in his expulsion from Guilford. Indeed, Pernell responded by threatening to "blow the lid off this place" if administrators pressed the matter.

After learning of the threat, a member of the committee informed athletic director Herb Appenzeller and invited him to take part in the hearing, which was convened in an oak-paneled room in the administration building. Sitting at a table facing the committee, Pernell brazenly attempted to carry through with his threat.

"Ever since I've been at Guilford, people have given me money," he said, knowing that such revelations, if made public, could bring censure and disrepute to the school's athletic program and to the college itself.

He took the big gold ring from his finger and held it up for all to see.

"One influential alumnus gave me this ring a few days ago," he said. "Another has given me a car...."

"Mister Chairman," Herb Appenzeller called out, interrupting the meeting. "May I request a brief recess so that I can speak privately to Mister Jefferson? It will take no more than five minutes, and then we can continue."

"Any objections?" the chairman of the committee asked. No one responded.

"Five minutes," the chairman said.

Appenzeller and Pernell retreated to a nearby room. Appenzeller did the talking. Forcefully.

"Pernell," he said, "I know you're lying. I expect you to go back in there and tell the truth, no matter what the truth is. If you keep lying there's nothing I can do to help you. If you tell the truth, I will do everything I can to help you get through this. Do you understand?"

"Yes sir," Pernell said, suddenly contrite.

"Then, let's go."

Pernell was a different person when he returned to the hearing room.

"The truth is," he told the committee, "a girlfriend gave me this ring. Another girlfriend gave me the car to use. It's not even mine. And no one has ever given me any money. I've worked in the summer and during the off-season for my money." Indeed, Pernell had become so proficient in the art of weightlifting that several Greensboro spas employed him parttime as an instructor for much of the year.

Pernell then admitted that he had persuaded a friend to pose for him in his German classes. He apologized and asked for another chance.

Pernell waited outside the meeting room while the committee discussed his case. It seemed to take much of the morning. When Pernell was called back into the room, he was let off with a light sentence. The committee expelled him but suspended the expulsion and allowed him to continue his classes during his final semester on condition that he take another German class, this time at Guilford. If he completed the course, maintaining a C average, the expulsion would be removed from his record. He quickly accepted the decision.

While Pernell had won a reprieve, Susan had not.

When she came to Greensboro driving a car Pernell did not recognize, he asked her about it. She attempted to sidestep the question. Later, though, he confronted her about it.

"I know about your car," he said. "I found out what happened."

Susan said nothing.

"Get your coat on," Pernell ordered.

"Where're we going?" she asked.

"We're going to Chapel Hill."

Outside, the early spring day had turned leaden and the temperature was dropping. Freezing rain began falling as Pernell followed Susan to Chapel Hill, and ice began forming on power lines and tree limbs. By the time they arrived, even the ground was frozen over.

Susan was filled with dread, but when they got to her apartment, Pernell said little. It was as almost as though he had forgotten why they had made the trip. Still, Pernell was in a dark mood, and that always made her wary. She settled in a chair and picked up a book.

"Where's your car?" Pernell asked a few minutes later.

"I thought you said you'd found out what happened to it," she responded.

"I want you to tell me about it," he said.

"I let a friend borrow it."

Pernell let the subject drop for a while, but he soon returned to it.

"When's she going to bring your car back?"

"He," she said, correcting him.

"What did you say?"

"I said it's a he, not a she."

"Who is he?" Pernell pressed.

"Just a friend of mine."

Susan realized that the conversation had gone too far. She knew the pattern all too well. First questions. Then anger. Then calm, followed by gentler questions, as if she were a child and he the father. Then anger again. And violence. Inevitable violence.

"Well, when's *he* going to bring your car back?" Pernell asked.

"Pernell, it'll be a while," she said, trying to diffuse the issue.

"Call him and tell him you want it back right now."

"I can't."

"Why not?"

"He can't bring it home right away because there was a little accident. He wrecked the car."

Pernell exploded.

"You stupid bitch!" he shouted into her face. "You nigger whore!"

He ranted on before suddenly calming himself.

"Okay," he said. "Let's go over this again. What, exactly, did you do?"

"I loaned my car to a friend."

"And what happened?"

"He had a little wreck."

As his inquisition continued, Pernell grew angrier and angrier, the veins in his neck bulging, and as Susan steeled herself for the inevitable, he yanked her from her chair and tossed her across the floor. Quickly he was on her, pinning her shoulders to the floor with his knees.

He slapped her, then hit her again, this time with his fist. Once more his fist smashed into her face. This time the ring on his right hand, a ring Ruth had given him, cut into her flesh just above her left eye. She felt searing pain as she struggled to free herself. Suddenly, she broke away, made a dash for the door, and ran down the steps toward the parking lot. But Pernell was right behind her. He caught her on the small lawn and threw her to the ice-coated ground. The hit was vicious, but Pernell didn't stop with that. He grabbed her head and ground her face into the ice. She felt as if a dozen knives were slicing her brow, cheeks and nose.

Still enraged, Pernell lifted her from the ground, spun her around to face him, and saw the blood streaming from her face. She wanted to cry. Instead, she stared into Pernell's face, not bothering to wipe the blood away, forcing him to see what he had done. Even as the blood began to flow into her eyes, she did not blink. She saw Pernell's rage evaporate from his face almost instantly, and she started to cry. He lifted her sobbing into his arms, carried her to his car and drove her to the nearby university hospital, where an emergency room doctor stitched closed a gaping wound over Susan's left eye.

"How'd this happen?" the doctor asked as he worked.

"Just a little disagreement."

"Your husband or boyfriend?"

"Boyfriend," she said after a moment of hesitation.

"You'll have quite a scar there," he told her when he had finished. "But almost all of it will be hidden by your eyebrow and I don't think anyone will be able to see it."

"Thanks," she said but she was thinking something else: *I have lots of scars nobody sees.*

"Now, I'm not going to admit you to the hospital, but I want you to remain here in the room for a while until the anesthesia wears off," the doctor said. "A nurse will be by in a bit to check on you."

Excusing himself, he left the room. Within 30 minutes, a Chapel Hill police officer arrived and began to question Susan. Reluctantly, she told him what Pernell had done.

"Where is he now?" the officer asked.

"I think he's in the waiting room."

The officer told Susan that he had to charge Pernell with assault, but she pleaded with him not to do it. "If you do, he'll beat me. I won't testify against him, and I won't press charges."

The the officer told her that he had no choice. He arrested Pernell in the waiting room and took him to a magistrate's office, where he was quickly released on his own recognizance. He returned to the hospital and drove Susan home, but he didn't beat her.

"It was as though he had done what he had to do and it was over," she recalled years later. "He didn't talk about it. That's the way it always was. It was as though I had behaved in a way he felt was not appropriate, and he had had to punish me."

Two weeks later, Pernell returned to Chapel Hill, where a judge found him guilty of assault and fined him $200. Susan paid the fine.

10

The Pro Treatment

Pernell thought that his football career had ended, but soon after the incident in Chapel Hill, Tommy Saunders called to tell him that two National Football League scouts, one from the Cleveland Browns, the other from the New York Jets, had asked to see game films featuring him.

"Stay ready," his former coach told him. Pernell had continued his weightlifting, but now he intensified his daily workouts, adding 40-yard sprints to his regimen. Excited that he might become a professional football player, Susan occasionally timed his sprints and ran with him, encouraging him. Pernell also adjusted his daily intake of steroids, adding to the stack, reaching for more strength.

Within a day of each other, the two scouts arrived on campus. Each discussed Pernell's abilities with his coaches, then met with Pernell and timed him in the 40-yard dash, a standard procedure in the NFL.

Both the Browns and the Jets had been attracted by Pernell's ability to return kicks, but both saw his potential beyond special teams work. The Jets talked to Pernell about moving to the offensive backfield as a halfback. New York's star running back, Freeman McNeil, had suffered an injury late in the 1984 season, and the Jets were looking for someone who could back him up. Pernell would be used primarily on third-down situations, he was told.

But the Jets' scout had something else he wanted to talk about.

"How long you been on 'em?" he asked.

"On what?" Pernell said, trying to appear innocent.

"Steroids."

Pernell never had been honest with his college coaches about his steroid use, but this was another matter. His future, he now knew, could be riding on his answer.

"How'd you know?" he asked, choosing not to dodge the issue.

"Oh, there are always signs. Your build. Your stamina. The puffiness in your face. That sort of thing. Adds up to steroids; probably for a long time."

"More than two years," Pernell confessed. "Closer to three."

The Browns wanted to use Pernell to return kicks, an area in which their needs were acute, and as a weak-side defensive back. If their scout detected steroid signs, nothing was said.

Pernell was uncertain about his chances after meeting with the scouts. He was certain that he had ruined his chances with the Jets by admitting his steroid use, and he didn't want to let his hopes get too high about the Browns. But Saunders thought he had a chance as a kick returner and encouraged him to stay ready. On May 4, only days after his meeting with the scouts, both teams telephoned contract offers through Saunders within 15 minutes of each other. Though both offers called for a $45,000 base salary, there were substantial potential differences. The Jets would write Pernell a check for $1,200 for signing and would include production clauses, most based upon games played and yards gained. The Browns would pay $1,500 for signing and would add $10,000 if Pernell were on the roster on opening day, another $5,000 if he earned a place on the NFL's all-rookie team, plus various incentives based upon performance. Both teams said they needed a quick decision.

Saunders called Pernell's dormitory room, where he and Lamar were packing for summer break. Pernell was getting ready to go to Benson to visit his son, and he and Lamar were talking about getting together afterward when the phone rang.

"It's for you, Pernell," Lamar announced. "Coach Saunders."

Saunders couldn't contain his excitement.

"Both of 'em want you," he practically shouted into the phone.

Pernell excitedly jotted down the figures as Saunders read them off. Saunders had to remove the phone from his ear when his star defensive back yelled the news to Lamar. Pernell was soon on his way to Saunders' office, where he called his mother.

"Mama, I've got a chance to play in the NFL," he told her.

"Where?" she asked. Pernell could hear the excitement in her voice.

"Cleveland or the Jets," he answered.

"Where are the Jets?" she asked, almost breathless.

"New York, Mama."

There was a brief silence on the other end of the line. "You sign with Cleveland," she said, surprising Pernell. "I don't want my baby in a big city like New York."

Pernell also tried to call Susan at the food brokerage office where she worked but couldn't reach her.

For the next 30 minutes, he and Saunders weighed his options. In the end, Pernell chose the Browns, not because his mother had wanted to keep him out of New York, but because the Browns played on grass and wanted him for the position he had played at Guilford.

At 11:30, he called home again.

"Mama," he said, "I'm signing with the Browns."

"I'm proud of you, Pernell," she told him, then laughed. "You can take care of Mama for a while now."

Quickly, Pernell had his agent, Tom Martinelli of Yonkers, N.Y., phone his decision to both the Jets and the Browns. Within minutes, the Browns were on the phone to Saunders. They had made a reservation for Pernell on a 1 p.m. flight to Cleveland through Charlotte. Pernell grabbed a bag from his room, and Saunders rushed him to the nearby airport for the short hop to Charlotte.

When he boarded a second plane at Charlotte and took his seat, an athletic-looking young man in the seat beside him introduced himself.

Unable to hide his pride, Pernell told him that he'd just signed with the Browns and was on his way to Cleveland.

"Maybe we'll make the team together," said Greg Allen, an acclaimed running back from Florida State who'd been chosen as Cleveland's No. 1 pick in the second round of the draft. When the plane landed in Cleveland, TV cameras and reporters were waiting for Allen and Pernell basked in the deflected attention.

A white limousine whisked the two young football players to comfortable rooms in the Helmsley Hotel in Berea, Ohio, and that night Pernell called Susan in Chapel Hill.

"Guess where I am," he said teasingly.

Sensing the excitement in his voice, she tried to be imaginative, but nothing unusual came to mind, and after a couple of lame guesses, Pernell suddenly blurted, "Ohio."

"The Browns flew me up this afternoon. Tomorrow morning I sign a contract with the Cleveland Browns and I'll be here for the rest of the week in their mini-camp."

Susan shrieked with joy. "She was so, so proud of me," he later wrote to a friend. "She really loved me."

Browns players were required to be in mini-camp for three days, but could stay as long as five. Pernell stayed for the full five and spent much time talking with two of the NFL's best defensive backs, Hanford Dixon and Frank Minnifield, hoping to get tips that would help him make the team. "They even taught me how to cheat by holding the jersey of the receiver," Pernell said. "Those two guys took a liking to me."

Chris Rockins and Don Rogers, second-year defensive backs from Oklahoma State and UCLA respectively, also took to Pernell, inviting him to parties twice.

When the camp ended, Pernell flew home with the $350 he had been paid for the five days, plus his $1,500 signing bonus.

"I sent part of it home to Mama," he later recalled.

Back in Greensboro, Pernell drove immediately to Chapel Hill, and that night he took Susan to their favorite Chinese restaurant and told her about his week. She'd never seen him so excited or happy. This, she thought, might be the start of a new life for her and Pernell.

11

The End of Dreaming

Susan had regularly reminded Pernell how important a college degree would be after his football playing days had ended, but at the end of his senior year, Pernell still needed six credit hours to complete his degree in physical education. Until the offer had come from the Browns, he had planned to attend summer school with his friend Lamar, but his pro contract changed that plan. His degree would have to wait.

After the mini-camp, Pernell moved in with Susan in Chapel Hill. He had eight weeks to get ready for rookie camp, which would open at Lakeland Community College in Mentor, Ohio, in late July. Susan became his personal trainer, accompanying Pernell almost every evening to the soccer fields on the campus of the University of North Carolina, where she pushed him like a drill sergeant.

Although he was anxious about training camp, with Susan's encouragement, Pernell was growing more confident by the day.

"I did not have any doubt about making the team," he said years later.

Big changes lay ahead for Susan as well as Pernell. A little more than a month after he was to report to training camp, Susan would be moving to Miami to work on a master's degree in sports administration at St. Thomas University.

She saw her move as a chance to start over. Her feelings about Pernell were in conflict. She wanted to be away from him and make a life of her own, but she still loved him, too, and knew that she would miss him.

On the night before Pernell was to leave, he and Susan had dinner at the Chinese restaurant where they had become regulars and spent the evening talking about where the future might take them. It was clear that Pernell saw her as part of his life for a long time to come, but she was careful not to make any long-term promises.

The next morning, Pernell held Susan in a long, intense embrace.

"I'm proud of you," she whispered, then stood watching as he drove off to
Greensboro to catch the flight to Cleveland.

Pernell thought the Lakeland campus where rookie camp was being
held looked a lot like Guilford's. But here he was no hero; nobody paid him
any special attention. Yet, after a quick assessment of his competition, he
thought his chances of making the team were good.

During the 1984 season, former Boston College star wide receiver
Brian Brennan had been used as Cleveland's primary punt returner. But the
Browns, the last of the great tight end teams (the incomparable Ozzie Newsome
gained more than 1,000 yards as a receiver in 1984), wanted Brennan to take
a bigger role in the team's offensive plans. He was too valuable as a wide
receiver to risk injury as a punt returner.

Running back Earnest Byner, whose college career Pernell had followed at East Carolina University in Greenville, N.C., had been Cleveland's
workhorse on kickoff returns. The Browns entered training camp hoping to
find a return specialist who could save wear and tear on him as well.

Pernell had done both at Guilford College, and on at least one level,
he had done it better than anyone in the nation.

The Browns also had brought in free agent Todd St. Louis out of tiny
Augustana College in South Dakota as a kick return candidate. Nebraska's
Shane Swanson, who had been drafted in the 12th round, was also a potential
punt returner.

Wide receiver Bruce Davis, a nine-year veteran out of Purdue, had
been the team's second leading kickoff return specialist in 1984 and was still
there if needed. Wide receiver Nate Johnson, who had played briefly in the
Canadian Football League, rounded out the list of players who would get
chances to return kicks in training camp.

In the early days at camp, Pernell also worked as a defensive back
just as he had done in mini-camp back in May, taking his turn with Minnifield,
Dixon and the rest of the veterans.

His first phone calls to Susan were hopeful, full of enthusiasm. He
had broken up a pass to Ricky Feacher, and the coaches had noticed, he reported. And he had stepped in front of Dwight Walker for an interception in
another practice session.

"I'm having a good camp. I think they're beginning to notice," he
told her one night in late July. "I've figured this thing out. Know what I do? I
study one of the wide receiver's playbooks. So when they come on a pass
pattern, I know about where they're going to make their move and where
they're likely to break off a pattern. And I get there.

"I've been jumping their bones. I got 'em wondering how in the world

70

a rookie free agent from little Guilford College can run man-to-man like that." Susan loved the boyish enthusiasm that now filled Pernell's voice.

All those evenings back in Chapel Hill when perspiration had poured from his body as he prepared for this week were now paying off, he told Susan. He knew that he was in the best condition of his life, and his confidence was at a peak. He felt strong enough to control his own destiny. Indeed, he felt so strong that he made a remarkable decision. For the first time in almost five years, he quit using steroids. Cold turkey.

All NFL players had been warned that concern about the use of illegal drugs might soon prompt drug testing, and Pernell wanted to make certain that if testing came about, a positive finding wouldn't threaten his budding career. Steroids had helped get him to this point, he reasoned, but he would do it on his own from here. It would be years before he would learn that stopping use of the drugs suddenly could have serious, even devastating consequences.

Marty Schottenheimer, the Browns' head coach, reminded Pernell of his college coach, Charlie Forbes. They both were about the same size, on the short side, like Pernell. Both were well built, even though their playing days were long past; and both had the same fair complexions and sandy hair, neatly trimmed. Neither smiled much. Quiet and strong, Schottenheimer, like Forbes, was a man who talked little but seemed to miss nothing. Pernell wondered if Schottenheimer even knew his name, until an incident in the training room following practice one day.

"Jefferson!" Schottenheimer called out forcefully. Everyone in the room turned to look.

"Yes, sir," Pernell responded loudly, as if he were a Marine recruit.

"Do you love football, Jefferson?" the head coach shouted, his voice echoing.

"Yes, sir!" Pernell responded enthusiastically.

"Attaboy, Jefferson," Schottenheimer said, then was gone. Some of the veteran players only smiled. At that moment Pernell felt like a rookie and wished Schottenheimer had not chosen him.

For two weeks, the Browns practiced twice daily in the hot Ohio sun, scrimmaging several times each week, and day by day, Pernell's optimism waned. He was beginning to feel weak and a step too slow. At first, he blamed the pace of the practice sessions, and the dining room conversations he had with other players made him feel that he was not alone.

When Schottenheimer gave his team a two-day break in the middle of training camp, Pernell flew home. His brother Willie met him at the airport.

"Man, this is different," he said on the drive from the Raleigh-Durham Airport to Benson. "I don't think I can make it. All these guys are bigger and faster than I am. This is a different league."

Willie had never seen his brother like this. For as long as he could remember, Pernell had been an optimist. For years, Willie thought there was nothing Pernell could not do. But this was a different Pernell. He had suddenly changed, and he seemed almost fearful.

Pernell visited for only a few hours, then began the long drive back to training camp in a new gold Pontiac Fiero that he had purchased in late spring when he had been so full of hope. After he left, Willie told his mother, "Pernell's going to quit."

"No, son," she said. "Pernell has never been a quitter."

"He will be this time, Mama. I just don't think Pernell would have taken that car if he thought he was going to make the team. I think he took the car because he's thinking about coming back home."

Back in camp, Pernell felt homesick for the first time in his life. He felt alone, and he began falling into a depression that grew deeper and darker as the days went on, but he didn't connect it to his abstinence from steroids.

As his depression worsened, Pernell began to think that he didn't belong. He thought about P.J., Susan, Lamar and wanted to see them. He began to wish that he'd stayed in Greensboro, gone to summer school and finished his degree. His legs felt heavy on the field, and he worried that his strength was failing. After practice one day, Nate Johnson, a second-year wide receiver who was battling Pernell for one of the kick return positions, fell in beside him.

"How ya doin'?" Johnson asked.

"I ought to be doing better," Pernell said, not bothering to hide the pessimism he felt.

"Rookie," Johnson said, "you looked around yet?"

"What do you mean?" Pernell asked.

"I mean, take a look at who's here," Johnson said, speaking low, as though he wanted no one else to hear. "We're all superstars up here, man. Guys from big schools. Guys who have played pro football. Where'd you say you went to school?"

"Guilford College," Pernell answered.

"Where?"

"Guilford College, in Greensboro, North Carolina."

"What's a Guilford College, man? Never heard of it. Listen, guys from small schools like that just ain't going to make it here." Johnson said.

Unaware that Johnson himself was from tiny Hillsdale College, Pernell felt his spirits sinking. He never knew if the conversation with Johnson was a classic rookie put-down, or if the former Canadian Football League veteran was merely practicing a bit of reverse psychology in an effort to lead him out of the doldrums. At the time, Johnson's motivation didn't matter, his words sent Pernell's mood spiraling downward.

"Susan, I ain't going to make it," he said over the phone that night.

"You've got to give yourself a chance," she said, pleading. "It's only been — what — two weeks?"

Even through the long distance line, she could feel the depression in his voice. She had seen it coming, mentally charting his moods that had been growing darker with each call. Now this. This was a Pernell she had never known. Something had changed drastically.

For more than three years, Pernell had told her again and again that she wasn't good enough, that he was the important one, because athletics made him special. Now he was saying that he wasn't good enough and the sound of it frightened Susan. Pernell, she realized, had lost all his swagger. Susan took no joy in the realization that the tables were now turned.

"Listen, you've got what it takes," she said, attempting to encourage him. They talked for a long time, Pernell mostly listening. But nothing Susan said seemed to lift his spirits.

As soon as she had hung up, Susan called Lamar.

"I'm worried," she said, going on to fill him in on her conversation with Pernell. "Call and see if you can cheer him up."

Later that night, in separate calls, Susan and Lamar offered to drive to Ohio and stay as long as necessary to see Pernell through this crisis, although doing so could endanger Lamar's standing in his senior season on the football team and Susan would have to postpone her plans to get her master's degree. But Pernell rejected their offers. Over and over, they reminded him that he was at an important crossroads in his life, but he seemed not to hear them.

The Browns already were making the first roster cuts, and as Pernell dressed for practice each morning, he couldn't help but notice the freshly emptied lockers that stood as symbols of lost dreams.

He imagined what it would be like to be told that there would be no place for him on the team, and he couldn't help but wonder if he truly loved football as much as he had assured Marty Schottenheimer that he did.

"What if I get cut?" he asked Susan on the phone. Until now, Pernell had been a star athlete all his life, from the very youngest baseball teams back in Benson through his three-sport high school career at South Johnston High School, and on through four sometimes rocky seasons at Guilford. Until now, however, the possibility that he might not be good enough had never occurred to him. Now it seemed to haunt him, spoiling his sleep and stealing his appetite.

"That's probably not going to happen," she said. "But if it does, you'll make it with somebody. Cleveland's not the only football team. The Jets offered you a contract, too. If you get cut at Cleveland, give the Jets a call. You'll be all right."

For the first time since she had known him, Pernell seemed to be a frightened little boy filled with uncertainty.

"I'm coming home," he told her.

"No, you're not, Pernell. You can do this." Susan tried to sound strong, insistent, almost parental.

"I'll try," he said without enthusiasm. That night, Pernell tossed sleeplessly in bed, wondering how he would react when the knock came at his door and the runner said, "Coach wants to see you, and bring your playbook," the cursed words of certain failure in NFL training camps.

Well before dawn, he decided that he would not allow that to happen to him. He climbed from bed, pushed his belongings into a bag and walked out of the dormitory without awakening any of the other players. In the dead of night, Pernell drove away from his dream.

"I had to cut myself before some coach cut me," he said years later. "I'm not sure I could have taken it if somebody had told me I wasn't good enough to make the team."

Years later, Willie Jefferson reflected about his brother's decision that night.

"Pernell carried not only his hopes, but the hopes of all of us when he went to training camp," Willie said. "The deal was that he got some money to sign — not a lot like a draft choice gets, but a little money. And if he made the team, he'd get $55,000 his rookie season.

"In Benson, $55,000's a lot of money. I'd hate to think how many years Mama would have had to work to earn $55,000. But that's what Pernell walked away from."

For a moment, Willie fell silent.

"He needed his Daddy," Willie said softly. "He needed a male figure in his life right then more than he ever needed it before, and I was too young to fulfill that role. He needed a man to talk sense to him, somebody to say to him, 'Pernell, you can't quit now because this is what your mother walked through rain and sleet and snow to run two jobs for, just so you could go to school and play sports and get a chance at something a lot better.' But there was no one to say that."

It would be years before Pernell learned that the Browns were close to a decision to keep him. Indeed, hoping that he might change his mind, the team had carried him on its protected list through the 1986 season so that no other team could sign him.

But by the time the coaches realized he was gone, he was well on his way to Greensboro, where later that day, he pulled into a parking space in front of a familiar fitness center where he used to train and where he had been a part-time instructor. Through the plate glass windows he could see perhaps a dozen people straining against weight machines, the very machines upon which he had grown strong.

Thirty minutes later, he emerged from the building carrying a small box containing a fresh supply of anabolic steroids.

Then he drove to Chapel Hill, waited for Susan's work day to end and knocked on the door. In spite of their intense telephone conversations of recent days, she had not expected to find him there, and in anger and disappointment, she slammed the door in Pernell's face.

12

"Daddy, Don't Hurt Susan"

Soon after Pernell returned to North Carolina, his agent, Tom Martinelli, tracked him down by phone in Greensboro.

"Pernell, what happened?" Martinelli asked.

"I just walked, man."

"Well, it's not too late. I've been talking to the Browns and they want you back. You've got twenty-four hours to get back to camp."

"I just don't have it, man," Pernell said. "Whatta they want to do, get me back into camp just so they can cut me?"

"I think you're wrong, Pernell," Martinelli said. "The Browns said I should remind you that they have the rights to your contract this year and next."

Although he had already started a new steroid cycle, Pernell still felt slow and weak.

"Tell them that I won't be coming back," he said.

As the Browns were finishing their camp, Pernell had gotten work in Greensboro with a business card company. He also took a part-time job at a trucking company. For the first time since P.J. had been born, Pernell now had time to get to know his son better.

Despite Susan's reaction to his quitting camp, she had taken Pernell back, as she always did, and one weekend, he took her to Benson to visit his family. Pernell's mother insisted that Susan sleep in her bed. Pernell slept in the bedroom in which he and Willie had grown up.

While they were there, Joann reminded her son of the incident in high school when Sarah's father had come looking for him for hitting his daughter.

"Now, Pernell, I don't ever want to hear that you laid a hand on Susan," she said. "You understand?"

If only she knew, Susan thought, but she wasn't about to tell her the truth about Pernell, who made light of the admonition.

"See," he told Susan with a laugh, "She likes you better than she likes me."

But he didn't make any promises.

In mid-August, less than two weeks before Susan was to leave for Miami, Pernell took P.J. to Chapel Hill for an evening with Susan, and, as usual, an argument soon erupted.

"I could feel the tension building," Susan remembered. "Then he started criticizing anything about me he could find to criticize. Then he became extremely polite. It was like he was just waiting, just looking for a reason, because in his eyes whatever we argued about had to be my fault."

The pain came in a flash. Pernell's right hand landed squarely against the left side of her face, staggering her. As she began to sob, P.J., frightened, also broke into tears.

Suddenly, Pernell was aware that his young son had witnessed the scene and his mood changed.

"P.J., come to Daddy," he said softly.

P.J. didn't move.

"P.J., come to Daddy."

Only reluctantly did the child move into the open arms of his father. Pernell held him close, saying nothing, until in a whimper, P.J. asked, "Daddy, do you love Susan?"

"Yes, P.J., Daddy loves Susan."

P.J. turned to Susan.

"Are you mad at Daddy?"

Still crying, Susan did not answer.

"Daddy," P.J. finally said.

"What is it, P.J.?"

"Don't hurt Susan anymore."

"I'm sorry," he said.

But the apology failed to stop his abuse. The threats and violence began to come with even more frequency, and with each new episode her will to resist grew weaker. She no longer felt that she would ever be free of Pernell, not even more than 800 miles away in Miami, and she screamed, "Either kill me or let me go."

"At that point," she recalled years later, "I would have gladly accepted either alternative."

Strangely, on that occasion, Pernell seemed to take the ultimatum with the seriousness with which it was intended. He drove her back to her apartment.

Still, Susan felt trapped by her fear of Pernell.

"He told me, 'If you leave, I'll kill you and everyone you know. If you do anything, I've got a gun.'"

Susan never knew when Pernell might show up in one of his violent moods.

She had the memory of an incident earlier that summer as confirmation. It began to develop when her company dispatched her unexpectedly to Elizabeth City, more than 150 miles from Chapel Hill on the North Carolina coast, for an emergency meeting with a group of grocery retailers.

It had been an important, spur-of-the-moment trip and Susan had not had time to let anyone know she would be away for the day. She arrived in Elizabeth City just in time to hurry into a meeting room where the grocers already had gathered. An hour into the session, the door burst open and Pernell barged into the room, his eyes darting about for Susan. In front of more than a dozen startled businessmen, he began angrily accusing her of disloyalty, chastising her for leaving Chapel Hill without telling him.

Then, as suddenly as he had come, he was gone. After a brief adjournment called to permit Susan time to gather her emotions, the meeting continued, though awkwardly.

On the long drive back to Chapel Hill, Susan kept a wary eye on her rear view mirror, expecting to see Pernell's gold Fiero appear in the darkness, but it never did.

Her despair over the hopelessness of her situation caused her to think about taking her own life. Indeed, she made what she later called "minor" attempts at it, first by cutting her wrists and later by taking an overdose of sleeping pills. Just before taking the overdose, Susan told Pernell that she was considering ending her life. "Sure," he responded without emotion. "Go ahead. That would end my misery, too."

That was not what Susan wanted to hear. More than once in recent months, Pernell had told her he, too, was thinking of suicide. Each time, she had pleaded with him not to talk foolishly. Despite the abuse, she felt that she could not live without Pernell. And now she remembered those phone calls from Ohio when Pernell thought about leaving camp and her attempts to talk him through his crisis.

As if things weren't bad enough, Susan began to suspect that she was pregnant, and an obstetrician confirmed her fear. Fearing reprisal from Pernell, she kept the news to herself. Pernell would not know for months.

Pernell had worries of his own now.

Word came that summer that Willie Thomas Jefferson, Pernell's and Willie's father, had been admitted to the University of North Carolina Hospital at Chapel Hill suffering from an incurable cancer.

For the only time in their adult lives, both Pernell and Willie visited their father together. Susan accompanied Pernell and Willie's girlfriend,

Michelle, the woman he would later marry, made the trip from Benson with him.

For a time, the four maintained an uneasy vigil in the room with the dying man. Then Pernell and Willie were alone with their father.

"I want to say something to the two of you," the father said. "I want to apologize for not being around for you when you were growing up. Your mother did a good job with you, your mother and Aunt Katie.

"I sent money when I could, but I should have been there for you. I hope you will forgive me and I hope you will do good. Just don't smoke and don't drink wine."

Though Willie would speak with his father briefly on the phone before he died in November 1986, this would be Pernell's last conversation with him.

After the visit, Pernell and Susan spoke briefly with Willie and Michelle, then walked toward their car.

"Didn't you think my Dad's a handsome man?" Pernell asked Susan.

It had been a comment Susan had not expected. "Pernell, that's the man who abandoned you and Willie and your mother a long time ago," she said. "How can you say nice things about him?"

"I know, but didn't you think he was handsome?" Pernell pressed.

"I thought he was handsome," Susan answered.

Within the month, Susan checked into a clinic and underwent an abortion. It became an important turning point in her relationship with Pernell.

"Pernell always thought that I couldn't leave him if I was pregnant," she recalled. "I'd be stuck forever."

Now, in late summer with her classes at St. Thomas drawing ever closer, she thought about the abortion from which she had quickly recovered and about what she saw as its implications for her relationship with Pernell. Severing herself from Pernell's child, she felt, perhaps meant that she could eventually end her relationship with Pernell as well. The thought gave her new hope.

Early in the third week of August, Susan backed her loaded car from its parking place in front of her Chapel Hill apartment for the last time. This time Pernell was saying goodbye to her, and as he stood watching her go, a feeling of release rushed through her.

Later, as she drove southward on I-95, she began to feel that at long last, she was leaving her tormented life behind one wonderful mile at a time. She knew now that she never wanted to see Pernell again, and the thought of leaving him forever in her past filled her with hope.

Although graduate students at St. Thomas normally lived off-campus, a room had become available in a dorm, Sullivan Hall, and Susan took it. She shared the room — 109 — with a member of the St. Thomas women's softball team, Ellen Barber.*

The change in scenery was all that Susan had hoped it would be. She felt alive again, no longer the self-imposed social outcast she had been at Guilford College. She was quickly gathering a new set of friends, something that had not happened since Pernell had come into her life. Among her new friends, in addition to Ellen, were Terri Gilmore,* Erin Collins* and Barbara Pegues,* who shared the room across the hall, Traci Vandermire,* from room 103, and Andrea Hastings* from room 105.

She learned the neighborhood surrounding the campus, the nearby shopping centers, the best Chinese restaurants. And because of her old fears, she got to know one of the St. Thomas security guards, although she thought she was being overly cautious in that. Pernell called occasionally, but there was comfort in the realization that he was far away in North Carolina. For the first time in years, days passed when she didn't think about Pernell at all, and as the months went on, she began to believe that Pernell was out of her life for good. Then on a spring day in 1986, she returned from a brief shopping trip to find a note taped to her door.

Just stopped by to see how you're doing. P.J.

Her heart dropped. "It was as though he was just in the neighborhood and thought he'd drop in," she said years later. "You know, the old neighborhood, eight-hundred miles from the neighborhood."

A day later, Pernell called to say that he was coming to see her. It wasn't a good time, she told him, trying to discourage him, fighting the feelings of dread she had not felt in months. Exams were coming up, she said, and she needed to study. Another time, maybe.

But Pernell would not be dissuaded, and she tried to make the best of it when he arrived on campus. None of her new friends, she reminded herself, knew anything about the years of terror and degradation she had known at his hands. Susan pretended that she was happy to see him, and Pernell was on his best behavior, as friendly and charismatic as he had been when she first met him. It annoyed her that her new friends liked him immediately. "They thought he was wonderful," she recalled. "I didn't tell them any different because this was my new life."

She reasoned that Pernell was only visiting and would soon be returning to North Carolina. But when she learned that he had come to Florida in hopes of finding a job, the old panic hit her. She knew that in a sense she had only herself to blame. Months earlier, during those summer days after Pernell had dropped out at the Browns camp, she had helped him blanket the southeast with resumes in a search for a high school or small college coaching job. So it should have been no surprise that he had come to Florida to follow up. After all, he had been born in Stuart and still had relatives in the state. And with Susan now in Miami, he thought that this just might be the perfect place for him.

He had several leads for high school coaching jobs, he said, and he would be around for a while. Lamar had come with him, taking a vacation, and the day before they had called at the offices of the Miami Dolphins. Pernell had introduced himself as a former player for the Browns, and said that he was looking for a tryout. The Dolphins' personnel director had thumbed through a loose-leaf binder and found Pernell's name.

"You're still under contract to the Browns," he had told him. "You're not supposed to be here, and I'm not supposed to even be talking to you. We have nothing to discuss. I suggest that if you want to try again, report to the Browns."

Susan didn't know what to do about Pernell's renewed presence, and her worry turned to desperation when he called a few days after his visit to say that he was returning for a two-day stay on Thursday, April 10, and expected to sleep in her dorm room.

"Not Thursday," she said. "Pernell, it's really not a good time."

But once again Pernell would not be put off. He would arrive sometime Thursday afternoon, he said firmly.

Suddenly, Susan had no choice but to reveal her past to two people who had become important to her. First, she called Ian James,* a fellow student and a pitcher on the university's baseball team. They had become friends and recently had begun dating. Now she told him that she would have to cancel their Thursday night date, telling him why and offering a brief description of her long and turbulent relationship with Pernell.

"I'm coming anyway," Ian said.

"Ian, please don't," she pleaded. "He's crazy. He's not normal. He'll create a scene here in the dorm if you do."

Reluctantly, Ian promised to stay away.

Now Susan closed the door to her dorm room and had a long conversation with Ellen, her roommate.

"You've got to do something for me," Susan said. "Something really important. You've got to stay right here in this room with me all the time he's here. You can't leave me. Pernell's crazy. You've got to be my rock. He won't do anything if both of us are here together."

The request presented a problem to Ellen, a member of the school's softball team. The team was in the heart of its season and was scheduled to leave Saturday morning on a two-day trip for games at other schools in South Florida.

Ellen would stay as close as she could, she promised, but had no choice but to travel with the softball team.

A day earlier, Susan had started a letter to her mother back in Winston-Salem, but interrupted by Pernell's call, she had slipped it unfinished into the top drawer of a chest in her room. That was where Pernell found it late Friday afternoon when he was alone in the room. In the letter, Susan had mentioned that a new man had come into her life.

"His name's Ian," she had written. "He's a pitcher on the baseball team and he's such a nice man. He's good to me and we enjoy being together...."

Pernell had read enough. In a jealous rage, he jammed the unfinished letter back into the drawer, slamming it shut.

Susan and Ellen had left the room only briefly. The visit had been going well, Susan thought, but she returned to the room to find that Pernell's mood had changed. She saw the anger in his face as soon as she stepped inside the room. Reaching past her, he slammed the door, barring Ellen from her own room, and without speaking, he began slapping Susan until she fell to the floor screaming.

"Why are you doing this, Pernell?" she wailed. "Why are you hurting me again?"

Susan's friends in nearby rooms heard the commotion, and Ellen finally pushed her way into the room.

"Are you all right, Susan?" Ellen called.

Screaming, Susan ran past Ellen and down the hall, with Pernell close behind. Doors sprang open up and down the hall as startled students emerged to see what was going on. Pernell caught Susan from behind, sweeping her from her feet as she continued to scream..

Terri rushed to Susan's aid, but Pernell pushed her against the wall, while he secured Susan under one strong arm.

"We're leaving," he said, sweeping Susan off the floor, "and if anybody tries to stop me, I'll kill her."

Susan's frightened friends stood back as Pernell carried her to the maroon 1981 Datsun 240 SX she had given him several years earlier. A minor traffic accident had left the fender of his gold Fiero crumpled and he had left it in Benson.

"We're going to see that boyfriend of yours," Pernell said as he pushed Susan into the car. "Where is he?"

For a moment, Susan didn't speak.

"I said, where is he?" Pernell demanded.

"He's at a baseball game," she said weakly.

"What baseball game?"

"I think they're playing at Miami Dade," she said, fear in her voice.

He sped away from the St. Thomas campus and into early evening traffic. Back in the dormitory, Andrea was dialing the number for the Metro-Dade Police Department. Moments later she was telling detective Cynthia Griglen what she and a half dozen fellow Sullivan residents had just witnessed.

Griglen sought to calm Andrea so that she could be sure what had happened.

"Who was abducted?" she asked

"Susan. Susan Demos."

"Do you know who took her?"

"Yes, ma'am. His name's Pernell Jefferson. He used to be her boyfriend."

"What does he do?" Griglen continued, rapidly jotting down the responses.

"I'm not sure," she said. "I think he's a football player."

Griglen noted the occupation. Seven months after he had walked out of the Browns training camp, Pernell once more was being called a football player by the Metro-Dade Police Department.

On the north campus of Miami Dade College, Pernell pulled into a parking lot near the baseball field.

"Okay," he told Susan, "go get Ian. But listen to me. If you make one false move, I do have a gun and I'll kill him. Do you understand?"

Susan only nodded. As she walked slowly toward the baseball field, trying to determine what to do to keep Ian from a confrontation with Pernell, no solution to her dilemma would come. She found Ian watching the game from the bullpen. He had not been scheduled to pitch on this Friday, and he was enjoying the game and the warmth of the spring sun.

"Ian," Susan called in a low voice from beyond the chain link fence against which he had been resting. He turned and immediately saw Susan's fear.

"What's wrong?" he asked urgently.

"I'm in trouble. My former boyfriend's waiting in a car. He wants to talk to you."

He went to a nearby gate and followed Susan to the parking lot, his spiked shoes clicking on the pavement. Pernell was still in the driver's seat, smiling strangely as they approached the car.

"Hi, Ian," he said, "I'm Pernell Jefferson."

Ian didn't acknowledge the greeting, instead turning to Susan and asking, "Are you okay?"

"I'm fine," she lied.

"Ian, I want to ask you something," Jefferson said. "Are you dating Susan?"

"Yeah, I guess I am," he said, trying to feel his way through this conversation in which he had unexpectedly found himself. Again he turned to Susan. "Are you sure you're all right?" he asked again, this time with more urgency.

"Yes, Ian. I'm okay." But this time Susan did not raise her eyes to meet his.

Susan thought about running, but she was held by Pernell's earlier warning that he had a gun. She worried that Ian would be killed.

"Well, Ian," Pernell said, "I just want you to know that Susan's my woman and she won't be seeing you any more."

Ian looked once more at Susan. He didn't want to make the situation worse than it already was.

"I'm not afraid of you," he finally said with an evenness that gave Susan a moment of hope. "I'm as strong as you and I'm as big as you. I won't see Susan for a while, but not for your sake, for hers."

With that, Pernell ordered Susan back into the car, revved the engine and roared away. Stunned by this eerie confrontation, Ian watched the car until it disappeared into the distance.

He turned and began a slow, thoughtful walk back to the baseball stadium where the lights were beginning to push back the night. Suddenly, as rapidly as they had departed, Pernell and Susan were back, speeding through the parking lot and coming to a skidding stop beside him.

"I've changed my mind, Ian," Pernell said, never leaving the driver's seat. "Susan's nothing but a whore and a slut and I don't want her. You can have her."

Then Pernell stamped the accelerator and they were gone again, leaving Ian puzzled by the strangeness of the encounter. He would remember later, when questioned by Detective Griglen, that Pernell's car had been a Datsun, maroon in color. But even though he had twice watched the car disappear into the distance, he had not noticed the distinctive license plate — NAIA-AA.

As Pernell turned the Datsun north on Interstate 95, he ordered Susan to remove her jewelry. After she had handed it to him, he put it into an envelope and threw it from the car.

Moments later, he hit the brakes, skidded to a stop on the shoulder and backed up until he saw the envelope. Quickly retrieving it, he shoved it into a compartment and sped northward again, finally exiting near Fort Lauderdale. Thirty minutes later, he pulled into a faded old tourist court with an ancient neon sign that had lost most of its glow.

For Susan, the terror had only begun.

13

The Solitary Rose

"Check us in," Pernell ordered.

He waited in the car while Susan walked into the office. She had a splitting headache from the beating she had taken in the dormitory room, and it had grown worse from the tension of the confrontation with Ian. Her pain and the stress over what was to come were so great that she had to fight back tears as she inquired about a room. She knew that she looked terrible, frightened and frazzled, but the desk clerk asked no questions. She returned with the key to a room at the distant end of the dark, decrepit motel, a room too isolated from the rooms of other customers, she thought. Pernell pushed the key into the lock and opened the door. He pushed Susan inside ahead of him. She could hear him sliding the security latch into place behind her. Susan had never seen such a sad and squalid room, clearly a perfect place to play out a sad and squalid relationship.

Still in a rage about Ian, Pernell began shouting insults at Susan, then slapped her repeatedly across the face before driving his fist into her midsection, causing her to double over in pain so overwhelming that she no longer could think clearly. The sickening throbbing inside her head, the spasms in her stomach had prevented her from realizing that she needed to find a way to make herself bleed so that Pernell would stop. She thought she was going to die, and she didn't care. She only wanted death to come quickly.

Now Pernell took a coat hanger from a closet. Susan thought he was going to hang his clothing on it, until he whirled and began beating her with it. With one hand, he ripped off her blouse. She felt straps digging into her back as he tore at her bra.

"Undress," he ordered.

Obediently, she pushed her shorts to her ankles, then her panties, nudging them from one small foot with the other, trembling at his gaze, feeling more exposed than she had ever been.

Without taking his eyes from her, Pernell untwisted the coat hanger and thrust one jagged end under Susan's nose.

"Now, you're going to make love to me for as long as I want you to," he said in a voice more evil than she'd ever heard, "and if you disappoint me, I'll put both your eyes out with this."

He shoved her onto the soiled bed, and she curled on her side, away from him. After he'd undressed, he grabbed her shoulder, forcing her onto her back.

"Don't hurt me," she said plaintively.

"Just do everything I tell you to do," he warned.

For hours, it seemed, he penetrated her again and again, using his brief respites to insult her as he had done so many times before.

"You're nothing but a nigger," he told her, his face in hers, then loudly demanded, "What are you?"

"Oh, Pernell, why?"

"What are you?" he yelled even louder.

"I'm your nigger."

Spent at last, Pernell rolled to the side of the bed.

"Now, get out of here," he ordered.

Susan reached to gather her clothes from the filthy, cheap carpet.

"Leave 'em," he said forcefully. Leaping from the bed and grabbing her by the arm, he pulled her toward the door, opened it and shoved her outside.

"Now find your way home. See if Ian likes you like that," he shouted.

She heard the door lock catch behind her. Holding her arms over her bruised breasts, Susan stood at the door trying to decide what to do. Then she started toward the lights of the office, but had taken only a few steps when the door swung open and Pernell shouted, "Get back in here."

She considered running but hesitated. She had thought of running from Pernell many times in the past, but fear, or something more fearsome inside her, always kept her from doing it. Whatever force had held her in the past prevailed again. She dutifully returned to the room. Pernell began beating her anew as soon as she stepped inside, her reward for obedience. After she crumpled to the floor in pain she thought she couldn't bear, Pernell fell across the bed, as if exhausted, and was soon asleep. Trying to muffle her sobbing so as not to awaken him, Susan made her way slowly to the only chair in the room and crawled into it. There she remained for the rest of the night, awake, weeping softly, bound by fear, fighting her pain. The pain seemed to be so deep inside her head that it penetrated her very soul, and it grew more intense by the hour.

At times, she listened for sounds outside, hoping for rescue, but heard none. She wondered if her friends were searching for her. Had they called the police? Had Ian perhaps noticed Pernell's distinctive license plate and reported it? Did anybody really care what was happening to her?

As she listened to Pernell's regular breathing, she looked at his dark, naked body and thought about all the money and time she had lavished on this man, about the clothing she had bought so that he would fit in at Guilford College, about the apartments she had helped furnish so he would be comfortable, about the car that she had bought for his use. She realized how wrong her judgment had been and how she hated him. Hated him for all the years she had lost. Hated him for the pain she felt in her head. Hated him for this night, especially for this night.

"I was so ashamed," she later recalled. "I was really ashamed of getting beaten. Only trashy people allow themselves to get beaten up. I wasn't a trashy person with five kids and an alcoholic husband. But I was allowing myself to be treated like a trashy person."

A thought entered her mind that she never had dreamed she could think, a thought alien to all that she had known before she knew Pernell. A thought that ran so counter to all she had been taught growing up that for a moment she found it remarkable that it even could have occurred to her. It was a simple thought: Could she kill Pernell? Kill him as he slept. And if she did, would a judge and jury understand? And if they didn't, could prison be worse than the hell she had known for the past five years? What was this very room but a prison, a torture chamber? Deep down, she knew she never could do that, but now she could understand those who did.

She watched morning break through the dirty, drooping drapes, and still Pernell slept, his strong, naked body at rest on a filthy bed. After another hour or so, he stirred, raised his head and looked at her sleepily.

"You didn't run away," he said in a way that told her this was not so much an observation as a reminder of his control.

"No, I didn't run," she said with an evenness that surprised even her.

"Get dressed," he told her after he had arisen and gone to the bathroom, and as she pulled on her clothing, trying to piece together her torn blouse, he tossed her the car keys and ordered her to get him some breakfast.

She knew that this was a test, and as she left the motel, she actually thought about driving away and never coming back, but she knew, too, that he had found her before and he would find her again. She returned shortly with coffee and an Egg McMuffin from a nearby McDonald's.

After he had eaten, Pernell withdrew a ring with a small stone from his trousers pockets, a ring he had given her before but had taken back.

"I love you," he said, holding the ring out to her.

For a moment, she didn't react, then she took it, held it in her hands and looked at it, but said nothing. It was ten in the morning, Saturday, April 12.

Now he handed her the telephone, instructing her to call her friends in the dorm and tell them exactly what he told her to say.

Andrea Hastings was first to grab the ringing dorm phone. Susan's friends had been up all night, frantic to hear something after reporting her abduction to the police. They had searched their brains for clues that might help lead the police to her and were angry at themselves that they could come up with nothing useful, not even the make or color of the car that Pernell had been driving.

At first, Andrea didn't know what to say or do as Susan recited the litany Pernell laid out for her, telling Andrea that she and her other dormmates had failed her, were no friends of hers and that she particularly never wanted anything to do with Ian again. In the background, Andrea could hear Pernell directing Susan.

"Susan," Andrea finally said, taking a chance that Pernell could hear only Susan's half of the conversation, "are you okay?"

For a moment, Susan lost control, beginning to cry, drawing an angry rebuke from Pernell.

"No," she said sternly, regaining control of her emotions, hoping that Pernell would not realize that the answer would provide Andrea some idea of her true situation.

"Can you tell me where you are?" Andrea asked.

"Of course not," she said through her tears, trying to sound hateful for Pernell's benefit.

"Is Pernell there with you?" Andrea pressed.

"What do you think?" Susan responded, pleased that she could keep a bite in her voice when she wanted so desperately to cry out for help. This was a turn in the conversation that suddenly gave her more hope than she had had in hours.

"I think he's there."

"You can count on it, Miss Hastings."

"I want you to know the police are looking for you."

"Okay, Andrea, if that's the way you feel," Susan said.

"Does Pernell have a gun?"

"I wouldn't know."

"You don't know?"

"That's what I said," Susan answered.

"Ask her if anyone has any warrants out for me," Pernell said in a loud whisper.

"Andrea, has anyone sworn out any warrants for Pernell?" she dutifully asked. Andrea knew of no warrants, nor did she know that a statewide all-points bulletin had been issued.

"Hang up," Pernell suddenly ordered.

Without saying another word, Susan placed the phone in its cradle.

"What'd she say?" he asked.

"She just said some police officer came and asked some questions but there are no warrants. Don't worry. They don't know where we are."

For a long time, Pernell was lost in thought. Though the car Ian had partially described sat outside in the small, dusty parking lot, police officers had passed along Highway A1A in front of the motel without slowing.

Pernell took his time considering his options. Noon came and went. Near one, he decided on his next move. He ordered Susan to dial the number in Sullivan Hall once again.

This time Erin Collins answered.

"Tell them that I'm going to drop you off at the Button in Fort Lauderdale," he said, referring to a well-known Fort Lauderdale oceanside park that takes up most of the 800 block of Highway A1A South.

"Erin, he's going to take me to the Button in Fort Lauderdale and let me out there," she said.

"Tell them no police. Do you understand?" Pernell said.

Susan's voice was pleading as she stressed that the presence of police might endanger her. Erin agreed.

Pernell drove, but he seemed to have no particular destination in mind. He talked little. At one point, he stopped at a flea market, asked for somebody named Ed, and talked privately with the man for nearly 30 minutes while Susan waited in the car. Together, the two men returned to the car, still talking, until they drew near enough for Susan to hear.

"What if they come to my house?" Susan now heard Ed say to Pernell.

"Who?" Pernell asked.

"The police. They'll be looking for you."

Susan could not hear Pernell's response, because he started walking away, heading for a men's room, where he left Ed waiting outside.

Susan called to the man, and he came to the car.

"You've got to help me," she pleaded. "I've got to get away from Pernell. Please do something."

"That's between you and Pernell," he said firmly. "I can't get involved."

Back in the car, Pernell drove more deliberately, finally turning south on A1A in the direction of the Button. As they neared the beachfront park, Pernell slowed, searching for signs of police. He spotted Ian James in the distance, scanning the traffic, and as he came closer, he noticed two police officers in an unmarked car not far away. Andrea, watching from a nearby vantage point, was the first to see the car with Susan inside and hurried to the waiting police to point it out. It was not yet three o'clock.

"That son of a bitch!" Pernell shouted, speeding up, bypassing the park.

"I thought you told them not to call the cops," he screamed at Susan.

"I told them, Pernell. You were sitting right there. You heard me tell 'em."

For Susan, the presence of Ian and the policemen was a frightening development and she kept looking back as Pernell weaved and dodged through traffic, hoping to outmaneuver any pursuers, but she never saw a police car coming after them. While Pernell drove aimlessly, weighing his options, Susan did something she hadn't done in recent memory. She said a silent prayer. "If You will give me the strength," she promised without speaking the words aloud, "I am not going to fear Pernell Jefferson any more. I know that at some point, I've got to make a stand and this is it...."

Pernell interrupted her thoughts.

"I've decided what we should do," he said. "We're going to get married."

"Married?" she said, startled at the suddenness of his announcement.

"Yes, married," he said excitedly, wheeling the car around.

"When?"

He smiled broadly, obviously pleased at his decision. "As soon as we can find someone to do it."

Panicking at the thought, she searched her brain for a way out.

"Pernell, you shouldn't marry me looking the way I do," she said. "You deserve a pretty wife. Give me a chance to get some nice clothes for the ceremony. I need some makeup, too. Just look at me. I'm a mess. My clothes are torn. I haven't had a bath in more than a day. I need to do something about my hair. No girl wants to get married like this. Besides, if I show up for my wedding looking like this, people are going to ask questions."

She thought that she probably was laying a foundation that would have one of only two possible results — either Pernell would release her under the pretext of preparing for the wedding, or he would kill her.

For a long time, he said nothing, dragging out the suspense.

"Okay," he finally said. "Maybe you're right."

Suddenly, he slowed and pulled into a parking space. "I'll be right back," he said, jumping from the car.

She watched Pernell disappear into a nearby shop. A few minutes later, he returned, carrying a package.

Not far from the shop, they stopped again at a 7-11 at the corner of 168th Street Northwest and 37th Avenue. Pernell handed Susan a quarter and told her to call her dormitory once more to tell her friends that he was bringing her back and didn't want to see any police.

Erin answered. "He says he's going to bring me back to the campus," Susan told her.

"Great!" Erin responded. "When?"

90

"I don't know, but it won't be very good if he runs into police when he gets there."

Despite the warning, Erin quickly dialed the Miami-Dade Police Department and told Detective Griglen about the call. Rushing, Griglen arrived at the campus at 3:30 and took up the vigil with half a dozen of Susan's friends and dormmates.

Pernell, meanwhile, was driving through neighborhoods several miles from the campus, talking about his marriage plans. He spoke excitedly about the ceremony they would have, the honeymoon they would take, the house they would buy eventually.

A cautious block at a time, he moved closer to the campus, ever on the lookout.

At five, Griglen was called back to her office. An hour later, Pernell pulled to a stop outside the main entrance at St. Thomas University. He took hold of Susan's arm, gently this time, delaying her freedom.

"I love you very much," he said, thrusting the package he had picked up earlier into her hands, "and I'm looking forward to marrying you."

"Thank you," she said softly.

Tentatively, she reached for the door handle, and when he made no effort to stop her, she opened it.

"I'll be in touch and we'll make plans," he said, as she stepped from the car to precious freedom. She closed the door, and he drove away, leaving her standing on the street with her bruises, her tattered clothing, the small package he had handed her, and the splitting headache that had never gone away. She opened the package as she walked across the lush grass of the campus toward her distant dorm. Inside was a solitary red rose.

"One rose," she said bitterly. "One stinking rose. That's all I get for what I've been through. One stinking rose."

She tossed it into a trash container.

14

A Change of Scenery

As Susan walked toward her dorm, one thought was on her mind.

"You've read all these stories about rape victims and the fact that the first thing they want to do is take a bath?" she remarked years later. "I can tell you it's true. I thought if I could get to a shower, I'd stay there with that warm water running over my body for hours."

She climbed the stairs at Sullivan and turned down the long corridor toward her room. The dorm, too, seemed deserted, but then Andrea and Erin appeared in the hall and rushed toward her, grabbed her in hugs and began asking questions.

"I survived," Susan said.

"What can we do?" Erin asked.

"I don't know," Susan answered. "I just want to get to my room."

"We called your mother to tell her that he had been here and that he had taken you," Andrea said. "We told her we'd let her know any news as soon as we could."

"I'll call her," Susan said tiredly.

Now other friends began gathering around, all asking questions but getting few answers.

Back in her room, Susan fell onto her bed exhausted and reached for the phone to call home.

Her mother picked up on the first ring.

"It's me," Susan said. "I'm back in my room."

She did not go into great detail about what had happened but did tell her mother about the severe pain in her head.

"Do you want me to come down?" Irene asked.

"Yes, please," Susan answered. "You know you always make things better, Mom."

Although Susan's parents had been keeping an anxious vigil by the phone since Erin had called the day before, Irene was now alone. Her husband had left only minutes earlier for a meeting at his church that was to be followed by a dinner in his honor. Irene had urged him to attend the dinner. So much planning had gone into it, she said, and he deserved such an honor. George had gone reluctantly, telling his wife to call the church if any news came. He had been gone only a few minutes and couldn't have reached the church yet.

So after Irene called an airline and learned that there were two evening flights to Miami through Charlotte, she booked herself on the earlier flight, her husband on the second and called his church. He still had not arrived, but she left a message that Susan had called and was safe. She also left word of the travel arrangements, then rushed to the airport to catch her flight. She would arrive in Miami at ten that night. George, who would leave the church as soon as he got the message, missing the dinner in his honor, would get the later flight and arrive near midnight.

While Susan had been on the phone with her mother, Erin had stepped across the hall and called Detective Griglen, who waited on the line while Erin returned to Susan's room.

"I've got Detective Griglen of the Miami-Dade Police Department on the phone in my room," Erin told Susan. "She's been trying to find you since yesterday evening. I told her you're back. She wants to talk to you."

"I'm so tired," Susan said weakly. "Tell her I can't come to the phone right now."

Erin returned to her room and delivered the message, but Griglen became insistent. "Tell her to come to the phone," she said sternly. "I have to talk to her."

This time, reluctantly, Susan walked across the hall and picked up the phone.

"This is Susan," she said.

"I need for you to come down to the station right away," the detective instructed her. "Is there anyone there who can give you a ride?"

Susan replied that she was too tired, that she needed a bath and that she needed to wait for her mother to arrive.

Later, Susan would recall that Griglen became angry and yelled at her, insisting that she have someone drive her to the police department for questioning.

"Lady," she recalled telling the detective pointedly, "I'm not moving one foot until my parents get here. I don't want to talk to anyone but my Mom right now."

In her report, Griglen wrote: "Victim...was very uncooperative.... Victim stated she did not want to talk to me at this time and that she was

93

awaiting her parents' arrival in town. Victim stated she would decide what to do about this incident after talking to her parents."

Years later, after learning about Susan's experiences with Pernell in greater detail, Griglen would have more sympathy for Susan's reaction. "Now, almost ten years later, I understand why. But at the time, I didn't have the advantage of that understanding."

Near eight that night, the telephone in Susan's room rang.

"Susan," said the voice on the line, sending a chill through her.

"Pernell," she said, fighting back her rising anger. "Where are you?"

"Corky's," he said. "Corky's Restaurant in Miami. You know where it is?"

"I know where it is, Pernell," she said. "What do you want, Pernell?"

"I just thought I ought to remind you that I can still watch you. I can keep up with everything you do."

"That's fine, Pernell."

She hung up the phone.

Irene caught a cab to the campus, and after Susan's friends directed her to her daughter's room, they stepped back as Susan rushed into her mother's arms, crying like an injured child. Irene wanted to take Susan to an emergency room to see a doctor, but Susan resisted.

"It'll be all right," she said, though she wasn't certain it ever would be. "I just need a chance to rest. Besides, Dad's plane will be landing before long."

Susan went with her mother to the airport to pick up her father and he embraced both at the same time. He put his hand lovingly on Susan's head making her feel for an instant as though she were eight years old again.

"You know some strange people, Susan," he said, gently patting his daughter's head. "But be thankful you don't have to live in Pernell Jefferson's mind."

They returned to Susan's room, where Susan finally fell asleep in her bed, while her mother napped on her absent roommate's bed and her father attempted fitful sleep on the floor.

Susan slept until mid-morning, and she and her parents spent most of Sunday talking about what had happened, although Susan withheld many details of her ordeal, details she wouldn't share with anyone for years. Her mother continued to worry about the persistent pain in Susan's head. The flesh around Susan's ears was already showing the dark signs of bruising, but Susan insisted that she didn't need medical treatment.

Satisfied that his daughter was safe and whole, George took a Sunday evening flight back to North Carolina. Irene checked into an on-campus motel to be with her daughter for as long as she was needed.

On Monday, Irene finally talked Susan into visiting the college's physician, who found no critical injuries. A few day's rest probably would alleviate the pain in her head, he said.

On Tuesday, three days after Detective Griglen had insisted that Susan come to the police station, Irene convinced Susan to talk with the detective, but Griglen was now dubious about her story.

"At the time, I thought it didn't happen the way she said," Griglen recalled. "I suspected that there was money and drugs involved and that she really was where she wanted to be."

In her report, Griglen wrote: "Victim stated she let subject stay with her in the dorm on Thursday night....Victim states subject repeatedly struck her about the face and head, but no visible injuries were seen." Griglen also noted that Susan had not attempted to escape when she and Pernell checked into the Fort Lauderdale motel. "Her reason was that she tried once (unknown when) before and she knew what would happen if she tried it again."

"At the time, I felt there was no escaping Pernell," Susan explained years later. "I always figured that if he could find me in less than a half day in a meeting room in a motel in Elizabeth City, North Carolina, he could find me just about anywhere. Pernell always wanted to be a bounty hunter anyway. He'd have been a great one because he'll just wait you out."

Griglen, however, saw Susan's failure to attempt an escape as an indication of willingness to remain with Pernell.

On the same day that Susan met with Griglen, she also made another visit to the school doctor. The pain in her head had not gone away and at times was as intense as ever. The doctor referred her to a specialist who found that she had suffered a shattered eardrum and needed surgery. "He told me that in all his years of practice, he had never seen so much inner ear damage administered by a blow like that," Susan said.

On Thursday, with her mother at her side, Susan reported to an outpatient clinic for surgery to repair her eardrum. She was sent to her dorm to rest through the night.

"She has suffered at least a twenty percent loss of hearing in one ear," the physician told Irene, "and perhaps some diminished hearing in the other."

"Permanently?" Irene asked.

"I'm afraid so," the doctor said.

On Friday, Susan reported once more to the police station as she had promised Griglen earlier in the week and submitted to a polygraph examination.

"All I know about that," Susan said years later, "is that they told me I passed."

On Saturday, however, Griglen informed Susan and her mother that Carmen Puig-Domingues of the district attorney's office had studied Griglen's report and decided not to prosecute Pernell on abduction charges.

For Susan, the decision was startling.

"Why?" she asked, her disbelief obvious.

"Frankly, we see this as just a domestic dispute, a boyfriend-girl-friend disagreement," Susan would remember Griglen telling her.

"Let me understand this," Susan said angrily. "Because it's girlfriend against boyfriend, you're not going to do anything about this?"

"That's right."

"Could I swear out a warrant against Pernell on my own?" she asked.

"You could," she was told, "but we don't think it would do you much good."

Years later, Susan confessed that she did not fully understand her rights, that she indeed could have forced law enforcement agencies in Florida to seek Pernell and to arrest him if he could be found.

"The police told me there were indications I was making it all up," Susan said years later. "And they told me that the laws in the State of Florida don't have rights for girlfriends."

Griglen had one further addition to her police report. She dutifully recorded the Puig-Domingues decision to drop the case and added one further thought.

"But if the victim could provide any other evidence," Griglen wrote in her report, "the State would consider filing charges of simple battery against the subject."

In capital letters at the end of the report, Griglen typed:

"DISPOSITION: EXCEPTIONALLY CLEARED."

For the police, the case was closed.

"I always took my cases on an individual basis," Griglen said in a 1995 interview. "I'm a people person and all I can go by is what the word is. In every case, you gather all the information you can and that's all you can do."

The information to which she did not have access at the time, particularly Susan's long history of abuse at the hands of Pernell, would have made a difference, Griglen said.

"In this line of work, you encounter a lot of domestic abuse cases," she said. "The way she is described to me now is very plausible. I have worked many cases in which the woman was helpless to escape the man who was beating her. You hear it all the time. 'Oh, he loved me so much that he was willing to abduct me. He beat me, but what would I do without him? He's all

I've got.'

"If that's all they know, how can they expect to do anything better than that? It's a cycle women fall into and sometimes they never get out of it. In this case, Pernell was her life and Pernell was going to be her death."

After the learning of the decision not to prosecute, Susan's mother called a Quaker friend in Miami.

"I need a lawyer," she said after exchanging pleasantries, going on to describe briefly what had happened.

"What you need," her friend said, "is a good female lawyer. A woman would probably pursue this case with a little more enthusiasm than a man."

"Do you have someone in mind?" Irene asked.

"Got a pen?"

Irene wrote down name and number and got an immediate appointment.

"Okay," the lawyer said to Susan when they met a few hours later, "why don't we begin from the beginning so I'll know what we're talking about here."

Susan told her about her long relationship with Pernell and described what had happened. The lawyer questioned her closely.

"And where was this gentleman from the time he arrived on Thursday until this happened late Friday afternoon?" she asked.

"With me, most of the time," Susan responded. "We'd had a good visit until he got jealous about someone I was dating and started beating me."

"Where did he spent the night Thursday?"

"In my dorm room," Susan answered.

"I don't think I want to have anything to do with this case," the lawyer suddenly said and proceeded to deliver a lecture on morality.

Susan was startled by the turn of events. "This means you will not represent me?" she asked uncertainly.

"That's exactly what it means. And I'd advise you that you need to review how you choose your friends and how you live your life."

Susan and Irene left the office in stunned silence and drove back to the campus. "I guess I just ought to be happy that the pain in my head is going away now a little at a time," Susan finally said.

Still fearful that Pernell might return, Susan and her mother came up with a plan to make certain that there would be no repeat of Susan's ordeal. They reasoned that the danger was less great while classes were in session, because others would be around to help if she needed it. But on weekends when many students were off campus, Irene would fly from North Carolina to stay with her daughter. Only six weeks of classes were left before Susan would be spending a two-week break at home.

Those two months passed with no more trouble from Pernell, and Susan felt safe enough for her mother to stop the weekly commutes when she returned to start summer school classes.

Susan's relationship with Ian had ended with the spring quarter. They had dated a few times after her abduction, but the romance was gone. None of Susan's dormmates was taking summer classes, and she was without a social life when she returned to campus. That gave her plenty of time to study and bring up her grade point average.

Twice during summer school, letters arrived from Pernell in Greensboro, neither mentioning the ordeal he'd put her through, nor his proposal of marriage. But one letter did indicate that he might be planning another trip to Florida. Susan put it out of mind.

She was studying late on a hot July night when she heard a knock on her dorm door near midnight.

"Who is it?" she asked pleasantly without opening the door.

"Guess," said a familiar voice that caused her heart to sink. Despite her fear and anger, she opened the door.

Pernell looked more powerful than ever, the result of his intense weightlifting routines.

"Aren't you going to ask me in?" he said.

"Come in," she said, "but I've got a lot of studying to do, you know how summer school is."

This was going to be another long night for Susan, but decidedly different from her experience in April. Pernell wanted to talk, and he was on his best behavior.

"We talked all night long," Susan remembered. "He talked about how he didn't mean it when he hurt me in April. He told me again and again how sorry he was. And he kept saying, 'Let's be friends, just friends.'"

Through the long night, Susan refused to be swayed. And that was a new experience for her. Since those early days at Guilford College, she had always taken him back. But this time, she felt a resolve she had never known before.

It's *over!*, she told herself jubilantly. And the thought gave her courage.

Pernell was still talking when the sun rose, giving no indication of leaving, and Susan was trying to think of ways to prod him.

It was about ten before she finally suggested that he might need to be going, adding that she needed to do some shopping.

"I'll take my car and you can take yours and we'll say goodbye at the mall," she said.

Driving the maroon Datsun that was still registered to Susan, Pernell followed her MG through the busy morning traffic to a mall in Hollywood.

Susan found a parking space near Marshall's, a department store. Pernell had pulled into another spot nearby and hurried to the MG. As Susan was getting out of her car, he grasped her by the arm and began pulling her forcefully toward the Datsun.

Suddenly, Susan could picture all the horrors of April returning, and she began screaming — frightening, piercing screaming.

"Don't do that," Pernell told her. "I'm not going to hurt you. We're just going to go to my car and talk."

But Susan continued screaming, struggling to get away from him, and she attracted the attention at last of an elderly couple who were emerging from their car a short distance away. The couple hurried toward them.

"Hey, what are you doing?" the man called out, coming closer. Pernell looked momentarily uncertain, then released Susan.

"Just remember that I still know where you are and I can watch you," he said before he ran to his car and sped away.

Susan watched him go as the elderly couple hurried to her. She was trembling, trying to catch her breath.

"Thank you," she said. "You may have saved my life."

"Can we do anything for you?" the man asked.

"Just let me walk with you to the mall."

Flanked by two brave senior citizens, Susan entered the mall. After thanking the couple again, she found a phone and called home.

"Mom," she said. "He came back."

Following Irene's instructions, Susan left the mall and after making certain that Pernell wasn't lurking nearby or following her, she drove to a hotel, checked in and called her mother again.

"I'm on the next flight to Miami," Irene told her.

This incident caused Susan to resolve anew to take charge of her life. Her test came within a week after her mother had returned home and she had gone back to classes. She answered the phone and heard Pernell's voice.

"Where are you?" she asked firmly.

"Does it matter?" he shot back. "I moved in with a friend of mine up here in Hollywood just so I can keep an eye on you. I just called to tell you that I know everything about you, where you're going and what you're doing."

"That's it, Pernell," Susan said, her anger rising. "I've had enough of you and your threats. If you ever come close to me again, I'm going to the police. Do you understand that?"

"I understand," he said, suddenly meek, surprising her.

During this conversation, Susan discovered that Pernell thought he was a wanted man, that there were warrants for his arrest and that, through cunning and daring, he was staying one step ahead of the police. She decided to take advantage of his paranoia.

By threatening to expose his location, she could control him, and by allowing him to call or write occasionally, she could keep track of him.

"I decided I'd have a lot more peace if I knew where he was instead of wondering where he might be," she said later.

Pernell agreed to her terms.

Late that summer, Pernell completed the classes he needed to complete his degree at Guilford, but he never attended a graduation ceremony. His diploma was mailed to his mother in Benson, and years later it still hung on her living room wall. Surprisingly, he kept his word to Susan. He didn't bother her any more while she was at St. Thomas. She received her master's degree in the spring of 1987 and went to work in the marketing department of a professional soccer team in Fort Lauderdale. That fall, she called her former roommate, Ellen, at St. Thomas to see how things were going.

"You'll never believe who showed up on campus yesterday," Ellen said.

"Who?" Susan asked.

"Pernell."

That night, Susan wrote a strongly worded letter to Pernell reaffirming her demand that he never attempt to visit her again. Although they continued to speak occasionally on the phone, Susan would see Pernell just once more.

During a visit home late in 1987, she ran into him in a shopping center parking lot. Pernell pulled the Datsun alongside Susan's car and they talked through open driver's side windows, neither getting out.

Pernell told her that he'd bought a dog, but Susan revealed little about her life. They said goodbye and drove off in different directions. Afterward, Susan called Greensboro lawyer Pella Stokes, a former football player at Guilford College, and asked him to contact Pernell about returning the Datsun. Stokes suggested to Pernell that Susan was willing to take him to court over the matter. Two days later, the Datsun was left in her mother's driveway in Winston-Salem with a note under the windshield wiper.

"Here's your old car," Pernell had written. "I don't need it any more. I've got a new sports car."

15

The Champion

After getting his degree, Pernell had remained in Greensboro. He found a job selling athletic shoes in an outlet store in Greensboro's Cotton Mill Square and continued to haunt his old college hangouts. Still committed to one steroid cycle after the other, he spent his evenings becoming bigger and more powerful, stronger than he'd ever been as a football player.

He left the health club where he had trained for years and moved to a gym known for its emphasis on competitive lifting.

"This was a hard-core gym," Pernell remembered. "Anything goes."

He occasionally introduced himself to people at the gym as a former Cleveland Browns football player.

During his junior year at Guilford, Pernell and Joey Monsay, another football player, had entered a lifting competition at Rehobeth Beach, Delaware, and Pernell had finished seventh. Now he began to train for serious competition.

For two hours five days a week, Pernell stuck to his routine: Monday was for bench presses, Tuesday for squats, Wednesday for accessory work, Thursday for bench presses again, Friday for deadlifts. His diet, he later would boast, consisted of proteins, carbohydrates and steroids.

Pernell used his best lifts as a college senior as his bench mark. In 1984, he had succeeded at 425 pounds on the bench press and had set a record for defensive backs at the college with a squat of 630 pounds.

He matched that squat twice in 1986 competitions, first in Winston-Salem, again at the Greensboro YMCA. He had bench presses of 435 pounds and 415 pounds, winning that title on both occasions.

Pernell's former teammate Lamar Boykin had taken a job with a paper company and moved to Virginia Beach. Pernell had been visiting him regularly and began entering weightlifting competitions in the Tidewater area, where by 1987 he was becoming known as an accomplished power lifter. He won one bench lift competition with a dozen repetitions at the 315-pound weight and then had a stunning victory at a fitness center in Virginia Beach with a bench press of 445 pounds and a squat of 705, both records.

Impressed by his own success, Pernell now decided to move up a level competitively and entered the North Carolina Powerlifting Championships held in Charlotte in September 1987.

"The competition was so intense that on my first squat of more than 500 pounds, blood came from the pores on my forehead," he said.

He was named the novice state champion in the 198-pound class, but that turned out to be his last big success in competition.

"It was okay to be a champion," he said years later. "But I thought this type of full power training was too stressful. I didn't take it seriously after that."

At work, Pernell had become friends with an attractive young woman named Judi,* who worked in another store at Cotton Mill Square, and they soon began dating. Like all of Pernell's girlfriends since he had entered college, Judi was white. Pernell occasionally took her with him to spend evenings at the home of his college coach Tommy Saunders and his wife Betty.

It didn't take long for Judi's relationship with Pernell to fall into a familiar routine of verbal abuse and violence, but for the first time, Saunders became aware of this side of Pernell's character. Judi began to confide in Saunders and his wife and they were startled by her revelations. In college, Pernell had babysat with their children, and he still seemed like a son to them.

"He was playing games with Judi," Tommy remembered. "Most of the time, he knew where she was and what she was doing. Today we'd call it stalking."

One night late in the summer of 1987, Judi called the Saunders home distraught.

"She was hysterical," Tommy said. "She said that Pernell was outside her apartment waiting for her and she was scared to death."

Saunders drove to her apartment and searched the parking lot for Pernell or his car. Seeing no sign of him, he took Judi back to his house and she remained there two days, too frightened to leave.

Shortly before Christmas, Judi again called the Saunders home. She was even more frightened than before. "I don't know what to do," she said. "He's scaring me and I can't get away from him. I have nowhere to go."

This time, she remained with the Saunders for three days. Pernell never thought to look for her there.

"She called me one other night," Tommy recalled years later, "and I went over and found that her apartment had been broken into. Pernell had kicked the door down to get in and had taken all the trophies he had left there and a lot of other stuff."

This time Tommy called Pernell at work.

"We've got to talk," he said pointedly.

When they met that evening, Saunders said, "Pernell, I've got something to say to you and I want you to listen. You need to get away from Greensboro and Guilford College. You're not a college kid any more. You don't need to be hanging around the campus. You're still living in the past. You're still trying to be somebody's hero. That's over. Your football days are gone. You need to accept that and move on, go somewhere and get started on your life. Find something to do."

Then he brought up Judi, warning Pernell about bothering her. Pernell was startled that he knew about it.

"When I started talking to him about Judi," Saunders recalled, "Pernell started backing off in a big way."

Clearly, Pernell did not want to discuss his relationship with Judi, and he soon stopped coming to the Saunders house. He didn't stop bothering Judi, however, and on Valentine's day, 1988, she swore out a warrant charging him with aggravated assault. The case was later dismissed, primarily, Pernell later claimed, because Judi had filed similar charges against two other men in the past.

By the time the charges were dropped in March, Pernell had taken Saunders' advice and left Greensboro. Later, he claimed that Judi got his number from a friend, called and begged to see him again, and they met at a Burger King in South Hill, Virginia. "We ended up staying the night at a local motel," he said. "Then we went our separate ways."

Judi later married and moved to Atlanta. She made friends in Greensboro swear to keep her new name and address secret. She never wanted Pernell to be able to find her again.

Pernell had moved in with his friend Lamar in Virginia Beach. He also had renewed acquaintance with Mike Reardon, the former Guilford College running back with whom he once had gotten into a fight on the practice field in Greensboro. Reardon had become an officer in the K-9 section of the Norfolk Police Department and worked out regularly at a fitness center to keep in shape. He told Pernell about an opening there for a trainer, and he was pleased when Pernell landed the job.

16

"Looking Good, Baby Girl"

Denise had started working out with Jeannie and Jeannie's new friend, Mike Reardon, and she was there the night Mike introduced Jeannie to Pernell Jefferson.

Mike had described Pernell on the way to the center that evening. "He's a body builder," Mike had said. "And he's got a body most people would kill for."

Denise thought that Mike's description was apt. Pernell stood almost six feet tall and weighed 200 pounds. Jeannie looked tiny beside him. Pernell was well groomed, Denise noted, and his bronze skin seemed to glow. His arms and shoulders bulged from beneath his knit tank-top shirt, and his snug knit shorts showed off his well-developed legs. He moved gracefully, and when he squatted to instruct Jeannie, the large muscles in his upper thigh flexed in an interesting manner. Denise knew that Jeannie would notice that. She never failed to notice such things.

"Jeannie always went for the Mister America types," Denise said years later, "and Pernell was certainly built like a Mister America."

Jeannie was so taken with Pernell that she failed to introduce him to Denise until they were halfway through her training session. "He was very pleasant, very nice," Denise recalled. "He seemed well-educated, well-mannered, and he was really built."

Jeannie talked about Pernell a lot after that first night. She believed that he was going to transform her body, and in coming weeks she looked forward to her training sessions with increasing eagerness. Even when Mike couldn't go, she was always there, and Denise was usually with her. Denise always worked out nearby, close enough to hear that Pernell increasingly raised his voice at Jeannie, especially if Jeannie spoke during a lift.

"I thought he was like a drill sergeant," Denise said later. "He wanted things done exactly his way; he wanted perfect silence except for the sound of the weights, and he was a task master. I just didn't think that sort of intimidation was necessary."

Such treatment was in marked contrast to Mike's gentle manner when he had tried to instruct Jeannie, but she didn't seem to mind. Within a month, Denise had begun thinking of Pernell as mean-spirited, demanding, a prejudicial tyrant.

"C'mon, Baby Girl," he would say, pushing her. "You can do it, Baby Girl. Make it hurt, Baby Girl! Looking good, Baby Girl!"

Though Jeannie seemed not to mind being called "Baby Girl," Denise came to hate the expression. To her, it was the ultimate male putdown of women, machismo at its chauvinistic worst. But Jeannie didn't mind it at all.

The more she saw of Pernell, the more Denise disliked him. She thought he was phony. "The first clue was that he kept telling people he had been a big time football player," she said. "He kept talking about all he was and all he had. He kept telling people he had played for the Cleveland Browns, and he told Jeannie he had checks from the NFL he hadn't even cashed yet.

"When people start telling you all they have and all they are, they're usually the people who don't have, aren't and never have been. And that's the way I saw Pernell."

But Jeannie didn't see Pernell that way. She clearly thought that he was wonderful, and Denise kept her opinions of him to herself.

"What do you think of my black guy?" Jeannie asked one night after a workout.

The question caught Denise by surprise, and she wasn't certain how to answer. It bothered Denise that Mike had quit coming to workouts with them and had stopped calling Jeannie, and that Jeannie had been so wrapped up in her training sessions with Pernell that that hadn't bothered her at all. Denise liked Mike and thought that he was good for Jeannie, but she didn't like Pernell at all and had been concerned that Jeannie might be developing personal feelings for him.

If she's looking for my approval to have a relationship with a black guy, I have to be careful, Denise thought, as she considered how she should answer.

"Jeannie, it really doesn't matter what I think of him, does it?" she finally said. "What do you think of him? That's what counts."

"I think he's good for me. He tells me I look good. He says things I need to hear. He pushes me."

Denise wanted to tell Jeannie that she was worried that she might be venturing into a dangerous relationship. She wanted to say that every time Pernell said, "Looking good, Baby Girl," it was like a slap in the face. She wanted to say that he was not the knight in shining armor that Jeannie seemed to think he was; he was a jerk with little or no respect for women. But she kept her opinions to herself.

*   *   *

Jeannie's parents knew little about her relationship with her fitness trainer. Though Jeannie had mentioned Pernell's name a few times, she had volunteered little about him.

"Jeannie was always worried about what her mother and dad, especially her dad, would say if they found out Pernell was black," Denise said. But curiosity would lead to that discovery.

In early May, Jeannie went with Pernell on a weekend visit to his mother's home in North Carolina, where she met Willie, Pernell's brother, who admired her shiny Nissan 300 ZX. Willie had become an expert at automobile detailing and offered to add some small, tasteful pinstripes to highlight the sports car form of Jeannie's vehicle. But it would take him several days to do the job, he said. He would deliver the car to Virginia Beach when he finished.

Since she had purchased her dream car shortly after her divorce from Tony, Jeannie had been so particular about it that she washed and waxed it every Saturday morning and kept it immaculately clean. No one but Jeannie was allowed to drive it. Now she was leaving the car she loved in the hands of a man she had just met so that he could spend a week painting designs and lines on it. That made no sense to Denise.

The arrangement also left Jeannie without a car for more than a week. But Pernell offered to pick her up in the morning and drive her home in the afternoons. To keep Pernell's identity from her parents, Jeannie devised a plan to meet him a block away from the Prickett home and have him drop her off at the same place.

The plan stirred curiosity in her father, who, close to a week into the arrangement, purposely timed a leisurely walk in the neighborhood to the hour Jeannie was expected home. He watched from a discrete distance when Pernell pulled to the side of the street and let Jeannie out. Though he didn't get a good look, he realized that Jeannie's friend was of a different race, and later he asked her about it.

"Jeannie, this guy Pernell, is he black?" Ben asked, going straight to the heart of the matter.

"Yes," she answered.

"Jeannie, you know I don't tolerate that," he said.

Nothing more was said and Ben and Jeannie never discussed the matter again.

"You have to remember that I am a Southern boy, raised in the South in the forties and fifties," Ben said years later, recalling this brief exchange with his daughter. "Times have changed, I guess, but they have never changed that much for me."

Ben and Carrie talked at length about the situation, trying to decide if they should do something. Carrie already had asked Jeannie if she were getting serious about Pernell and Jeannie had said they were only friends, but the Pricketts suspected otherwise. Should Ben talk to Pernell? Did they have the right to do or say anything? They had to remind themselves that Jeannie was almost 30, no longer their child, no longer bound to their commands.

"Remember Tito." Carrie said during one of their conversations. "We didn't think Tito was right for Jeannie either, did we? But we decided then that you don't own your children; they're yours to keep for only a little while. And you love them for all the decisions they make. I guess I still think that approach is best."

Ben nodded. He'd let his daughter know how he felt, and that would have to do. He would not interfere.

The Pricketts' suspicions about Jeannie's relationship with Pernell deepened shortly afterward when Jeannie told them that she was renting an apartment and moving out of their house. Denise had been trying to get Jeannie to move in with her for months. It seemed the sensible thing for both of them. Denise shared her home only with her daughter, Dawn, who loved Jeannie and had called her Aunt Jeannie from the time she could talk. Jeannie loved Dawn as well, and the house was plenty big for all of them. Still Jeannie had declined her offers. Why would she take an apartment of her own now if not to be with Pernell?

The apartment was at 1216 Level Green Boulevard in Virginia Beach, just four miles from her parents' house but more than eight miles from Denise's house in Chesapeake. It was on the second floor, and it had only one bedroom, a living room and a small balcony off the kitchen-dining area.

Jeannie was excited as she moved into her new place, but Denise knew that she was more excited about Pernell's impending 25th birthday. Denise went with Jeannie as she searched for a gold chain to give to Pernell. Again and again, Jeannie had sales clerks remove chains from display cases so she could examine them, but each time she looked in dismay at the price tags.

"I just can't afford that," she would confide.

As June 4, Pernell's birthday, drew closer, Jeannie arranged for a small dinner celebration at Captain George's, a seafood buffet restaurant at Lynnhaven Mall in Virginia Beach.

"You'll come, won't you?" Jeannie asked Denise.

"Sure," she said without enthusiasm.

Only a few couples, friends of Pernell's, would be there, she said, all dutch treat except that she planned to pay for Pernell's dinner.

Denise came with a friend from the bowling league and was astonished when Pernell opened a small package from Jeannie and drew out a gleaming gold chain. Jeannie helped him with it, latching it into place around his strong neck.

"When did she buy that?" Denise said under her breath.

"What did you say?" her friend asked.

"Just talking to myself," she said.

Because the only large table available was crowded, Denise and her friend volunteered to move to a table for two near the back of the restaurant and told their waitress to keep their bill separate from the rest. Her friend took the bill when it was presented and Denise looked to the table where Jeannie sat surrounded by Pernell's friends. She witnessed the awkward moment when the bill came and no one reached to pick it up. Finally, Jeannie pulled it toward her and handed the waitress a charge card. No one else had offered to pay part, or to even pay their own share. Jeannie was stuck with the tab, dinner for eight.

As the small group was making its way out of the restaurant, Denise hurried to catch up with Jeannie, pulling at her elbow. "Why'd you do that?" she whispered. "Why'd you let them do that to you?"

"It's all right," Jeannie told her.

"It is not all right," Denise said.

But Jeannie turned cheerfully to the others. "Anybody for Rogues?" she asked, referring to a favorite nightclub at the beach. "Why don't we all meet there?"

Denise and her friend, Jeannie and Pernell arrived at the night spot, got a table for eight and waited. No one else came.

"Let's get out of here," Denise whispered to Jeannie as acquaintances began coming over to speak them. "I don't like doing this. There are just too many people in here that we know."

Denise thought that Jeannie also had grown uncomfortable as people she knew realized that Pernell was her date and obviously began talking about it, but when she suggested that they leave a short time later, Pernell balked.

"I'm staying," he announced. "You can go if you want to. I'll find a way home."

Disappointed and hurt that her evening was not turning out as she hoped, Jeannie got up to go, following Denise and her friend out, leaving Pernell behind.

Early in Jeannie's relationship with Pernell, Denise and Jeannie had maintained their old routines, still going to clubs on Friday nights, still spending time at the beach on Saturday afternoons, but all that changed without notice.

"Jeannie and I talked on the phone at noon just about every day,"

Denise remembered later. "When she got her lunch break, she'd always call me. If it was early in the week, one of us would ask if we were going out on the weekend and we'd always agree that we would stay home for a change.

"But as it got later in the week, we knew we'd change our minds. And it was always the same. It would get to be Wednesday or Thursday, and Jeannie would say, 'We going out this weekend?' And I'd say, 'I don't know. What do you think?'

"'Yeah,' she'd say. And then there would be silence on the phone because neither one of us wanted to ask what the other one was going to wear. Then one of us would do it and we'd spend the rest of the week fussing about that and getting ready to go out."

And so it was into the third week in June. But this time when Denise arrived at Jeannie's apartment to pick her up, Jeannie was not ready to go.

"Aren't we going out?" Denise asked.

"No," Jeannie said in a strange tone of voice.

"Why?" Denise pressed.

"Pernell might call."

For a moment, there was silence. Denise wasn't sure how to handle this situation.

"Where is Pernell?" she finally asked.

"He's gone out with some friends."

The conversation was making even less sense to Denise, and she had become annoyed.

"He's gone out with some girl, and you're sitting here at home waiting for him?"

Jeannie now did not look up to meet Denise's gaze.

"What happens if we go out like we'd planned?"

"I'm afraid he'll come looking for me," Jeannie answered.

"So what?"

"I'm afraid he'll be mad."

Now, unexpectedly, Jeannie extended her right leg and flexed her small calf muscles. "You think my legs are showing any muscle yet? Pernell would like it if I was finally showing some muscle definition in my legs."

Denise had been concerned about the spell Pernell seemed to be casting over Jeannie, and now she was sure that he'd succeeded in taking control of her. There was nothing logical about this conversation, she thought.

"Jeannie," she said, "think about what's happening."

But Jeannie only continued to look at the muscles in her legs, as if she hadn't even heard Denise. Denise left fearful of what was happening to her friend.

* * *

During the week that followed, however, Jeannie called regularly, as usual, acting as if nothing had changed, and once again they went through the old routine of deciding whether to go out on the weekend. In the end, Jeannie told Denise to pick her up at eight Saturday night.

Denise arrived on time, but when she knocked on the door, no one answered. She could hear someone walking inside, so she knocked again, still getting no response.

Now she went back downstairs to the back of the building and looked up, trying to see past the trellised balcony to get a glimpse inside. The apartment was dark. Once more, she returned to the door and rapped on it, this time more insistently. This time, she could hear whispered voices inside.

What on earth was going on?

Denise returned to her car and stood there, trying to decide what to do. Should she call someone? The police? Ben and Carrie? She looked to see if Jeannie's 300 ZX was there and spotted it parked just across the lot. Finally, she climbed into her Jeep and drove slowly through the parking lot looking for some clue to as to who might be in Jeannie's apartment with her, though she suspected Pernell. Who else but Pernell?

Twice she circled through the complex, then began a slow drive through the nearby neighborhood. Two blocks away, parked along the curb, was a gold Pontiac Fiero that Denise recognized as Pernell's.

Though she was worried and dialed Jeannie's number numerous times that night, Denise got no answer until Sunday.

"Jeannie, I've been worried sick," she said. "What happened?"

"I heard you knocking," Jeannie said matter-of-factly, "but he wouldn't let me answer the door."

Denise didn't have to ask who he was. And she was annoyed that Jeannie now seemed to think of her out-of-character rude behavior as nothing important, not even requiring an apology.

Some aspects of Jeannie's life remained unchanged since Pernell had come into it, however, and Denise saw that as a hopeful sign.

As she had always done, Jeannie still visited on the phone with her mother two and three times a day. She continued meeting her mother for Saturday lunch after Jeannie's regular visit to the hairdresser. Her appointments at a nearby tanning salon were faithfully kept.

Despite this, by mid-summer, Jeannie's relationship with Pernell worried her mother, who thought that Jeannie's personality was changing. During one of their Saturday outings, Carrie carefully broached the subject.

"Baby, is there anything I need to know about you and your friend, Pernell?" she asked.

110

"Mama, I know how Daddy feels," she said. "But how do you feel?"

"All I can say, Jeannie, is not in my lifetime," said Carrie, who feared that the relationship might be leading to marriage. "Please, not in my lifetime."

Jeannie smiled at the response. "I swear to you, Mama, we're just good friends," she said and reached to hug her.

17

The Christmas Visitor

By late July, Pernell had left his job as an instructor at the fitness center and had begun selling cleaning supplies in the Tidewater area. He stopped supervising Jeannie's training and only occasionally visited the fitness center. Jeannie continued training on her own, and Denise thought it was becoming as much an obsession with her as Pernell seemed to be.

On August 5, Jeannie's 30th birthday, her mother made a cake for a small family celebration. Denise called with birthday wishes while the party was going on.

"What did Pernell give you?" Denise asked.

"Well, he didn't have any money," Jeannie said, almost apologetically. "You know he took that new job and he's having it a little tight right now."

That made Denise angry. She remembered the gold chain Jeannie had bought for Pernell on his birthday only two months earlier, even though Jeannie couldn't afford that either. Nor could she afford the dinner tab for Pernell and his friends.

"What about all those NFL checks he's never cashed?" she wanted to say, but kept it to herself.

"He got you nothing?!" she said instead. "Didn't even mention it, didn't say 'Happy birthday, Jeannie,' or anything?!"

Jeannie started to make another excuse but Denise cut her off.

"Jeannie, even if he had no money, he could have found a pencil and piece of paper and made you a little card that just said 'Happy Birthday, Jeannie'. Sometimes those are the best of all anyway. And he didn't even think to do that?"

"I guess not," Jeannie said, as if embarrassed.

"Jerk," Denise said, not bothering to hold back her opinion any longer.

Still, Jeannie remained under Pernell's spell, often waiting alone in her apartment while he was out on the town, fearful of stirring his anger.

Denise had never known Pernell to have his own apartment. He kept

112

moving in for extended stays with friends and acquaintances. When Pernell first came to the Tidewater, she knew, Lamar and his new wife had taken him in. He'd had a couple of other temporary addresses since then. Denise saw him not as an All-American football player, but an All-American moocher, and she suspected that Pernell had now moved in with Jeannie, no doubt with Jeannie paying all the bills, though she didn't inquire. "Any time I'd call or stop by," she recalled years later, "he seemed to always be there."

That troubled Denise deeply, because Jeannie had once told her that Pernell had angrily pushed her against the wall and held her so she couldn't move. True, that seemed to have been a solitary incident, for Jeannie hadn't mentioned any others. Still, Denise worried that something like it, or worse, might happen again.

In September, Pernell quit his job selling cleaning supplies and with little warning moved away. He was going to share an apartment with his half-sister, Blondie Richardson, at 2347 Brady Street in Richmond, two hours away, he told Jeannie. Within days, he called to say he had a job in Richmond at Remco, an appliance rental store in Southside Plaza where he worked as a delivery man and chased down deadbeat debtors. His massive body and intimidating appearance made him perfect for the job.

Denise thought Pernell's departure was good news for Jeannie. "Let's go out this weekend, maybe a little celebration," she suggested.

"What are you going to wear?" Jeannie asked, more cheerful, Denise thought, than she had been in months.

"I don't know. What'll you wear?" Denise said, going along with the silly game the two had always played.

It was like old times once again. Jeannie called Denise at the photo lab promptly at noon every day, making plans for the weekend. Maybe she would buy something expensive this week, she said, perhaps a $10 scarf, maybe even a new pair of shoes.

Denise thought this weekend would be special, and she really looked forward to it.

"You look great!" Denise said when Jeannie answered her knock Friday night.

"Guess who came in from Richmond," Jeannie said, opening the door wider so that Denise could see Pernell sitting in the living room, settled in for the evening.

"Are we still going out?" Denise asked uncertainly.

"Oh, yes," Jeannie said. Turning, she called out to Pernell, "See you in a few hours." She got her purse and they left in Jeannie's car.

Jeannie wasn't the old Jeannie that Denise was hoping she would be that night, not nearly as lively and cheerful. Still she had gone out despite Pernell's sudden reappearance, a good sign, Denise thought.

When they returned near midnight, Denise declined Jeannie's invitation to come in. "I'll call you tomorrow," she promised. She had climbed inside her Jeep and put the key into the ignition before she noticed a pattern of bullet holes in her windshield.

Trembling with fright, she was uncertain what to do. Finally, she hurried to Jeannie's apartment and got her to the door.

"Somebody shot out my windshield," Denise said, loudly enough for Pernell to hear.

Pernell came to the door. "Did you hear any shooting while we were gone?" Jeannie asked him.

"I thought I heard something," he said. "Must have been the kids across the street." Denise took the inappropriate grin on Pernell's face as a smirk. She knew that the kids across the street were all under ten years old, and it wasn't likely that they'd been shooting. She was sure that Pernell had shot her windshield to get back at her for taking Jeannie out, and as she drove home in a dark mood, she was frightened more than ever for Jeannie.

Pernell's move to Richmond turned out not to be the blessing for Jeannie that Denise had hoped it would be. It soon became clear that even from two hours away he was still controlling Jeannie's life.

"He called constantly," Denise remembered. "All hours of the day and night. Even when Jeannie wasn't home, there would be four and five telephone messages from Pernell waiting for her return.

"They'd all be the same. You know, 'It's me. I know you're there. Pick up the phone.' Or, 'Me again.' Or he'd say something like, 'Just calling to let you know I have ways of keeping up with you.' By their very nature, the messages he left were themselves intimidating."

Almost every weekend, Pernell showed up without invitation, stifling any plans that Jeannie had made. After a while, she just quit making any and began to withdraw from her family and friends.

"Jeannie was worried," Denise recalled. "Actually, from the time she first met Pernell, there wasn't a day she wasn't worried. In the beginning, she was worried because she didn't know how her parents were going to react to the fact that he was black. But now she had a different reason to worry. Now she was worried about how she was ever going to get away from him."

A telephone call changed everything. It came a few days after Thanksgiving, 1988. Tony, her former husband, called just to say hello.

"She lit up," Denise remembered. "If there had been a way to harness that glow, Jeannie would have lit up Norfolk."

Tony's work in Pennsylvania was going well, he said, but his third marriage had broken up. The news had not surprised Jeannie. For as long as

Jeannie had known Tony, he had little tolerance for people who were over-weight. When Tony had married his third wife, a woman Jeannie and Denise had known from a distance, she had been slim and trim, but Jeannie and Carrie had spotted her at a Virginia Beach shopping center a few months after the marriage and both noticed that she'd had gained weight.

"She's getting a little fat," Jeannie said, sounding pleased. "Tony's not going to like that."

"That sticks in my mind," Carrie said in 1995, "because that's the only catty thing I ever heard Jeannie say about anyone."

Now Tony was telling Jeannie that his divorce soon would be final.

"I guess it's my fault, in a way," he said. "I should have known more about her before we got married."

Tony went on to say that he would be coming home at Christmas to visit his family and would call when he got to town.

"I'll be here," Jeannie said.

Jeannie called Denise to tell her about Tony's call and impending visit.

"And how do you feel about that?" Denise asked.

"Great," Jeannie responded. "He's going to call me when he gets here."

Denise now felt like a wet blanket.

"Jeannie, be careful," she said. "You know Tony wasn't the best thing in the world for you when you were married to him. You just can't go back. You can forgive, but you can't forget. Just be careful."

But Denise knew it didn't matter what she said. It was clear that now, more than ever, Jeannie was looking forward to Christmas, always her favorite time of the year.

Tony's reappearance made Pernell's presence in Jeannie's life an even more pressing problem. He still called at all hours and continued to show up when Jeannie least expected him. But come the holidays, he told her, he would be in North Carolina with his son.

More than a week before Christmas, Pernell showed up without notice at Jeannie's apartment. Jeannie had decided that she wanted Pernell out of her life, she had told Denise, but she didn't know how to accomplish it. Pernell's mood was mellow when he arrived, making Jeannie think that this was the time to try to break away from him. She opted for an easier, partial solution.

"She told him that they could be friends, even best friends if he liked," Denise recalled, "maybe talk on the phone once in a while, but not every night and not every week, maybe a letter occasionally, but that their relationship had come to an end. She told Pernell that he was a nice guy and that he ought to find him the kind of girl in Richmond that he deserved and marry her. That's the way Jeannie was. She never wanted to hurt anybody's feelings. Other people will give almost as much as they take, but Jeannie would just give. And Pernell was a taker. There was nothing mean about Jeannie.

"Pernell was real nice about it. He told her that was fine, that he had made a few new friends in Richmond and maybe something would work out."

Before leaving, Pernell gave Jeannie a Christmas gift, a bracelet with a strange gold bear charm attached to it. The charm was encrusted with three tiny white gemstones, one for each eye and another where a belly button should be. Jeannie loved teddy bears. She'd collected them for years.

When Pernell left a short time later, Jeannie thought it was for good, and she was happy that she had chosen the gentle approach in breaking off with him. Pernell had taken it so well, she later told Denise.

Joy returned to Jeannie's life as Christmas approached. She had always embodied the spirit of Christmas to her family and she spent most of the days leading up to the holiday with her parents, as usual taking charge of decorating the tree and the house. She also bought another Christmas teddy bear, this one dressed in a sweater with "1988" woven into the fabric. It joined the rest of her collection beneath the tree.

A few days before Christmas, Jeannie taped a cluster of small golden bells to the top of the decorative mirror in the foyer of her parents' home, and on Christmas Eve, when her sister Carrie and her brother Sam came home, the whole family posed for a snapshot beneath the bells. Sam's arm was on Jeannie's shoulder. Ben was hugging his older daughter to him. In the middle was Carrie, the mother, with a happy expression on her face. Jeannie was smiling and from her wrist dangled her new teddy bear charm bracelet.

Tony had arrived from Pennsylvania a day earlier, and having him home for Christmas, her family knew, was the best gift she could have hoped for. They spent hours together talking, remembering their high school days, recalling the best days of their marriage. Within days, they already were talking of remarrying.

"They had even decided that they would go to Mexico for their honeymoon," Denise said. "They were making plans."

Jeannie and Tony were in bed at her apartment a few days after Christmas when they heard a sharp rapping that seemed to be coming from the back of the apartment in the area of the living room. Tony started to get up to investigate, but Jeannie realized that Pernell surely had returned, and panic struck her. She couldn't afford for Tony to find out about Pernell, and she told Tony to stay put and she would see what was going on.

Jeannie pulled on a robe and went outside. She found Pernell on her balcony. He had climbed there on a trellis. He knew Tony was inside, he said, and he threatened to break into the apartment and confront him.

Unbeknownst to Jeannie, Tony had called the police, and as she begged Pernell to leave after talking him down from the balcony, a police car turned into the parking lot. Pernell saw it and ran off into the night.

Two officers came to the apartment, and Jeannie told them that she had heard a noise at the back of her building but had found nothing. After searching the area, the officers left. Jeannie returned to Tony with relief, but she knew now that Pernell did not intend to make an easy exit from her life.

Through January, Jeannie's telephone stayed busy. Tony called frequently from Pennsylvania, and Pernell called just as often from Richmond, now leaving messages even more chilling than before.

"Pernell was telling Jeannie that he would never hurt her," Denise remembered, "but that he had friends who might. He bragged that he had had a girl down in North Carolina put in the hospital one time."

She begged Pernell to leave her alone, but he began showing up unexpectedly at her apartment and in the courthouse parking garage even more frequently. She was terrified of him now, but she didn't know what to do about it.

Tony was her counter balance. When he called, it was always about pleasant, hopeful things — their remarriage, their honeymoon, finding a house in Pennsylvania.

"If things don't work out with Tony, what will I do?" she asked Denise during a long, emotional conversation one night.

Denise tried to be positive. "You'll do just fine," she said. "You've always been able to bounce back and there's no reason you wouldn't do it again. You've got a lot to offer somebody, and if it's not Tony, then it will be somebody else, some wonderful man."

But Denise kept her true feelings to herself. She wasn't at all certain that Jeannie would be all right. When she called Jeannie's apartment now, she discovered that on most days Jeannie was in bed by six in the evening. Clearly, Jeannie was deeply depressed. She ate very little.

In late January, Tony asked Jeannie to come to Pennsylvania for a week, and she eagerly accepted. Despite her depression, she tried to put herself in an optimistic mood before the trip. And she was filled with anticipation and excitement when she left in the third week of February, 1989.

But only a few days after Jeannie had left, Denise's phone rang.

"You heard from Jeannie?" Pernell asked without preliminaries.

"No, Pernell, I haven't," Denise said flatly.

"Listen, do you know where she's staying in Pennsylvania?" he went on pleasantly.

"I sure don't. I didn't ask her and she hasn't called."

"C'mon, Denise," he said teasingly. "You and Jeannie are like sisters. She wouldn't leave town without telling you where she's going to be."

"We may be like sisters," Denise answered, "but she sure didn't tell me where she's going and I didn't ask."

"Why don't you give me the number? I won't tell her how I got it."

"Maybe you don't understand, Pernell," said Denise with growing anger. "I don't have Jeannie's number."

"She's with Tony, isn't she?" he said, surprising her.

"Like I said, she didn't tell me what her plans were."

"I really need to talk to her," Pernell said. "I can't just let her go. I just don't know what I'll do without her."

Denise didn't respond.

"She means a lot to me, you know."

Denise's silence continued.

"Denise, you there?" he asked.

"Yes, Pernell, I'm here."

"I know you have her number, Denise. So, why don't you go ahead and give it to me? I only need to talk to her for a minute."

"Pernell, I don't have her number. I don't know where she is. I don't know where she's staying, and even if I did I wouldn't give that information to you."

Without another word, Pernell hung up. The call, Denise knew, did not bode well for Jeannie's future.

Jeannie Butkowski refused to press charges when her former boyfriend abducted, raped and beat her. When she turned up missing again two months later, her front door kicked off its hinges, her family thought that the police in Chesapeake, Va., were not interested in looking for her.

Jeannie's last Christmas with her family. Left to right are her sister, Carrie; her father, Ben; her mother, Carrie; her brother Sam, and Jeannie.

Jeannie's roommate and closest friend, Denise Edwards, knew that Jeannie was dead as soon as she discovered her missing, and she knew who had killed her: Pernell Jefferson. Denise's daughter Dawn now has faint memories of her "Aunt Jeannie," recalling only that her mother once spent a lot of time searching for her.

Jeannie's grave in Rosewood Memorial Park in Virginia Beach. Her mother goes there every Tuesday to polish the bronze marker, clip the grass and replace the flowers.

The church in Benson, North Carolina, where Pernell Jefferson sang in the choir with his family.

Pernell's mother, Joann Richardson, knew that athletics could take Pernell out of the poverty of his childhood, and she was right. He became an All-American football hero and was recruited by the Cleveland Browns.

Willie Jefferson was a football star at South Johnston High School, but he was far outshone by his older brother Pernell, who starred in three sports and once participated in two simultaneous events, running in a track meet between innings in a baseball game.

121

Guilford College's 1984 football team was not expected to win a single game, but under Pernell's leadership, it rose to be Number 3 in the nation. Pernell (22) poses with other backfield defenders: his close friend Lamar Boykin (37), Tim Everhart (10) and Kieran Byrne (13).

As a sophomore in 1982, Pernell opened Guilford's homecoming game with a dazzling 80-yard kickoff return for a touchdown. Cheering him in the stands was a girlfriend he was abusing just as he later would abuse Jeannie.

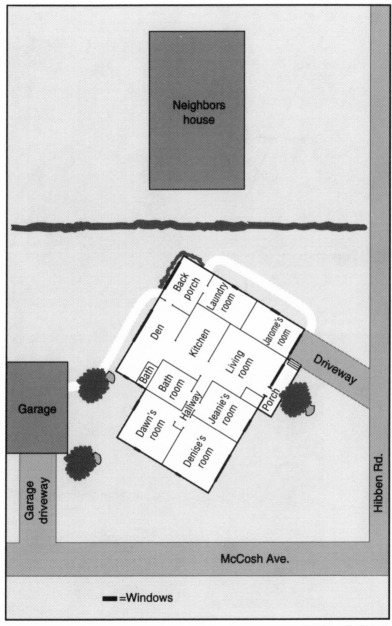

Drawing — Tim Rickard

Diagram of the house on Hibben Rd. in Chesapeake, Va., from which Jeannie was twice abducted by Pernell, the second time with deadly result.

123

Jimmy Weaver, the sheriff of Amelia County, Va., resented that his county had become a dumping ground for murderers from nearby cities. He became determined to put Pernell into prison.

Wes Terry, chief deputy of the Amelia County Sheriff's Department, was the lead officer in the investigation of Jeannie's murder. He had come to Amelia at the request of his old friend Jimmy Weaver.

Photo credit — Amelia Monitor-Bulletin

Pernell later said that he was in shock after his conviction for Jeannie's murder. Soon after he was taken from a back door of the Amelia County courthouse, his brother Willie stood on the front steps, Bible in hand, shouting that Pernell had not received a fair trial.

18

The Miracle Tape

Jeannie returned from her visit with Tony brimming with happiness and plans for the future. Although they hadn't set their wedding date, they had planned their honeymoon to Mexico and looked at houses. Jeannie even had talked with the clerk of court in the town where Tony lived about a job. Things could not have gone better. But as she was struggling to get her suitcase out of the car on her return to her apartment, a neighbor came over.

"I'm not being nosy," he said, "but I was just wondering if you gave anyone permission to stay in your apartment while you were gone."

"Well, no," Jeannie said, suddenly wary. "Did you see someone in my apartment?"

"A black man," her neighbor said. "He seemed to have a key. Stayed several days."

"Is he still there?" she asked.

"Haven't seen him today," he said.

Jeannie's glanced around the parking lot for Pernell's gold Fiero but didn't see it, and declining the neighbor's offer of help, she climbed the stairs to her apartment.

She opened the door only a crack at first, then cautiously wider. She was shocked by the sight before her. Her neat, tidy apartment and been ransacked. Clothing was scattered, furniture overturned, food scraps and dishes spread about. She stepped inside in disbelief, and when she did Pernell was instantly upon her, pushing her against the wall and pinning her there.

"Miss Butkowski," he said, his angry face pressed close to hers, "don't you know that if I can't have you, nobody's going to?"

"Pernell, you're hurting me," she cried out. His grip on her wrists was like vises. Suddenly, he released her arms and grabbed her by the neck with both hands. He was choking her, and she fought vainly to break his grip. Just as she thought she was going to lose consciousness, he hurled her to the floor, pounced on her and began hitting her as she struggled for breath. Later she would withhold many of the gruesome details about what followed, telling Denise only that Pernell had alternately beaten and raped her throughout the night. He had left at dawn, she said, with a warning that he could have her killed with a single phone call.

Jeannie had thought about going to her parents' house after Pernell left but decided against it because she feared that her father would try to kill Pernell and get himself in trouble. Instead she had gone to Denise's house. Denise had come to the door sleepy-eyed and was shocked at Jeannie's appearance. Her mouth was cut, her eyes and temples were beginning to blacken, and handmarks could be clearly seen on Jeannie's throat.

"You still need a roommate?" Jeannie said sheepishly, trying to smile. Denise had been running a want-ad for a roommate and had already interviewed several people.

"What happened to you?" Denise said, reaching out to her, and Jeannie fell crying into her arms.

"Pernell?" Denise said as she comforted her.

Jeannie only nodded.

"It's time we called the police," Denise said after Jeannie had sobbed out her story, but Jeannie quickly objected.

"No, we can't. He says he can have me killed and if we call the police, I'm afraid he will."

"So, what do we do, wait until this happens and maybe he kills you himself the next time?"

She was beginning to lose patience with Jeannie.

"I don't know," Jeannie said, still sobbing.

"Well, one thing we can do," Denise said. "We can move you in here where I can keep an eye on you."

"Thank you," she said.

After sleeping for a few hours on Denise's couch, Jeannie went back to her apartment with Denise to pick up a few things. They circled carefully through the neighborhood first to make certain that Pernell's car wasn't there. When Jeannie walked into her bedroom, where Pernell had strewn all the underwear from her clothing drawers, she was quick to spot her personal phonebook lying amidst the clutter. It was open to the B page.

"He's got Tony's number," Jeannie said.

Denise knew the implications of that, and she saw the panic rising in Jeannie.

"This is probably how he got my number, too," Denise said, "and where he called me from that night."

She reached for the telephone and pushed the redial button thinking that the last number called might have been her own and she soon would be hearing her answering machine.

"Hello," she said warily when a female voice answered. "Who is this?"

"Susan," the voice said.

"Susan who?"

"Susan Demos. Who are you trying to reach?"

"I'm sorry," Denise said. "Must have dialed the wrong number." She put the phone back on the cradle.

"Do you know a Susan Demos?" she asked Jeannie.

"Who?"

"Susan Demos."

"No."

Jeannie picked out a few clothes and other items and left without bothering to clean up the mess. She just wanted away from that place and the memories of the previous night, she told Denise.

That evening, Jeannie called her mother and told her cheerfully about her trip, failing to mention her homecoming. Almost as an afterthought, she mentioned that she was staying with Denise and was planning to move in with her.

On Monday, Jeannie asked the telephone company to disconnect her line and send a final bill. That night, she and Denise took boxes to her apartment and began packing. When Denise reached to unplug the telephone and answering machine, she pressed the review button first. The machine beeped to life.

"Jeannie. You there?" It was Pernell's voice. "You'd better pick up because I know you're there...."

Denise jerked the plug from the wall, silencing the machine.

Denise left first in her loaded Jeep, and Jeannie followed shortly. Halfway to Denise's house, Jeannie looked into her rear-view mirror and saw a gold Fiero closing fast. The Fiero rode her bumper for a short distance before pulling alongside and swerving toward Jeannie's Nissan. Jeannie turned sharply right, nearly going off the road but managed to keep control. The Fiero fell back and remained on her bumper, so close that she couldn't see the headlights. No matter how fast Jeannie went, the Fiero stayed there, until finally it pulled alongside and swerved toward her again, this time so close that she ran off the road and onto a grassy knoll before coming to a stop. Her heart had been pounding with fear, she later told Denise, and she was certain that Pernell would stop and yank her from the car, but she saw the taillights of the Fiero disappearing into the darkness. Shaken, she backed her car onto the road and made her way to Denise's house.

At the end of the week, Jeannie got her phone bill and discovered that Pernell had made more than $150 in long distance calls from her phone. The next day, Pernell called, and Jeannie angrily confronted him about the phone bill. She demanded the money and told Pernell that she wasn't going to tolerate his harassment and brutality any more. Denise listened in disbelief when in answer to a question from Pernell, Jeannie responded, "I'll have you killed, that's what!"

"Why'd you say that?" Denise asked after Jeannie had hung up.

"I had to do something," Jeannie answered. "What would you have done?"

"I don't know," Denise said.

Within 30 minutes of the call, Pernell swore out a criminal warrant in General District Court in Richmond for Jeannie's arrest. In a brief written report, he charged that Jeannie had "threatened to kill me on phone approx. 2:30 p.m. 2/27/89," and that she "have assaulted me with 12" army knife recently."

He also wrote that "...this lady being under...psychiatric treatment before can and will cause bodily harm to me. Did say she was going to have someone kill me."

Jeannie didn't find out about the warrant until it was served on her at work Monday. Two days later, on March 3, on the advice of a commonwealth's attorney with whom she had spoken about her problem, Jeannie wrote a cease-and-desist letter to Pernell and mailed it to his place of employment in Richmond.

This letter is to notify you, Pernell Jefferson, that you are not to harass me in any way therefore by not contacting me by phone or in person at work or at home. Also you are not to have anyone else harass or threaten me or damage any of my personal property. If this occurs legal action will be taken.

Jeannie knew the letter wouldn't stop Pernell, and she and Denise began taking extra precautions. They devised a way to use their telephone answering system as an electronic bulletin board, with both leaving messages about any changes in plans. They worked out a routine in which Jeannie would call at the end of her work day to make certain Denise would be at home when she arrived. If Denise were going to be late, Jeannie would go to her parents' house, or stop to visit Denise's mother until Denise arrived. When leaving work, Jeannie would arrange for escorts to accompany her to her car in the parking garage at the courthouse. And Denise would delay her morning departures to the photo lab until Jeannie was safely on her way to work.

Jeannie also decided that she would place weekend calls to Remco in Richmond. If Pernell came to the phone, she would know that she had at least two hours to shop or do her chores without fear. If he were not working, Jeannie would go to her parents' house and stay.

The plan quickly went awry, however. Just four days after Jeannie had mailed her cease and desist letter, Denise had to stay late at work. When she arrived and didn't see Jeannie's car, she assumed that Jeannie was at her parents' house and began putting away the groceries she had bought. After finishing in the kitchen, she went down the hall to her bedroom to change into something more comfortable. As she passed Jeannie's bedroom, she noticed that the bed was still rumpled, but Jeannie rarely made her bed. Denise had always thought it strange that someone as careful with appearances as Jeannie would leave her bed unmade for days at a time. Denise, on the other hand, who was never as obsessed with her clothes, makeup and hair as Jeannie, felt she was not ready to begin the day until her bedroom was in perfect order.

As Denise entered her own room, she realized it was not as she had left it that morning. A chair had been moved, and the bed seemed rumpled, though the cover and pillows still were in place.

Noticing that the memo light on the answering machine was flashing, an indication that Jeannie had left a message, she pressed the PLAY button.

"No! Leave me alone!" she suddenly heard Jeannie's voice screaming from the tape. "You're ruining my life.... Why are you doing this to me?"

"C'mon, let's go," said another voice that Denise recognized as Pernell's. "C'mon, get your purse...."

"Pernell, let go of me...."

"You're going with me. You ready to get in the car?... Let's go... Let's go...."

"You've already ruined my life," Jeannie pleaded. "What else do you want?... Leave me alone, Pernell. I'm not talking to you any more...."

"Do you want to die right here?" he asked. The question sent a shiver down Denise's spine.

She hit the STOP button, picked up the receiver and began dialing the number for the Chesapeake Police.

"I want to report a kidnapping," she told the dispatcher.

An officer was on his way, the dispatcher told her, after quizzing her for basic information.

Then Denise dialed the Pricketts' number and Jeannie's mother answered.

"Carrie, I think Pernell's got Jeannie," she said without bothering even to introduce herself.

"What do you mean?" Carrie asked. "How do you know?"

"Jeannie left a message," Denise said without describing the frightening exchange that had been captured on the telephone message tape.

"When did you find out?" Carrie asked.

"When I got home from work a few minutes ago. I've called the police."

"We'll be right there," Carrie said and hung up.

Denise removed the tape from the answering machine. She found her boom box, which she had not used in years, in the closet. She plugged it in and inserted the tape. She pushed the rewind button to cue the frightening exchange between Jeannie and Pernell for the police. Then she went to the living room and waited.

She heard a car door being closed in the back driveway off McCosh Avenue and was relieved to see that it was the tall construction worker named Jerome to whom she recently had rented a fourth bedroom that had been added to the house while she was still married. He had started across the back porch to his room when she called to him.

"I think Jeannie's been kidnapped," Denise said.

"How do you know?" he asked.

"It's all right here," she said, patting her boom box. "The police are on the way."

Shortly, the headlights from a police car illuminated the front of the house as the uniformed officer turned around and parked on the street in front. Denise met him at the door.

"Somebody's missing?" said officer Charles Winslow.

"My roommate." Denise quickly told him about finding the tape.

"I can play it for you," she offered.

Winslow listened intently to more than seven minutes of Jeannie's terror. Denise wept as the tape played. The recording ended in a crescendo of screams, followed by 20 seconds of silence and a low, mournful female sob.

Winslow asked to hear it again, frequently getting her to stop and rewind it to repeat particular sections.

"Who is this Pernell?" he asked, and Denise told him how Pernell had assaulted Jeannie and had been stalking and harassing her.

Winslow went to his squad car and requested a detective before returning to the house to look around. Denise was sitting on the couch, limp with shock and fear for Jeannie, when Winslow asked her to come to the den at the back of the house.

"You know when this happened?" he asked.

The floor was covered with shattered glass from the door to the back porch.

"I don't know," Denise answered. "This is the first time I've been in here since I got home. All I know is it wasn't that way when I went to work this morning."

Denise was impressed with Winslow, she recalled years later. "You could tell he was worried, like he cared, like he was a real person, not just a police officer doing a job."

Upon learning that no detective was immediately available, Winslow said that he would take the tape to the police station, discuss the situation with a detective and return.

Where were the Pricketts? Denise wondered after he had left. But more importantly, where was Jeannie? And was she still alive?

Ben was angry as he drove toward Denise's house as fast as possible in the heavy, frustrating traffic. Angry at Pernell. Angry at his daughter for getting involved with such a person. Angry at the traffic that now blocked him from getting to Denise's house and finding out what had happened.

Denise thought the Pricketts would never arrive.

While she waited anxiously for them, the phone rang, jarring her from her thoughts. She rushed to answer and heard only sobbing from the receiver.

"Jeannie!?" she said. "Jeannie?"

"Yes." came a whisper.

"Where are you?" Denise asked. "Are you all right? Are you hurt?"

No response was forthcoming.

"Jeannie!" Denise said forcefully.

"Yes." Another strained whisper.

"Are you in Chesapeake?"

"No."

"Are you in Norfolk?"

"Yes."

"Are you all right?"

"I'm okay," Jeannie answered, but her voice said differently and Denise realized that Pernell must be listening.

Silence followed until Denise said, "Jeannie, I'm here," hoping to encourage her to talk. Still nothing came from Jeannie.

"Jeannie," Denise said firmly, "you tell Pernell that I've got enough evidence to put him away. I've got everything that happened here in this house this afternoon on tape."

Suddenly, the line went dead, confirmation to Denise that Pernell had been listening. She placed the receiver back in the cradle and stood staring at the phone, uncertain what to do next, wondering if she had done the right thing in mentioning the tape. She wished the Pricketts would arrive.

She jumped when the phone rang again.

"Jeannie!" she said into the receiver.

"Pernell wants to know how you have it all on tape," Jeannie said in a flat, emotionless voice.

"Y'all must've hit the phone, or something, because the memo button was on."

"I didn't leave a message," Jeannie said.

"You left a message," Denise assured her. "The whole story. Everything's on the tape. And you can hear Pernell on the tape, too."

"But we were never in your bedroom," Jeannie said.

"Well, somebody was in my bedroom because it's all on tape, and you tell him I've got it and I'll put him away."

Again the line went dead.

Denise sank onto the edge of her bed to stay near the telephone. Big, easy-going Jerome stood at the door to her room, virtually filling the frame. Denise was glad he was there. He asked no questions, only waited. A few minutes later, just as Denise had expected, the phone rang again.

"I'm on my way home," Jeannie said. "Don't call the police."

"I've..." Denise started to say, but now she could only hear the dial tone buzzing in her ear.

Finally, Ben and Carrie were there, the front end of the Ford dipping as Ben hit the brakes in front of the modest house. He and Carrie hurried across the yard. Denise had heard them arrive and met them at the door.

"She's on the way home," Denise told Jeannie's frantic parents. Inside, she related what had happened but did not go into detail about the contents of the tape the police officer had taken. The tape had been difficult to listen to for Denise, and she saw no need to distress the Pricketts with its frightening details, especially Ben.

Still, after listening to Denise and seeing the shattered glass from the back door, Ben became even angrier.

"I'll find him and I'll kill him if he's hurt Jeannie," he said.

It was nearly half an hour before Jeannie's car pulled into the driveway, and everybody rushed outside. Jeannie's hair was wildly disheveled, her clothes soiled and torn, her face battered.

"She was scared to death," Ben said years later, remembering the scene a father could never forget. "She was pale looking, and she had bruises on her neck." Jeannie said nothing as she rushed sobbing into her mother's arms.

Still keeping her silence, she hugged her father, all the while looking with frightened eyes past them to Denise.

"I have to talk to you," she finally said to Denise, speaking for the first time. She led the way to Denise's bedroom at the far end of the hall, clearly not wanting her parents to know what she had to say.

"Pernell let me go to talk you out of going to the police," Jeannie said, closing the door as she did. "He said he'd do something to you and Dawn if you do."

The thought that this violence could spread to her child sent a chill down Denise's spine.

"Jeannie, it's too late," Denise said. "The police already have the tape."

"There really was a tape?" Jeannie said.

"Yes, there really was a tape."

19

No More Miracles

While Jeannie and Denise talked in Denise's bedroom, her father pondered what he should do. His instinct was to find Pernell and take care of the matter himself, but he didn't know where to begin to look for him. He was still considering his options when Jeannie returned from the bedroom. She was moving as if in a daze, and as he watched her, Ben suddenly knew what he had to do.

"It's time to go," he said to her, trying to sound strong.

"Go where?" Jeannie asked.

"To the police station."

"I can't," she protested.

"Jeannie, you have to."

Too weak and defeated to resist, she nodded her acquiesence. Ben put his arm around her and walked her to his car. Denise came with them. At the Chesapeake Police Department, Jeannie was taken to an interview room to talk with Charles Winslow, the officer who had come to the house earlier. After half an hour, Winslow and Jeannie emerged and Winslow took photos showing Jeannie's bruises.

"May I speak with you?" Winslow said to Ben after taking the photos. This time, Ben accompanied him to the interview room, while Jeannie waited with Denise.

"She's been through a lot," Winslow began.

"I know," Ben said.

"Do you know who this Pernell Jefferson is?"

"He's this black guy who's been tormenting Jeannie for months. Used to live in Virginia Beach. I guess he lives up at Richmond now," Ben answered. "Denise, the girl with us, can probably tell you more about him than I can."

"Well, your daughter says he took her out to the Hilton at the airport and checked into a room. She said he beat her pretty bad and tried to choke her and that he raped her, but she won't press charges. Unless she's willing to swear out a warrant, there's not much we can do."

"Let me talk to her," Ben said. This was the first time the possibility that Jeannie had been raped had come up, and he was upset that Jeannie would not press charges.

He took Jeannie aside, and being as gentle as he knew how to be, pushed her to swear out warrants for Pernell.

"I can't, Daddy," she said.

"Why can't you?" Ben asked.

"I just can't."

"But why?" Ben was growing exasperated.

"Let's just drop it," Jeannie said. "If I do anything, it'll just make him madder."

"I'm not worried about how it would make him feel," Ben said, bristling. "I just think it's time we did something about this."

"Daddy, I really can't," she persisted.

"You can, Jeannie," Denise said, though she was keenly aware of the reason Jeannie was hesitating.

"No," Jeannie said.

Ben finally gave up. Together, the three walked back to their car and pulled out of the parking lot. For a time, there was silence in the car.

"Jeannie, I've got something to say to you," Ben finally said as they drove along darkened streets. "I'm going to take care of this thing myself."

Jeannie turned and looked at her father. "What are you going to do?"

"No matter how long it takes me, I'm going to find Pernell Jefferson and I'll kill him."

"Daddy, you can't do that. You can't do that to me and you can't do that to Mother. You have to promise me you won't do something like that."

But Ben drove on in silence.

"Promise me," she insisted.

"Whatever you say, Sweetheart," he said.

Jeannie spent a fitful night in her old room at her parents' house. The next day brought more pressures, first from her father, then from a Chesapeake detective, Michael Slezak, to press charges against Pernell.

Slezak had conferred with Winslow the night before, but had not played a direct role until the following day when he called Jeannie and attempted to persuade her to file charges. He talked with her several times, but Jeannie remained adamant, declining even to give her reasons, and by sundown, Slezak had given up. He filed his summary as an addition to Winslow's report and at the end of it he typed in capital letters: EXCEPTIONALLY CLOSED.

"If you're with some guy and you don't mind that he's breaking your nose, what am I going to do?" Slezak asked years later, as he recalled the frustration of trying to persuade Jeannie to take legal action. He said Jeannie's reluctance was typical of domestic abuse cases. "When a victim's a hostile witness, we have a terrible time prosecuting someone. She made it very clear to me and others that she didn't want to prosecute."

Jeannie returned to work the following day and later told Denise that she got a call from Pernell.

"Just calling to find out if you were dumb enough to call the police," he told her.

"You can forget the police. They're not involved," she answered, and hung up the phone.

"I couldn't take the responsibility for taking somebody's life away and putting them behind bars," Jeannie later told Denise's mother, Arlene Bratten, whom she had known all her life. "I'm just not that kind of person." But Denise knew that the real reason was Jeannie's fear that Pernell might do something to Dawn.

Pernell knew that his threats had achieved the result he wanted. As long as Jeannie thought other people were in danger if she did not do Pernell's bidding, he held her in his spell.

Now the calls to Jeannie's new number at Denise's house came more frequently, and more threateningly, and at all hours of the day and night. He left five and six messages a day on the answering machine. In one, he said he had Tony's telephone number in Pennsylvania and was thinking about calling him about Jeannie's behavior. In another, he informed Jeannie that he had taken some of her panties and a favorite negligee when he had left the apartment the day she returned from Pennsylvania, and he was considering placing them in the mail to Tony. Several times, he taunted Jeannie about her April 27 court date in Richmond.

During this period, the only bright spots in Jeannie's life were the regular calls from Tony, who knew nothing about her troubles. He called to talk about plans for their wedding, called with travel details for their honeymoon in Mexico. Jeannie tried to sound cheerful for Tony, although she was becoming more and more depressed. When Tony sensed it and asked about her mood, she dismissed it by saying that the court calendar was crowded and she was tired.

Then, just two weeks after he abducted Jeannie, Pernell turned her life upside down with a single call. To Tony. He said that Jeannie was his woman and warned him to leave her alone. After two hours of troubled thinking, Tony called Jeannie.

"I just got a call from somebody named Pernell," he told her, and

Denise would later recall that the words took Jeannie's breath away. Her greatest fear had come true. Pernell clearly was intent on ruining her life.

Later, Jeannie would tell Denise that Tony had simply said that he couldn't handle this situation and thought it best that they suspend their relationship. After hanging up, Denise would recall, Jeannie stood for a long time looking at the phone, as if dazed. Then she replaced the receiver, ran to her room and buried her face in the pillow, weeping deeply. Denise tried to comfort her but only could caress the back of her head as Jeannie gave in to crushing emotion.

Jeannie's depression deepened drastically in coming days. "When Tony called and broke off their plans, that call just took the life out of her," Denise said.

From that point, according to Carrie, Jeannie began telling her parents that she feared Pernell was going to kill her. She rarely slept. She wept often. Her hands trembled. At her parents' house, she occasionally sat with her father's .22 pistol in her lap. At home, she kept a big knife between her mattress and box springs near the head of her bed within easy reach.

"She had gotten to the point that she felt she had no control over her life at all," Denise said. "She just didn't care what happened any more. She didn't smile. She almost didn't eat. I know that she felt that she might be better off dead. When Pernell made that call to Tony, it's like he took away her only reason to live. That was devastating.

"But Jeannie would not have killed herself. When I was going through my divorce and was so depressed, there were times I thought I was suicidal. I thought about killing myself. Jeannie knew that was happening to me and she'd always tell me that that wouldn't solve anything.

"Jeannie was under more stress than most of us ever have to face, but I don't think those beliefs changed for her. I mean, this was a deep-seated belief she had. When I talked that way, Jeannie would say to me, 'Denise, you'll go to hell if you kill yourself. God doesn't save those who kill themselves.'"

Few people other than Denise fully understood what Jeannie was going through. Jeannie's co-worker, Christine White, knew that Jeannie was having difficulty, although she had no idea of its extent, and she offered to loan Jeannie her dog for protection, but Jeannie declined.

Jeannie had talked with her brother in Richmond about her problems with Pernell, and he tried to help, as well. Twice Sam phoned Pernell at work to tell him that Jeannie no longer wanted to see him. Each time, Pernell had been cordial and accommodating and Sam felt he had reached an understanding with him.

Even after her abduction, Jeannie kept some things from her family, not wanting to worry them more. She didn't tell them about the warrant that Pernell had sworn out for her, and she explained her trip to Richmond by saying she had to attend a seminar. She drove to Richmond on April 26 and stayed the night at her brother's apartment so that she could be in court at nine the next morning.

Pernell failed to appear at the hearing, and the charges were dismissed. Only later did Jeannie admit to her mother the real reason for her trip. She told her that she had been charged with threatening Pernell's life and acknowledged that the threat was serious. Given the chance, she said, she would have killed him for all that he had done to her.

After the trip to Richmond, Jeannie became even more paranoid about Pernell, always making sure the knife was within easy reach when she went to bed.

"She even practiced grabbing it in a hurry," Denise recalled. "She'd lie on her bed and by placing the knife in various places try to decide what was quicker. She'd put it under her pillow just to see how long it'd take her to get it into her hands. Then she'd put it in the nightstand beside her bed, pretend to be sleeping, then suddenly she'd roll over and reach for the knife."

"The joy had gone out of her life," her mother said years later. "Jeannie had been someone full of life, fun to be around. But after she was kidnapped there was an emptiness about her, a kind of hollowness in her eyes."

Remembering how Jeannie had forced her back into life after her divorce, at one point taking her favorite party dress from the closet and ordering her to put it on, telling her she was going out whether she wanted to or not, Denise now attempted to do the same thing for Jeannie. Nothing seemed to work, however, and Denise despaired that Jeannie had lost all interest in living.

Early in May, Mike Reardon called. He had introduced Jeannie to Pernell, and after Jeannie had started dating him, she had quit seeing Mike and he knew nothing about her troubles with his former football teammate. Now he asked her out again. Reluctant at first, Jeannie accepted at Denise's urging, and Denise helped her select the outfit she would wear. Denise felt like a mother when she sent Jeannie off to meet Mike that evening.

"You look nice, Jeannie," she said. "Now just have a good time and don't worry about anything."

The evening went well. Jeannie seemed to have a good time, and Mike asked her out again for Friday night, May 5.

At work Friday, Jeannie began to feel achy. She had started sniffling and sneezing two days earlier, the first signs that she was catching her annual spring cold. She had worried that it might spoil her weekend. For the first time in perhaps a month, Jeannie had told Denise that she was actually looking forward to having Saturday lunch with her mother and touring the shopping malls with the $30 she had held out of her weekly check after making her first-of-the-month payments.

Scheduled to work only half a day on Friday, Jeannie left work at noon and went to her parents' home, where she fell asleep on the couch. Her mother later followed her home and remained until Denise arrived home. Both roommates planned to go out later. Jeannie had a date with Mike. Denise had for months been attending weekly ballroom dancing lessons and the last class was scheduled for that night, to be followed by a party.

When Denise arrived at home near 5:30, Carrie said her goodbyes and headed back across town to prepare dinner for Ben. Denise felt sleepy. She set her clock for eight and fell asleep in the recliner in the living room. Jeannie, feeling the effects of her cold, curled up on her bed and also fell asleep.

Both awoke with a start when Denise's alarm sounded. Denise took a quick shower and began to dress in a ballroom outfit. Jeannie slipped into jeans and a favorite blouse and fretted over her hair.

"See you later," Jeannie said as she started out the door.

"I'll probably be home before you are," Denise called. "If you decide to be out all night, just call and leave a message so I'll know."

"I will," said Jeannie.

"Be careful," Denise said as she watched Jeannie climb into the 300 ZX that she so loved so much.

"I always said to her to be careful," Denise said years later. "It was just a habit, just something I always felt I had to say. I knew she was going to be with Mike and she'd be safe with Mike."

Jeannie tooted her horn as she drove away.

At 9:30, Denise excused herself from her dancing lessons and called home to make certain that something hadn't gone wrong with Jeannie's date and that she hadn't returned to the house alone. She was reassured when she got no answer.

She called a couple more times later, each time with the same result.

But at 10:45, Jeannie's mother called the house as a safety check and was surprised when Jeannie answered.

"Why are you home so early?" Carrie asked.

"With this cold, I wasn't very good company," Jeannie answered and Carrie could hear the stuffiness over the phone.

"Are you by yourself?" Carrie asked.

"Yes," Jeannie said.

"Are you afraid?"

139

"Not really."

"Do you want me to come over?"

"No, that's all right."

"We're still on for lunch tomorrow, aren't we?"

"Sure are," Jeannie replied. "See you about noon."

Some time after one in the morning, Denise returned home, parked her Jeep in the back drive and entered the house through the back door. She walked through the den and kitchen and turned right down the hall to the bedrooms. She looked quickly into Jeannie's room as she passed. Jeannie wasn't there.

"Atta girl, Jeannie," Denise said to herself, as she climbed into bed. "She and Mike must be having a good time."

20

A Mother Knows

Denise awakened with a start on Saturday morning, May 6. She looked at the glowing numbers on the alarm clock beside her bed. It was almost 8:30. She had to work this Saturday, and she was going to be late.

She hurried to get ready and rushed toward the back door, calling out "Jeannie, I'm going," as she passed her friend's bedroom. Jeannie's door was open, but she wasn't there. Her unmade bed was empty. Denise figured she'd already gotten up and left. She knew Jeannie had a big day planned with her mother. Their housemate, Jerome, was away for the weekend and wouldn't be back until Monday night. As she did most weekends, Denise's daughter Dawn was staying with Denise's mother, Arlene Bratten.

As Denise sped off to work, Jeannie's mother was beginning a leisurely morning. Just before noon, she set out for the beauty shop to meet Jeannie. She arrived on time but Jeannie wasn't there.

"Jackie, has Jeannie already left?" Carrie asked her daughter's favorite hairdresser, who was her own as well.

"I haven't seen her yet," Jackie responded.

"Must be running late today," Carrie guessed out loud. "When she comes in, tell her I came by and when she gets through she can come on out to the house."

By one, Carrie had begun to wonder where Jeannie might be. She called her house and left a message on the answering machine. An hour later, when Jeannie still hadn't showed up or called, she called again.

"It's me again," she cheerfully told the answering machine.

Twice more she called that afternoon. Still no answer. But long-time family friend Nora Casey had invited Ben, Carrie and Jeannie to dinner that Saturday night and Carrie had that to look forward to. Jeannie would tell her then, Carrie reasoned, why her day had not gone as planned.

At 4:15 Denise arrived home from work. As usual, she entered the house from the back, where she parked. She went directly to her room, changed into jeans, a knit shirt and sneakers, then peeked into Jeannie's room to see if Jeannie had returned. *Still with her mother,* Denise thought. Leaving the back door open, Denise searched out a few gardening tools and began attending to some yard work along the back sidewalk leading to the garage.

At five, Denise heard the phone ringing and hurried inside.

It was Carrie. "Denise, let me speak to Jeannie."

"She's not with you?" Denise said.

"I haven't seen her," Carrie said. "When she comes in, have her call me."

Now Denise was worried. She returned once more to Jeannie's bedroom, stood in the doorway and looked for something that would tell her where her housemate was. She found nothing. And Jeannie had left no message on the memo device on the telephone answering machine in Denise's room.

For the first time since she had left for her dancing lessons the night before, Denise now walked toward the front of the house. The moment she saw the splintered front door leaning against the wall, Denise felt suddenly ill. Her trembling hands pressed against her cheeks as she stood in stunned horror, unable to move.

Despite her fear, she forced herself to the phone, and, fighting the panic that was welling inside her, she dialed the Pricketts' number. Carrie answered.

"Carrie, I'm scared," Denise said, breaking into tears. "Something's happened."

"What? What's happened?"

"I don't know. The front door's been kicked in."

Just as they had done two months earlier, Carrie and Ben rushed from their house. This time as they sped across town, Ben tried to think of ways to find Pernell. This time, he said to himself, Jeannie wouldn't talk him out of doing what he should have done earlier.

Back in the living room awaiting the arrival of the Pricketts, Denise stared in disbelief at the splintered door and wondered what had taken place there, and when. A deep feeling of foreboding swept over her. "It was the worst feeling in the world," she remembered years later. "I had a feeling that Jeannie was dead."

Attempting to overcome her fear, Denise paced. Down the hall to the bedrooms. Back again. Into the kitchen and then the den. To the closed door to Jerome's room. Several times she paused at the door to Jeannie's room. That room had always smelled of Jeannie, her favorite perfumes, her choice in powders, even the hint of freshness in her shampoo.

Now Denise realized that those comforting, familiar aromas were gone. "It was like confirmation that she was dead," Denise later recalled.

Denise paced some more, trying to gather her thoughts. Finally she

142

decided she could not wait for the Pricketts. She dialed the Chesapeake Police number and asked for Detective Slezak. The dispatcher reported that Slezak was out of the office but probably could be reached in his car.

"Please tell him to come to 123 Hibben Road. I think Jeannie Butkowski has been kidnapped again," she said, hanging up just as the Pricketts arrived.

Carrie and Ben stopped in astonishment at the sight of the splintered door that had been ripped from its hinges and now rested battered and broken against the living room wall. Both knew that this time something horrible had happened.

As she stood there, Carrie tried to envision Jeannie's face, she later recalled. She knew merely by closing her eyes how her older daughter Carrie looked, and how her son Sam looked with that red hair and that warm smile. But in her memory now Jeannie's features were blocked out.

"Ben," she said. "Jeannie's dead."

"Carrie, we won't know that until we find her," Ben said.

Then, calling on all her strength, Carrie said, "We've got to find her."

Yielding to his feeling that he ought to do something — anything — Ben tried unsuccessfully to restore the front door to its hinges. He struggled with it, trying to align the hinges that no longer would match up with the places they had connected to the frame. Finally, realizing the door was too badly shattered to be of any more use, he leaned it against an outside wall just as a TV news crew from WBEC, Channel 13 in Norfolk, arrived and walked into the living room without invitation. They soon were followed by a reporter from the Norfolk *Virginian-Pilot*.

The police were the last to arrive. Instead of Slezak, two uniformed officers had been dispatched. Slezak would not enter the case until Sunday morning, after reading the preliminary written report.

"It was mass confusion," Ben remembered years later. "The television people, the reporters, and here were these policemen walking around, talking, trying to figure out who else might have been involved.

"We knew who did it. We just couldn't prove it. The police just walked in and didn't do anything. They didn't even dust for fingerprints."

What Ben had not realized at the time is that by attempting to rehang the front door, it was possible that he had contaminated the best prints the intruders might have left.

The TV crew interviewed one of the officers, who said that he was not yet certain whether this had been an abduction, angering Ben and Carrie. Then the crew turned its lights and camera on Ben and Carrie. "Suddenly, I saw a side of Carrie I had never seen before," Denise remembered.

"Get out of here and leave us alone!" Carrie screamed.

Ben came quickly to his wife's side. "We don't have anything to say," he said, and ordered the reporters out of the house. Outside, the TV crew filmed the shattered door.

"Just leave us alone," Carrie screamed through the door, then collapsed in tears on the living room couch. Denise ran to her side and put an arm around her. "I didn't mean to do that," Carrie said. "Tell them I'm sorry. I just can't talk to anybody right now."

Though she thought it unnecessary, Denise made the rounds to the reporters apologizing for Carrie, explaining that the Pricketts were under a lot of stress.

The Pricketts and Denise got the feeling that not even the police knew what to do next.

"Maybe Mike knows something," Denise said but she had no phone number for him. She knew only that he was a police officer in Norfolk's K-9 unit. The information operator told her his number was not listed.

Out of desperation, Denise pushed the redial button on the phone in Jeannie's bedroom, though she had no way of knowing who had been the last person to get a call from Jeannie. Denise guessed it would be the Pricketts' own number.

The phone on the other end of the line was ringing. Once. Twice. Almost three times.

"Hello," came the strong voice of a man.

"Who is this?" Denise asked.

"Who wants to know?" Mike responded cautiously.

"I'm a friend of Jeannie's," Denise said just as cautiously.

"Denise?"

"Mike?"

Each had recognized the other's voice at almost the same moment.

"What's wrong, Denise?" asked Mike, now sensing the desperation in her voice.

"Mike, she's gone," Denise said, once again close to tears. She told Mike about the battered door, the missing car and Jeannie leaving no message.

"What do you think happened?" Mike asked.

"I think Pernell took her. He did this once before, a couple of months ago. That time he let her go. What do you think we ought to do?"

"I think you ought to call the Chesapeake Police," Mike advised.

"We already have," said Denise. "They haven't done anything."

"In the early part of the case, we didn't know if the victim was alive or dead," Detective Michael Slezak said in an interview in June 1995. "There was more information that she was alive than that she was dead, we felt."

"I guess the Chesapeake Police were going by the book," Carrie said. "But we weren't interested in the book. We wanted Jeannie found."

Through the long night, the Pricketts and Denise kept a sleepless vigil at the house, hoping for the phone to ring as it had before, with Jeannie on the line. Uncertain what to do, where to look, they could only wait.

Late in the evening, Carrie called her long-time friend Nora Casey, who had prepared the food for Jeannie's aborted wedding to Tito, and she came to offer whatever support she could. Carrie remembered Jeannie saying once that she and Pernell had visited some friends on New Market Road. Carrie and Nora drove out to the road looking for Jeannie's car, but couldn't find it and returned to the house.

Twice, Mike called Denise for updates, the second time near midnight.

"I decided I'd just go get Jeannie and bring her home," Mike said years later, recalling his thoughts about that night. Like the Chesapeake Police, Mike had not thought the battered door was a particularly ominous sign. "I still didn't feel like Jeannie was in a life-threatening situation," he said. "It's what we'd call a domestic situation. But I knew her mom, too, and I decided I owed it to her to go get Jeannie."

During his second call, Mike told Denise that he would do just that. He knew Pernell. He was certain that if he could find him he could persuade him to release Jeannie. Denise, however, was unable to provide Pernell's address, only his telephone number in Richmond, which she had found among Jeannie's phone records. She told Mike that Pernell would be driving a gold Pontiac Fiero.

Mike was scheduled to work later Sunday morning, but he arranged for his hours to be changed, and at two, he took his intensely trained German shepard, Lesko, and headed to Richmond. There he went to a police precinct, indentified himself as an officer from Norfolk and said he had come in search of a friend who had been abducted from her home. He asked if the Richmond police files held any information that would tell him where Pernell lived, but nothing turned up.

Mike didn't want to call Pernell's number and give him a chance to flee with Jeannie. He just wanted to knock on Pernell's door, tell him to hand over Jeannie and get back home in time for his delayed shift. He found a phone book at a convenience store and searched it for Pernell's number, hoping to find an address, but no number was listed for Pernell. He searched through all the Jeffersons in the book, hoping to match the number Denise had given him, but had no luck at that either. Then he remembered that Pernell's sister was named Richardson. Under that name he found a match for his number and jotted down the address. He stopped a passing policeman for directions and headed for a neighborhood on the city's south side, where he expected to find Jeannie with Pernell.

He located the apartment complex and spotted a gold Fiero nearby. He looked for Jeannie's charcoal gray Nissan ZX with the TIGRE Z license plate, but it was nowhere in sight.

Getting out of his car with Lesko at his side on a leash, Mike walked to the Fiero and placed his palm on the hood to feel for heat from the engine. It was cold. The car had not been moved in some time.

Cautiously, Mike approached the apartment and knocked on the door. He started to knock again but heard movement inside and waited. Soon the door opened and Pernell was standing before him in his undershorts.

"Mike," Pernell said, seemingly surprised. "What brings you here at this time of morning, man?"

"I'm looking for Jeannie, Pernell," Mike said. "I know y'all have been having some hard times and I wanted to come check with her. She's been missing for a while and her parents and friends are worried about her." As he talked, Mike looked for telltale signs of a struggle on Pernell's body, scratches, bites, anything, but he saw none.

"I guess I can't help you," Pernell answered. "Jeannie and I broke up some time ago. It's been two weeks since I saw her, maybe longer."

Pernell didn't invite him in, but Mike remained at the door for at least ten minutes chatting, hoping for some sign that Pernell knew something, but Pernell displayed no discomfort, no stress. Mike later recalled that Pernell was not acting like a man who had something to hide.

It was almost six when Mike headed back to Norfolk. He stopped just off the interstate to call Denise.

"I found Pernell," he told her. "Jeannie's nowhere around here."

He doubted that Pernell had anything to do with this, he said.

"Thanks for checking," Denise said.

"I'm on my way home. Let Carrie know. And let me know if there's anything else I can do."

Mike was not the only driver on Interstate 64 that morning worried about Jeannie's fate. At about the same time Mike was heading home, Jeannie's brother Sam was leaving Richmond for Chesapeake. He had waited at home hoping for good news about his sister, but it hadn't come, and now he was going to see what he could do.

"Have you heard anything?" he asked, when he arrived at Denise's house where his parents were still waiting an hour after sunup.

"Nothing," his mother reported. "Sam, I think she's dead."

"She was so scared of Pernell," Sam said. "Maybe she's hiding somewhere."

146

In desperation, Sam began to search the house, even climbing into the dark, dusty attic, but finding nothing that might lead him to his sister.

At mid-morning, the Pricketts decided they had to do something and launched their own search. Carrie and Nora in one car, Ben and Sam in another drove through the parking lots of every hotel and motel within a mile of I-64 from Chesapeake to Williamsburg looking for either Jeannie's distinctive Nissan or Pernell's gold Fiero. They searched for hours, calling Denise regularly to see if there was any news.

A friend of Denise's arrived with a new door and installed it. Unannounced, a TV news crew arrived for an update and trained the camera on the repair work. When Denise was alone again, she busied herself by sweeping the wood shavings from the new door out of her driveway. As she worked, a police cruiser stopped at the curb and an officer got out and walked over to her.

"Just between us," she later remembered him saying, "what's the real story? You can tell me. What really happened to your friend? You know where she is don't you?"

Denise flew into a rage. Screaming at the police officer, she ordered him from her yard. As he left, Denise ran crying to her house, slamming the new door behind her, and throwing herself onto her bed, no longer able to control her emotions.

Since her telephone conversation near dawn with Mike, Denise once again had been trying to decide what she should do. She was certain that Pernell was lying. Given the March abduction and the abuse he had heaped on Jeannie in recent months, there could be no other explanation. And if the police weren't going to question Pernell, Denise decided she was certainly going to try. She dialed the his sister's number in Richmond.

"Hello," a woman's voice answered.

"Is this where Pernell Jefferson lives?" Denise asked.

"Yes it is."

"May I speak to him?"

"Who's calling?"

"Denise Edwards."

"He's not here."

"I'll call back."

Twice more over the next two hours Denise called and got the same response. Growing frustrated, she dialed the number again late in the afternoon, this time changing her voice and mimicking jive talk.

"Hey, Mama, is ol' P.J. 'round?"

"Just a minute."

Denise heard the woman calling, "P.J., it's for you."

Then Pernell was on the the line.

"I don't know what you've done to Jeannie," Denise said, bristling, "but you'd better bring her home. And you'd better return her safe. Do you understand, Pernell Jefferson?"

"What are you talking about?" Pernell responded. "I didn't do nothing to Jeannie."

"Pernell," Denise said, raising her voice as anger rushed over her. "I'm warning you. You'd better not harm a hair on her head."

"You will get down on your hands and knees and beg for forgiveness for threatening me," Pernell shouted and slammed down the phone.

On the Sunday evening news, Channel 13 in Norfolk reported that Jeannie was still missing and so was her charcoal gray Nissan 300 ZX bearing the unusual license plate, TIGRE Z.

The Chesapeake Police Department also had issued a Crime Line alert for the Nissan, and suddenly calls began coming in. Cars matching the description had been seen traveling west on I-64 near Norfolk, in Virginia Beach and on U.S. 460 near Petersburg. At times the calls came in clusters, keeping the Chesapeake Police busy hurrying to various locations.

"That went on for several days, sightings all over the place," Slezak said in 1995. "We were doing all we could to hunt that car down and we were getting lots of reports."

Sunday night, Carrie, Ben and Sam returned home to rest. "We only slept from exhaustion," Carrie said. "We went for as long as we could, but after a while the body just shuts down on you and you have no choice but to rest."

On Monday morning, Carrie called her office to say she would be out of work for a while, and Sam phoned the computer service center where he worked in Richmond and asked to be excused for a few days. Ben went to work as usual but was unable to keep his mind on his job and came home early. "I went because I had to do something," he said later. "I had to keep busy if I could." He would not return to his job for three weeks.

By Tuesday afternoon, Ben was becoming a problem for the Chesapeake Police. He kept calling to ask if there had been a break in the case, if Pernell had been arrested, if he had even been questioned. He was growing more and more convinced that the case really was being treated as nothing more than a runaway.

Sam stayed until Wednesday afternoon and continued to search places in the Tidewater he knew had been familiar to Jeannie. Several times he turned around to chase passing Nissans, hoping they might be Jeannie's, but each time he was disappointed.

Denise had not been able to return to work either, and Jeannie's disappearance had changed her life in a more important way. She no longer felt the house in which she had once wanted to raise her daughter was a safe haven. She now left Dawn with her mother around the clock, seldom seeing her, while she kept a vigil at the house. "If Jeannie was still alive and called home," Denise said, "I was going to be there to answer the phone." She kept a loaded .22-caliber pistol in the hand-pouch of her baggy sweatshirt as she waited, and she jumped every time the phone rang, fearful of the news it might bring.

On Wednesday, May 10, four days after Jeannie had been discovered missing, the day Sam returned to Richmond, a call came with news she didn't want to hear.

"Are you a friend of Jeannie Butkowski?" an unfamiliar male voice asked.

"Yes! Yes!" Denise answered.

"Don't ask me my name. I can't give you my name and...."

"Okay, you didn't hear me ask, did you?"

"I want you to know that I'm Catholic, and I was raised right. And I just can't live with this on my conscience."

"Where's Jeannie?" Denise blurted, interrupting him.

"She's dead."

For a moment, silence dominated the line. Denise struggled to keep her composure. "Please," she finally said, "can you hold on for a few minutes?"

"I don't know. I can't afford to hold on long," the voice said.

"I've got to do something. It'll only take me a minute."

Again there was silence and Denise held her breath. "Just hurry," he finally responded.

"Good," Denise said.

Denise placed the receiver beside the phone, raced to a neighbor's house and called Detective Slezak. She told him she had a man on the phone who knew something about Jeannie's disappearance. Slezak said he would get there as quickly as he could. Then Denise called Carrie and told her to bring Ben and get to the house quick. She then rushed back across the street to the telephone.

"Are you still there?" she asked breathlessly, jerking the telephone to her ear.

"I can't afford this phone call," the man complained.

"Look, there are a couple of people you've got to talk to. They're on the way to the house," Denise said, worried now that she would scare him away. "Will you do that?"

"Who are they?" he asked.

"Well, the police for one."

Again there was silence, as if the caller were struggling with his decision. That worried Denise. Questions raced through her mind. Would he hang up? If he did, would this be the only chance to find out what had happened to Jeannie?

Finally, he spoke.

"You'd have to make a deal for me," he said.

"What kind of deal?"

"I know where the body is, but if Pernell finds out I told the police, he'll kill me too. I'll talk to the police if they won't say that I told them where to find her."

"I'll try."

"So, when will they be here? I can't hold on very long."

"You've got to," she pleaded. Keeping the anonymous caller on the phone had become a battle of wills.

"I can't," he responded.

Now Denise knew she had to take a chance on losing him. "Tell you what," she said, "why don't you hang up now and call me back in a few minutes when they've had a chance to get here."

"How long do you think that'll be?"

"Not very long, I hope. Half an hour at the most."

"I guess so," he said reluctantly.

"So you will call back in twenty to thirty minutes?"

Now he began to waver again. "I don't know," he said. "I can't afford any more phone calls."

"Call collect," she said quickly.

Another pause.

"But I told you I can't tell you who I am, so how can I call collect?" he said.

"That's okay," Denise told him. "Just say you're Mike."

He agreed, but without enthusiasm. She heard the click on the other end of the line. What if he didn't call back? How could she tell Carrie and Ben that Jeannie was dead?

Now Denise waited.

Once again Carrie and Ben arrived ahead of Slezak. They had just walked in when Denise's telephone rang again.

"I have a collect call for anyone at this number from Mike. Will you accept the charges?" the operator asked.

"Yes!" Jeannie said. "Hello!"

"It's me," the stranger said. Though a stranger with bad news, his voice was welcome.

"Will you talk to Jeannie's dad?" she asked.

"Sure."

Denise handed the phone to Ben.

"Yeah," Ben said gruffly as he put the phone to his ear. "What do you know about this?"

"I want you to know I'm a devout Catholic and I can't bear to have this on my conscience any longer," the caller began.

"So, get it off your conscience," Ben said. "What happened to Jeannie?"

"She's dead."

Ben later would recall that the words made his head spin. He fought to keep his emotions in check.

"Are you lying?" he said, clinging to faint hope.

"No, sir."

"You'd better not be lying because we're recording this," Ben said, lying himself.

Slezak arrived while Ben was on the phone and joined the others. "I'm just telling you what I know," the caller said.

"Where is she?"

"He buried her just outside of Richmond up here."

Ben had heard enough. "Would you tell this to the police officer? He's right here." Ben handed the phone to Slezak.

"This is Detective Slezak of the Chesapeake Police Department. You say you know that Jeannie Butkowski's dead?"

"Yes, sir."

"How'd it happen?"

"Pernell said he shot her."

"Where'd he shoot her?" Slezak pressed.

"I don't know. Somewhere here in Richmond, I guess."

"Do you know where the body is?"

"Yes, sir."

"How do you know?"

"'Cause I drove out there with Pernell when he went to bury it, that's how."

"Do you know where Pernell is right now?"

"Yes, sir. He's at work. At Remco in Southside Plaza."

"I'm going to have to come to Richmond and talk to you some more."

The caller balked. The woman who'd answered the phone had told him that he would be kept out of this, he told the detective, sounding frightened.

"If Pernell knows I've been talking, he'll kill me, too," he said.

"How about meeting me somewhere up there where Pernell won't know," Slezak suggested without getting a response.

"You've got to help us catch this guy," Slezak said. "I'll do everything I can to protect you."

"I don't know," he said, still reluctant.

"Look, we'll meet when and where you say," Slezak offered.

"Okay," he finally agreed.

"What's your name?"

"I told the lady I can't tell you that."

"Look, I've got to know who you are sooner or later. I'm not going to go running to Pernell and tell him I've been talking to you."

"Okay, it's St. Augustine."

Slezak jotted down the name. "You got a first name?"

"They call me Joey."

St. Augustine agreed to meet Slezak near downtown Richmond on Thursday morning. When Slezak arrived alone the next day, he saw a tall, thin man with Asian features and a light complexion waiting on the street. The man came to his car when he pulled up at the curb.

"St. Augustine?" Slezak said.

"Yes, sir."

St. Augustine climbed into the car and talked with Slezak for an hour. He said that Pernell had called him well before sunrise Saturday to tell him he had killed Jeannie and he needed help in getting rid of her car. When Pernell came for him, he said he had to bury Jeannie's body before taking care of the car. He drove Pernell's car to a construction site for a new church off Belmont Road where Pernell said he had hidden Jeannie's body, he told Slezak. There he let Pernell out and drove around for a while because Pernell was concerned that a strange car at the construction site might attract attention.

"You'll have to show me where the body's buried," Slezak told St. Augustine and he reluctantly agreed.

Slezak had his office in Chesapeake alert the Chesterfield County Police Department that he needed assistance in a possible homicide. Chesterfield investigator Ernie Hazard received the request and called Ray Williams, a detective with the Richmond Police Department, asking that he, too, join the investigation.

Williams and Hazard met Slezak and St. Augustine in southeast Richmond, and the four went to the construction site off Belmont Road. After they had searched the site and nearby woods without coming upon any sign of a body or a fresh grave, St. Augustine expressed bafflement.

Slezak felt that St. Augustine had led him on a wild goose chase and was not being truthful. He returned to Chesapeake, leaving Hazard and Williams to contend with St. Augustine.

Williams thought that St. Augustine had been telling the truth. He gave too many details to be making it up, Williams thought, and had no discernible motive for getting involved in something so serious if he weren't telling the truth. Also St. Augustine was clearly frightened of Pernell. Williams continued questioning him after Slezak left, and St. Augustine said that Pernell had told him weeks before the murder that he planned to kill Jeannie.

"When do you think you'll be seeing Pernell again?" Williams asked as they sat in Williams' unmarked car talking.

"He's supposed to come by my apartment tonight," St. Augustine answered.

"When?"

"About six-thirty, I guess."

"Good, we've got time to set up the wire," Williams said.

"The what?"

Williams said he wanted to put a listening device in St. Augustine's apartment and let St. Augustine lead Pernell into talking about the murder, hoping that he would say something incriminatory. St. Augustine was adamantly opposed to this idea. He was already in deeper than he'd ever planned to be, he said.

"If Pernell finds out I've been talking to you, I'm a dead man," he complained. "If he finds out I'm setting him up, he'll kill me on the spot."

"That's just the point," Williams said. "The quicker we get this man off the street, the safer you're going to be."

St. Augustine pondered that rationale, but still he was uncertain. "I don't know, man," he said.

Williams assured him that he would be able to hear everything taking place in the apartment and if any trouble started, he would be there instantly, but it took another hour and a half of persuasion to overcome St. Augustine's fear.

At mid-afternoon, Bill Showalter, a surveillance expert, arrived at St. Augustine's apartment in an unmarked van. By 4:30, the listening device was in place and the van in which the officers would be listening was parked across the street. Williams had a clear view of the apartment from the rear windows of the van.

It was almost seven before a Remco Rental truck arrived in the parking lot and parked near St. Augustine's apartment.

"There he is," Williams said, as Pernell got out and walked to the apartment. Showalter turned on the recording equipment, and both officers slipped on headsets.

They could hear Pernell tapping on the door, and St. Augustine opening it..

"Hi," they heard Pernell say.

"How you doing?" St. Augustine said.

But after that, the officers heard only low whispers, and they knew instantly that St. Augustine had betrayed them.

Pernell remained in the apartment for 22 minutes before emerging. They knew that he was aware that he was being watched, but he walked calmly to his truck and drove away.

Williams and Showalter waited after he left, making sure he didn't return, before they went to the apartment.

"What happened, Joey?" Williams said, his disgust and disappointment obvious.

"Man, I was scared to death," St. Augustine said. Williams could see he still was. "I just told him not to say anything."

Showalter retrieved the listening device while St. Augustine apologized repeatedly

Not only did the bugging fail, it also warned Pernell that the police were closing in. The next morning, he reported to work on schedule, but when he left for his lunch break, he never returned.

21

The Long, Lonely Vigil

Ben and Carrie were waiting anxiously for word from Slezak about his meeting with St. Augustine, and when he called and said that the mysterious caller had led the investigation into a dead end, it gave them some hope.

Still, the news left Ben with mixed feelings.

"I was hoping he was lying," Ben later said of St. Augustine. "I'm the kind who will always hold out hope until the very end."

Slezak told Ben only a little about the search for Jeannie's body and said that St. Augustine had backed out of helping.

Still, Ben had to wonder.

"Why would some guy get involved in that kind of thing if he didn't know something?"

Ben had become angry that Slezak had not gone to Richmond immediately after talking to St. Augustine instead of waiting for a day. He wondered if the trip and the search might have been more productive if Slezak had reacted more quickly.

The waiting soon turned from hours to days and finally to weeks, the Pricketts and Denise growing more frustrated and despondent with each passing day.

Denise kept her lonely vigil beside the phone for more than two weeks before returning to work at the photo lab. Ben missed three weeks from work and decided he had to get back to his job as a way of distracting himself from the anger and frustration he felt. Carrie was out of work for more than a month.

Sam had missed most of a week of work immediately after Jeannie disappeared. He had returned to his job more quickly than the rest, but spent all of his weekends now searching for his sister, sometimes with his mother and father, sometimes alone.

And he was in frequent touch with Detective Ray Williams of the Richmond Police Department and Detective Ernie Hazard in Chesterfield County, the two men who had searched the church building site for Jeannie's body. Although the investigation already was dragging by the end of May, Williams helped Sam keep up with whatever was going on and kept promising that the case would be solved, though he frequently admitted he was not certain when a breakthrough might come.

By early June, Carrie visited the family doctor "for my nerves." She was near exhaustion and her physician prescribed pills to help her sleep.

"When I got home," she said, "I took one of them and lay down on the couch. I fell asleep the way I was supposed to, but I had this awful dream and I couldn't wake up to get away from it. When I finally did wake up, I flushed the rest of the pills down the commode.

"Sleep becomes your enemy anyway when you're going through something like this. Sleep itself is like a nightmare. You don't want to go to sleep because you're always afraid something would happen and you wouldn't know about it. The phone might ring and you couldn't answer it. But mostly I was afraid they'd find Jeannie and I'd be knocked out and they couldn't get me to wake up. I didn't even want to think of sleep."

By now Carrie, if not Ben, had accepted that their daughter was dead, and late in June, Carrie asked Ben to visit Holloman & Brown Funeral Home in Virginia Beach to make arrangements for Jeannie's funeral. "When we find her, Ben," she told her husband, "neither one of us will be able to do that. I want her buried at Rosewood Memorial Park."

Though he still was not willing to accept the possibility that his daughter was dead, Ben made the arrangements.

Carrie called Jeannie's dentist and asked that he prepare a set of Jeannie's dental charts just in case they were needed. Within a week, the charts arrived in the mail.

After Carrie had returned to work with the Corps of Engineers, she was always so lost in thought that she had trouble remembering the route she took to and from work.

"All the time, you're asking yourself, 'Should we do this?' 'Have we done that?' You pick up ideas about things you can do everywhere. I'd watch one of those talk shows on television and somebody would talk about trying to find people and I couldn't do anything but sit down and watch, hoping that somebody would say something that we could do. And I wound up reading everything I could about how you find missing people."

One article she read was about a psychic from Greensburg, Pennsylvania, Nancy Czetli, who had helped police agencies solve crimes. Carrie leaped at the idea. She called Tony, Jeannie's ex-husband in Pennsylvania, and asked if he could find out how to get in touch with Czetli.

"Tony called back in a few hours," Carrie said. "He had her address, her phone number, the whole nine yards and he told me to call the psychic's secretary."

She did, only to learn that Czetli's fee was $60 an hour, that she worked only with police departments, and that she needed a sample of Jeannie's handwriting, the date and time she disappeared, the address of the house from which she disappeared, a picture of the house, a map of the area, and a picture of Jeannie.

Carrie gathered all the material and took it to Slezak.

"He let me know he didn't believe in that," Carrie recalled, and that angered her further.

"But at least I'm doing something," she snapped at him and walked out of his office.

Back at home, she phoned Sam and told him about Czetli. She asked him to call Ray Williams, the Richmond detective, and appeal to him to work with her.

Within the hour, Sam called back with the news that Williams was willing to cooperate and Carrie sent the material to him.

Czetli responded quickly.

"She told us she was dead," Carrie said. "She said Jeannie would be found close to a stream fed by the tides. She said there would be a windmill close by and there would be scrubby pines there. I already knew Jeannie was dead. The only thing the psychic did was give us an idea where to look."

From then on, the Pricketts used Czetli's readings as the basis for organized searches for their daughter.

"The point was," Carrie said, "I was dying slowly inside. I was trying to do something. This was just something else to try."

For weeks, the Pricketts plotted locations in Virginia that seemed to correspond to Czetli's descriptions, and on weekends and days off from work they made long, lonely automobile trips about the countryside searching out windmills and scrubby pines and streams fed by the tides. Regularly, Denise, too, made her own journeys to areas that had appeared on the Pricketts' list of likely spots.

A friend of the family remembered seeing a windmill in the Jamestown Plantation area, and for weeks the Pricketts covered the area, exploring every back road, all to no avail.

By early July, the private investigator Ben had hired had traced Pernell to Florida where, the investigator learned, Pernell occasionally visited with relatives in Stuart.

As soon as Ben got word of Pernell's whereabouts, he drove to the Chesapeake Police Department and marched into Slezak's office.

"He's in Stuart, Florida," Ben would later recall telling the detective.
"Who?" Slezak asked.
"Pernell Jefferson."
"What would we do with Pernell Jefferson right now?" Ben remembered Slezak replying. "We have no body, no weapon. We still don't know whether Jeannie's dead or alive. Her car hasn't even shown up yet. So what would we charge this guy with?"
"How about kidnapping?" Ben said, bristling.
"We're working on it," Slezak responded.
"Okay," Ben said, "I'm going after him myself. I can find him."
"You're not going after him," Slezak said, leaning across the desk, making it sound like an order, and that was how Ben took it. Years later, Ben said he had made the threat in the hope of pushing Slezak to action.
"Frankly, I just wanted him to get off his ass and do something."
In another moment of frustration in July, Ben phoned Slezak to find out if there were any new developments, and getting a negative answer, told Slezak just what he thought of his investigation.
"I don't like the way you're handling this case," he said. "You don't know nothing."

"It was evident that there were some individuals involved in this case who thought I didn't care," Slezak said in a June 1995 interview, while declining to name names. "It was said that I looked at it as just another case, and so be it. I'm not able to change what someone thinks. I'm sorry people think that way. And I'm sorry this whole situation took place.
"But the truth is that throughout this case, I had mixed ideas about what took place. With almost any case, there are a number of possibilities. What we were sure of was that she was missing. But there were other reports that she had been seen with him."
Among the reported sightings was one from a police informant in Pernell's hometown of Benson, who identified Jeannie from a picture Slezak took when he went there in June. The informant said that she had been seen in a drug house in Benson, and that she was with Pernell in Benson late in May.
Slezak thought that unlikely, since nobody had reported seeing Jeannie with Pernell in Richmond in the week after her disappearance, and Pernell had continued to work at the Remco store throughout that week.
One person in Benson offered Slezak no help at all: Pernell's brother, Willie. Slezak called him "uncooperative."
What Ben and Carrie couldn't understand was why Slezak had not gone to talk with Pernell while he was still at work at the Remco store.
"When I go in to talk with someone like that," Slezak explained in

1995, "I have had great success getting confessions because I don't go until I have something to pin on a suspect. If somebody came to me and told me you had just killed somebody, I wouldn't go rushing to talk to you. I'd want to talk to a lot of other people who might have seen that happened first. Then when I came to talk to you, I would be in a position to let you know that this isn't just a visit."

In the absence of witnesses other than St. Augustine, Slezak had concentrated on finding Jeannie's car, theorizing that it would lead him to her. He got plenty of reported sightings of the car.

"They came from all over," he recalled. From North Carolina, Florida, various points in Virginia, even one from Kansas City. "We didn't investigate the one from Kansas City," he said. "In a case like this, you have to use some common sense and not go chasing off after some lead that has very little promise.

"Obviously, locating the car became a problem. If you had to find a car in a situation like that, where would you go to look for it? There was a lot of Monday morning quarterbacking going on."

All the while, Slezak said, he was working informants as they became available.

"I have to admit that as time passed, there were days when I did nothing on this case. I had other cases to work and there were no new leads on this case. Information wasn't coming in every day any more after a while. But we were doing a lot that the family didn't know anything about, especially early on.

"In my business, you have to be careful when you talk to family members. You don't just give them all the information you have because at that time you simply don't know if some family member is involved or not. The bottom line is that I did everything I knew to do on that case, aside from a street-to-street search for the woman. It's hard to do that because the world's a big place."

In August, Jeannie's sister Carrie placed an emotional call to her mother.

"She had had a dream," Carrie said. "In the dream she saw Jeannie covered with dirt and calling out to be found. She said that everything seemed so real." So real, in fact, that her sister said she would know the location where the family could find Jeannie buried if she ever saw it.

Now Jeannie's sister became a part of the weekend searches. From Ray Williams, the Pricketts obtained directions to the church grounds southeast of Richmond where St. Augustine said Pernell had buried Jeannie. Again and again they drove along Belmont Road, out along Fairpines Street to Jessup

Street and back again. But none of the terrain matched the dream.

The search was taking Jeannie's mother away from her work, and she finally took a leave of absence to devote all of her time to it. She and Ben blanketed southeastern states with flyers seeking information. A man Jeannie had once dated in high school discovered that she was missing when he saw one of the flyers posted at a convenience store in northern Florida. All reports were passed on to the Chesapeake police including one from a husband-and-wife long-haul truck-driving team who called to say they had seen a 1985 Nissan 300 ZX with the license plate, TIGRE Z, racing north on a Florida interstate at high speed.

"My insides were like the San Francisco earthquake," Carrie said, remembering this period years later. "I couldn't put the pieces back together again. I made everybody's life miserable. It was taking all my energy twenty-four hours a day."

When sleep came, Carrie had a recurrent dream.

"Again and again, I'd dream that Jeannie's in this building, and the building has room after room after room, and they're all mostly empty. And Jeannie's in there and I'm trying to find her. And I'm down on my hands and knees crawling around everywhere trying to find her.

"I finally find her under a desk and I reach and grab her and I pull her to me and I turn her around to look at her, and I can't see her face. I always wake up trying to remember her face."

Jeannie's 30th birthday came and went in August without acknowledgement, and Thanksgiving was not observed in the Pricketts' home. As the days grew shorter and the weather colder, no news came from the police. It was as though the only people in the world still interested in what had happened to Jeannie were Ben, Carrie, their two children, Denise, and a few other friends.

As Christmas approached, the cluster of tiny, golden bells Jeannie had taped to the top of the mirror in the foyer of the family home the year before was still there. Carrie had vowed never to remove them. But her grief prevented her from putting up other decorations. When Jeannie's former co-workers at the office of the clerk of court called to ask if they could decorate in Jeannie's behalf, Carrie relented.

The tree, the bright lights and ribbons did little to boost the Pricketts' spirits. On Christmas Eve, Carrie's thoughts were elsewhere.

"You didn't love Jeannie as much as I did," she blurted to her husband, bursting into tears.

"I love Jeannie, Carrie," he replied.

"If you really loved her, Ben, you'd have gone to Florida and you would have found Pernell Jefferson and you would have killed him."

"If I knew exactly where Pernell Jefferson was," he said, "I'd have killed him a long time ago."

That evening, Ben and Carrie made the two-hour trip to Richmond to spend Christmas with Sam and his wife Lynn. On Christmas morning, Carrie broke down in tears again and her son moved to console her.

"Mom, you're going about this the wrong way," he said. "You're asking God to let us find her, but you're asking Dad to go and kill him. Why don't you say to God, 'Thy will be done, and if we can find Jeannie, I will find a way not to hate. And I will leave it all in the hands of the justice system'?"

Carrie looked into his face, still crying, and for long moments she couldn't speak. "I can't pray that prayer yet," she finally said.

"We may not find Jeannie until you can, Mama," Sam said, taking her into his arms.

"New Year's Day," she said softly. "New Year's Day. I'll pray that prayer on New Year's Day."

Ben and Carrie were back home on New Year's Day. Just before noon, Carrie went into her bedroom leaving Ben alone in the den. She made her bed. Then she lingered, thinking about what her son had told her on Christmas.

Quietly, she began to pray.

"If you let me find her, God, I won't be bitter. I'll let the justice system handle it. But I think it's time we find her. Not my will, God, but Thy will be done."

Near Amelia, about 160 miles away, hunter Randy DuClau, working his favorite dog, followed fresh deer tracks into low undergrowth and toward the distant tree line just off State Route 681.

22

The Telltale Charm

Central Virginia was cold and wet on January 1, 1990. Heavy, dark clouds made the holiday surreal, in constant twilight.

Near Nibbs Creek in Amelia County, deer hunter Michael Spain entered a growth of hardwood trees in their winter hibernation and worked his dog along the busy stream. Spain occasionally lingered over clusters of deer tracks trying to determine how fresh they were before moving on.

His partner, Randy DuClau and his favorite hunting dog, a wire-haired terrier, had followed another deer trail into low undergrowth perhaps 100 yards away. Just beyond a clearing where a power line cut a swath across the countryside, DuClau stood for a moment near a dry creek bed and tried once again to find the trail of fresh deer tracks in the gloomy light. Perhaps 15 yards away, along the side of the creek bed, his dog had become distracted.

Leaping to the distant bank, DuClau now had a small stream to negotiate and once past that he called to his dog to join him. Not far away, he could see the terrier playfully pushing about something that looked like an old ball. When DuClau called again and the dog still ignored his summons, he went to investigate. The terrier, its tail wagging excitedly, seemed proud of what it had discovered. DuClau quickly saw that the object wasn't a ball. It was a human skull.

He knelt for a closer look. Clearly visible was a ragged hole in the left temple of the skull and, as he pushed it around with his foot, he saw another hole opposite it at the rear, a few inches behind the right ear. Obviously, the holes had been made by a bullet. DuClau tentatively picked up the skull and heard something rattle inside. He shook it and again it rattled. Inside, amidst leaves and dirt he spotted what seemed to be a distorted slug.

But, he reasoned, if there were two holes, the bullet must have entered at one place and exited at the other. What else then besides the fatal bullet could this chunk of metal rattling around inside have been? It was too large to be a dislodged dental filling. So, was the small chunk of gnarled metal really what was left of a bullet? And if so, how did it get back into the skull?

He called to Spain. Getting no immediate response, he called yet again, this time more loudly, and Spain answered. "Come take a look at this," DuClau yelled.

As DuClau waited for Spain to cross Nibbs Creek and make his way along the creek bed that carried water only during torrential downpours, DuClaw thought once more about the deer tracks leading off into the distance and was annoyed that his day had been interrupted.

Finally, Spain was there staring down at the skull. "Found it right here," DuClau said.

"What are you going to do?" Spain asked.

"Take it to the sheriff's office, I guess," said DuClau.

They drove the three miles to the sheriff's office at the back of the courthouse in Amelia and parked near the big oak beside the sidewalk. DuClau carried the skull into the sheriff's office, being careful to keep the hunk of metal inside.

"Look what I found," he told Deputy Leonard Lee Wiggins Jr., the first officer he encountered. Wiggins had been enjoying a quiet, trouble-free holiday on patrol and had just stopped by the office for a break.

"Just hold it for a minute," Wiggins said declining the macabre offering. He disappeared into a nearby storage room and returned with a large plastic bag.

"Where'd you find this?" he asked as DuClau placed the skull in the bag.

"It was just laying there in a dry creek bed a few miles out of town, out where we were looking for some deer," DuClau answered. "I think the bullet's still inside."

Wiggins gently shook the skull in the plastic bag and could hear the distinct rattle.

"I'm going to have to take a statement from you and Michael," he said.

In ten minutes, Wiggins had DuClau's and Spain's brief statements, and he dialed Sheriff Jimmy Weaver's telephone number at home. He waited while Weaver's wife summoned him from the barn where he was attending his registered quarterhorses.

"Sheriff, there's something here you ought to see," he reported. "Randy DuClau just came in with a human skull. Said he found it in a field while he was out deer hunting."

Weaver told Wiggins to follow DuClau back to the scene to make sure no other hunters stumbled upon the area and disturbed any evidence. Then he called his chief deputy, Wes Terry, at home. Though it was noon, Terry was still asleep, resting up from a New Year's Eve party at which he had lingered long past midnight the night before.

"Wes," Weaver said, "better meet me at the office. Looks like our New Year's going to start out with a murder."

Weaver arrived at his office and picked up the gruesome evidence that had been left on a desk in the squad room. He took it into Wes Terry's tiny office and closed the door behind him.

The son of a West Virginia coal miner, Weaver stood six-feet-five-inches tall and weighed 250 pounds. An ex-Marine and a former member of John Kennedy's Presidential Honor Guard, he had been a detective for the Fairfax County Police Department and a chief investigator for the Virginia State Police before he and his wife moved to a farm near Amelia that had been in her family for generations. Police work followed him to his pastoral life. He had been hired as a regional investigator by the state before running successfully for sheriff in 1987.

This would be his first big case since being elected, he thought, as he placed the skull on Terry's desk so that it seemed to be looking at him. One of his favorite techniques for beginning an investigation was to close himself in a room where a crime had been committed and to sit in the middle of the floor pondering what had happened there.

"They used to kid me about the walls talking to me," Weaver later recalled. "The walls, the floors, the ceiling, the curtains. Sometimes it's like they all have something to say."

Now he sat staring at the skull. He had read Wiggins' hurried report and he, too, had shaken the skull and seen the slug inside, but it was no puzzle to him. He had seen such a phenomenon in murder cases he had investigated earlier in his career. "Tenting," he said out loud. "The bullet almost made it through, but not quite."

He shook the slug from the skull and looked at it through the plastic, moving it with the tip of his finger. "A thirty-eight," he said to himself. "Maybe a thirty-two."

He replaced the slug and spoke again to himself.

"It's not somebody from Amelia."

On his way in, he had searched his memory and knew that there were no missing person cases in Amelia. Hadn't been any since he'd become sheriff.

"Female," he said, judging from the delicate cheekbones, the fine line of the jaw and the size. "Small female. Adult, but not a large person." The structure of the bones told him it probably was a white female.

Now he looked closer, turning the skull as he did. "Red-headed female!" he said excitedly. Matted against the bone on one side was a long, solitary red hair.

"Talk to me," he said, turning the skull so that it faced him again.

He opened the bag and sniffed inside, detecting no odor of decaying flesh, no bad smell at all, and knew that this person had been dead at least four or five months, perhaps longer, considering how cold it had been since Thanksgiving.

A suicide? Not likely, he thought. Long experience had taught him that women who kill themselves almost always do it with pills, rarely with guns, and those who do choose firearms almost never shoot themselves in the head.

"They spend so much time trying to look good they usually find another way to end their lives," he explained years later.

This death seemed clear.

"It's murder," he said.

"What'd you say?" asked Wes Terry, who had just opened the door to his office.

"Murder," Weaver repeated.

"What else?" Terry asked, realizing that his boss already had begun analyzing the case.

"Probably a white female. Red-headed. Small, maybe five-feet-two, five-feet-four. Slight build most likely. Nobody around here knows her. Dead probably more than six months."

Like Weaver, Terry had an impressive resume in law enforcement. A native of Rich Square, North Carolina, he was 45, stood six-feet-one and weighed 250 pounds. He had been an agent with North Carolina's State Bureau of Investigation, The Florida Bureau of Law Enforcement and the Virginia State Police. He and Weaver had know each other since they had worked together for a chemical company in 1963. When Weaver had worked in Fairfax County, Terry had been a police officer in adjoining Arlington County. After Weaver had become an investigator for the Virginia State Police, he had recommended Terry for an opening in his department, and they had worked together on many cases before Weaver had moved to Amelia County. As soon as Weaver was elected sheriff, he called Terry and asked him to be his chief deputy.

Terry had always been impressed with Weaver's deductive abilities, even if he sometimes kidded him about them.

"Anything else?" he asked, only partially kidding.

"That'll get us started," Weaver said, reaching for the phone. He called an off-duty deputy, Les Moler, and told him to join Wiggins just off State Road 681 for a field investigation. Then he quickly called the state medical examiner in Richmond and the state police.

"Let's go," he said, turning finally to Terry.

*   *   *

By the time Weaver and Terry arrived at the scene, Wiggins already had taped off the area where the skull had been found. DuClau and Spain waited just outside that large circle.

After a quick look at the site, Weaver talked briefly with DuClau and Spain and sent them on their way. When he returned, he spotted a piece of denim protruding from the soft earth.

"Men," he said. "we've got some digging to do."

The officers dug carefully, using shovels Wiggins had brought from the sheriff's department. Turning up one small shovelful at a time, they carefully sifted each for any sign of evidence. Almost immediately, the creek bed began yielding its harvest. The piece of denim, apparently from jeans. A ring. Part of a necklace. A tampon. A cigarette butt. Bones. Lots of bones.

Weaver studied the bones and was struck by how delicate they seemed.

"Almost like a child's bones," he said later. Yet adult, he was sure.

While the other officers continued digging, Weaver walked along the creek bed almost to Nibbs Creek, some 50 yards away. He knew that animals had strewn the bones that they had been retrieving, and he was looking for clumps of hair, long red hair. But he found none.

Returning to help again with the digging, he stopped to pick up a sliver of cloth. It had the consistency, he thought, of a sheet with a small, delicate blue print pattern still visible. One edge of the cloth seemed to have been burned.

"Gentlemen," he announced, holding the fragment so that the others could see it, "This one was killed somewhere else and dumped here. And they tried to burn the evidence."

The burned sheet, Weaver felt, also explained why he had found none of the red hair he had expected to find. He reasoned that almost all of it had been destroyed in the blaze. Perhaps all but one strand.

This realization irritated Weaver, who already had begun to view his pleasant, rural county as a favorite dumping ground for murder victims. In the year since he had been elected to office, he had worked four murder cases. In only one had the victim been a local resident.

Weaver had a metal detector brought in and expanded the area of their search, leading to the discovery of an arm bone bearing a bracelet. On the bracelet was a charm of a bear with three tiny white stones, one for each eye and another where a belly button should be.

By mid-afternoon, Weaver and his men were joined by a state investigator and someone from the medical examiner's office, both of whom helped to catalog the evidence that had been discovered. Already Weaver was wondering who might wind up with this case. In the other cases in which bodies had been dumped in his county, he and his men had gathered evidence that other agencies had used to hunt down the killers. He thought that would be the situation with this case as well.

State investigators notified law enforcement agencies throughout Virginia of the grisly discovery in Amelia County late on New Year's Day. The remains were described as being those of a white female, five-feet-two to five-feet-four, slender, probably with reddish brown hair.

On the following morning, the Chesapeake Police Department became the first agency to respond, reporting that Regina Marie Prickett Butkowski, five-feet-two, slender, age 29, with reddish-brown hair, had been missing for eight months.

A television station in Richmond reported the discovery of the body on its evening news that day, and one of the people who saw it was Ernie Hazard of the Chesterfield County Police. He immediately called Jeannie's brother Sam.

"You been watching television?" he asked.

"Not today," Sam answered.

"Well, I just thought you ought to know that they just said on the local news that they've found some remains down in Amelia County and they think it's a white female."

"Do they know anything else?" Sam asked.

"That's all they said. If I hear anything else, I'll let you know."

Sam took a deep breath as he hung up. There had been so many false sightings of Jeannie's car, so much anguish for his parents for so long. This, too, could be a false alarm. He decided to wait until he knew more before calling his parents. He learned nothing else by staying up to watch the late news, however, and the next morning he decided to go ahead and call his mother.

"They've found something in Amelia County," he told her. "Do you have Jeannie's dental records just in case they're needed?"

"I have them," she answered. "I'll get them to you overnight."

Then she paused. "Sam, do you think we'll be bringing Jeannie home soon?"

"I don't know, Mama," he said, fighting back his emotions.

Later in the day, Hazard called Sam again, this time at work. "I've got a little more information," he said. "They've been able to recover a lot of stuff where the body was found, mostly jewelry."

He read through a short list of items that had been collected as evidence.

"Does any of that sound familiar?" he asked.

"My sister wore a lot of jewelry," Sam answered. "I'll see if I can find out what she was wearing that day and call you back."

As Sam dialed his mother's number this time, his fingers were trembling. He told her that some jewelry had been found.

"Do you know what Jeannie was wearing that day?"

Carrie knew the jewelry she usually wore. Six rings, including two pinkie rings and the engagement ring Tony had had made for her. A watch with a cloth band. Two necklaces. Carrie paused.

"Anything else?" Sam asked.

"A bracelet with a small bear charm...."

Sam started to speak. Instead, he burst into tears.

"Mama," he finally said, regaining control, "they found a bracelet with a small bear charm on it."

After trying to comfort her son, Carrie hung up and called Ben at work to give him the news. Only then did she cry.

After eight months of holding out hope that by some miracle Jeannie might be found alive, Ben finally had to accept reality. "That was the toughest time," he said later.

A day later, using Jeannie's dental charts, medical examiners in Richmond confirmed what the Pricketts already knew. Jeannie had been found.

23

The Rest of the Story

For three days, Jimmy Weaver and Wes Terry worked long hours writing reports and building a case file on the body that had been discovered in their county. When confirmation came from the medical examiner's office that the remains were those of Jeannie Butkowski, they finished their file and shipped it to the Chesapeake Police Department. The case, they thought, was out of their hands.

While it was clear that Jeannie had been murdered, nobody yet knew where she had been killed. The only indication was Joey St. Augustine's report that Pernell had shot her somewhere near Richmond, and Michael Slezak, the detective handling the case in Chesapeake, was dubious about that. Jeannie's car might yield some clues about her death, but authorities still hadn't been able to find it.

Under Virginia law, if the scene of murder cannot be established, the investigation and prosecution of the crime fall to the jurisdiction in which the body is found. Since the only thing certain about Jeannie's murder was that her body had been found in Amelia County, the file that Weaver and Terry had built was returned to them only a few days after they sent it away. For now, it was their case, but both knew that could change.

Weaver took charge with enthusiasm, nonetheless. Murder investigations stirred his juices, and this one not only intrigued him, it angered him.

"Somebody thought they could kill somebody and bring the body down here to Amelia and dump it and some hick sheriff would wind up with the case and it'd never be solved," he said later. "I'm no hick sheriff."

The eight-month interval between the murder and the discovery of the body left him with a cold trail to follow, Weaver knew, but he and Terry began with the paperwork that the case had created. They went first to Chesapeake to talk with officers there and try to get a feel for the scope of the investigation that lay ahead.

"From the very beginning, there was nothing but cooperation between the various law enforcement agencies involved," Weaver said later. "It was never a competition type thing."

Slezak opened his files on Jeannie, and Weaver and Terry heard Pernell's voice for the first time, when Slezak played for them an enhanced copy of the tape recording that Denise had found in her answering machine after Jeannie's first abduction. Pernell instantly became their chief suspect.

When Slezak said Pernell was thought to be in Florida, Weaver knew that he now had a finishing point as well as a starting point. He just wondered how long it would take him to close the distance between the two, and he was eager to get started. "That's just the way I am," he said later. "When I start investigating a case, I have no use for a clock. I work day and night until I've finished, sometimes twenty hours a day, sometimes longer."

Two weeks into his investigation, Weaver called the Pricketts, and afterward, for the first time, Ben and Carrie thought that the investigation of their daughter's disappearance and death was in the hands of somebody who would do something about it.

"He told us he would not let up until he solved the case," Ben said. "He said that his style was to go where he needed to go when he needed to be there. If he had to talk to a drug dealer and the only time he could get to him was midnight, he'd be there. We believed him. He just put us at ease."

Weaver got the break he needed, the one Slezak long had been hoping for, on January 16, when the Pricketts forwarded to him a letter that had been mailed to Jeannie. It was dated January 12, 1990, and was from the manager of the Newport Manor Apartments on Carnation Drive in Richmond, who reported that a gray Nissan 300 ZX bearing a vehicle identification number registered to Jeannie had been left abandoned at the apartment complex for six months. It gave Jeannie 30 days to claim the vehicle.

Weaver and Terry moved quickly. Within hours they met state law enforcement officers, including forensic experts, at the Newport Manor Apartments and found the 300 ZX. Weaver stood on a grassy knoll nearby as the forensics team worked over the car. Curious residents were coming and going, and several gathered at railings along second- and third-floor balconies to watch the police. From a nearby Richmond Police cruiser, Weaver heard one of the investigators asking for a check on the license plate the Nissan now bore, PNJ-720.

The report came back that the tag was registered to a Swansboro Baptist Church bus and had been reported stolen. The Richmond city inspection sticker on the car was discovered to have been stolen as well. As he listened, Weaver's eyes scanned the nearby apartments, although he later would say that he wasn't certain what he was looking for. "I figured I'd know it when I saw it," he said years later.

Finally, he noticed that at one of the second-floor apartments, the corner of a drape occasionally moved. Weaver turned away, but his eyes kept returning to the window. After seeing the drapes move, Weaver knew that someone who didn't want to be seen was peeking out at what was going on. He went to the apartment and knocked on the door, getting no answer. He knocked again, this time more loudly, and the door opened tentatively.

"You know anything about that car?" Weaver asked the man who stood in the shadows of the darkened room.

"Not much," he said.

"Tell me what you know."

"I just know that Sam and his cousin used to drive that car."

"Sam who?"

"Sam Washington."

"His cousin have a name?" Weaver asked.

"Probably, but I don't know what it is."

"And where do you think Sam Washington is now?" Weaver asked.

"Well, he used to live in one of these apartments, but he ain't been around in a while."

"You've got no idea where he is?" Weaver pressed.

"He might be in jail."

"But you don't know for sure?"

"No, sir."

A day later, on January 17, Weaver found Washington in the Richmond City Jail.

Washington said he had driven the car occasionally but it belonged to a man known on the street merely as JT. He had no idea where Weaver could find JT. But Richmond Detective Ray Williams knew.

"The thing is," Williams warned Weaver, "he lives in a tough part of town. Some of the people who live there would just as soon kill you as not."

"Just tell me how to get there," Weaver said.

Within half an hour, Weaver pulled his cruiser to a stop at the address in southeast Richmond. He could feel dozens of unseen eyes watching as he got out and walked to the door. An elderly woman answered his knock.

"How do you do, ma'am," Weaver said pleasantly. "I'm wondering if I can speak to JT."

"Won't you come in?" she asked, just as pleasantly.

She led Weaver toward the kitchen. Peeking from beside the refrigerator was a wiry man with a shiny gold tooth. Weaver guessed him to be in his early thirties.

"Why don't you come on out, JT?" Weaver told the man. "I'm Sheriff Jimmy Weaver from Amelia County and I've got a few things I want to ask you."

The man emerged from the corner but said not a word.

"You want to talk here?" Weaver asked.

"Might as well."

"I'll tell you what," Weaver said. "What I need to know from you can just stay between us. Why don't we just go sit in my squad car and talk?"

In the car, Weaver turned to him and said, "I hear you used to drive around in a little gray sports car, a 1985 Nissan 300 ZX."

"So?"

"So, I need to know where you got it."

The man hesitated. "Can't tell you," he said.

Clearly, this was a veteran of the streets, and after five minutes of questioning him, Weaver still was making no progress at all.

"Maybe I need to take you in so you'll feel a little more like talking," he finally said.

"You don't have a warrant," the man said flatly.

"I don't have to have a warrant to take you in for questioning," Weaver responded, "but I can take care of the warrant problem right now."

He reached for his radio. "Amelia, this is Sheriff Weaver," he said into the microphone.

"Go ahead, Sheriff," came the response despite the static on the line.

"I'm on my way in with a suspect," Weaver said. "I'm going to need a warrant real quick when I get there. Call the magistrate and ask him to stand by. Get back to me right away to let me know he'll be there."

The two men waited in silence.

"It's a shame," Weaver finally said, "a damned shame."

"What's a shame?"

"Well, you're smart. To tell you the truth, I kind of like you. You're strong. You're tough. Nobody pushes you around. But what we're dealing with here is murder. Just between us, I don't think you had anything to do with it, but I gotta take you in, and when we start asking you questions back in Amelia, no telling what'll come up. You know and I know that accessory to murder's pretty heavy stuff."

Weaver said nothing else, allowing silence to settle again in the car. Neither spoke until the radio crackled back to life.

"Sheriff, the magistrate says he'll be right here waiting."

"I'm on my way," Weaver answered. He reached for the ignition.

"Wait a minute," the man said quickly. "I got the car from Alphonso Brown. He said he needed some money and he wanted to sell it to me."

"What did it cost you?" Weaver asked, curious.

"I paid Brown a hundred and eighty-five dollars for it."

"Pretty good buy."

"Yeah, until I put it in the water and it got flooded," the man said with a little laugh.

172

"This Alphonso Brown. Where do you think I could find him?"

"I know exactly where he is," the man answered, surprising Weaver.

"You do?"

"They picked him up for shoplifting and drug possession. He's in Henrico County Jail right now."

"Thanks," Weaver said. "You're a good man."

As Weaver drove alone to the Henrico County Jail, he wondered how close he was getting. He knew he was working backward, but if the trail held together it would lead him to Jeannie's killer nonetheless.

At the jail, Weaver was shown into a small interview room. Within moments, Alphonso Brown sat across the table from him.

"Mister Brown," Weaver began, "you can help me with something."

"What's that?" Brown asked cautiously.

"I need to know everything you can tell me about that gray Nissan you used to drive."

Brown was silent, sizing up Weaver, wondering if he were about to become further entangled in the legal system. "Of course, you don't have to tell me," Weaver said, "but I wish you would. I'm investigating this case where a woman was killed, the woman who used to own that car. I'll bet you didn't have anything to do with that, but I'm not sure."

"Got it from Wayne Scott," Brown said quickly. "Met him on Thirty-sixth Street back sometime in May. It was Scott and this black man I didn't know."

"What'd this black male look like?"

"Well-built," Brown said. "Medium height, I'd say. Moustache. He was the guy driving the Nissan. And he was the guy trying to sell it. Didn't have no county or state tags."

"Did you ask this black male where he got the car?"

"He said the Nissan belonged to his girlfriend and he had to get out of town fast. He said he was mad at his girlfriend, so he just took her car. Wayne Scott said the Nissan came from down in Chesapeake. He said he and this other guy broke into a house and stole the keys."

Brown described the car as very clean, well-cared for, with a shiny coat of wax and an alarm system that Scott tried to demonstrate for him.

"What'd you pay for a car like that?" Weaver asked.

"Twenty dollars and a quarter of cocaine," Brown said. Brown said he then walked to Swansboro Baptist Church less than two blocks away, stole the license plate off a church bus and purchased a city sticker from a young man he did not know for five dollars.

"Shoulda known the car was stolen," Brown said.

"Why's that?" Weaver asked.

"'Cause that's what Scott does. Steals cars. He's been driving this red GT he stole. He likes that car. Scott does his business at night in that car. Then he takes it and parks it in this fancy white neighborhood and leaves it all day so nobody from the old neighborhood will bother it. If the police come around in the day to look for the car, they don't find it anywhere around where Scott's at. Scott's pretty smart."

"You don't know where Wayne Scott is, do you?" Weaver asked.

"Used to live with his grandmother. I guess he's still there."

"You know where that is?"

"No, sir," Brown answered.

Weaver had one more stop to make, at the Remco store in Southside Plaza where Pernell had worked. Eight months after Pernell had left town, a police officer was making a visit to Pernell's former employer for the first time. Weaver talked with Mike Thomas, the store manager, who told him how Pernell had gone to lunch on a Friday in May and never returned.

Sometime during his last days as an employee, Thomas said, Pernell had told him that his girlfriend was missing from her Virginia Beach home along with her car and that the front door of the house in which she lived had been kicked in.

Weaver asked about the people who had worked with Pernell. Thomas said that Joey St. Augustine had been a co-worker and a friend and that Sean Brooks,* who had become a Remco store manager in Macon, Georgia, also worked at the store at the time.

Late on January 18, Weaver called the Remco store in Macon and Sean Brooks answered.

"What do you remember about Pernell Jefferson and his last week at the store in Richmond?" Weaver asked after identifying himself.

At some point during that week, Brooks said, Pernell had asked if he would trade cars with him for the evening. "He said he had to move something and he didn't have much of a trunk in his Fiero," Brooks remembered. "I had a 1985 Mercury Topaz with a big trunk and I told him he could use that and I would drive his Fiero home from work that night."

Brooks said his Topaz was a two-door model with a light blue exterior and a royal blue interior. Brooks said that Pernell returned the Mercury near midnight of the day he borrowed it.

"Did you see Pernell after that?"

"Just Friday morning, the day he left. But I got a call from Pernell sometime in September."

"What'd he have to say?" Weaver asked.

"It was a strange phone call," Brooks remembered. "He wanted to know if I knew what Joey St. Augustine had told the police about his girl-friend."

"What did you tell him?"

"I told him I had no idea."

Early on January 19, Weaver returned once again to Richmond to the office of Detective Ray Williams who already had briefed Weaver on his in-terview months earlier with St. Augustine and the failed attempt to bug St. Augustine's apartment.

This time, Weaver told Williams he needed to find Wayne Scott, who apparently lived with his grandmother. Williams made two calls to informants and found out where Scott lived. "Let's go," he said.

Ten minutes later, the two officers knocked at the door of a house in an aging south Richmond neighborhood. An elderly woman answered.

"We're here to talk to Wayne Scott," Williams told her.

"Wayne," she called out.

Soon, a short, stocky black man with a thin mustache stood before them. At first glance, Weaver figured that Scott knew a lot about the streets of Richmond and how to survive there.

"If it's not too much trouble," Weaver said, "we'd like for you to come down to the police station to talk to us a little bit."

"Got nothing to say," Scott said.

"We think you do," Weaver said sternly, "and we think the best place to say it is down at the station. We can do this the easy way or the hard way."

"Be back later," Scott called to his grandmother. But on the ride down-town, he refused to respond as Weaver probed gently, hoping to learn what he was up against.

"This guy's not going to talk to both of us," Weaver told Williams when they arrived at police headquarters. "Why don't you just give me a shot at him first?"

Williams agreed and showed Weaver and Scott to an interview room. Weaver put a tape recorder on the table in front of Scott, turned it on, and began asking about Pernell Jefferson and the car the two had sold to Alphonso Brown.

But Scott only glowered, saying nothing.

Weaver got up and paced, searching his mind for more questions.

"I knew there would be a key to this interview and I knew I was going to have to find it somehow and turn it," he later recalled.

Warning Scott that this was a murder case wasn't it, however. Scott didn't scare easily.

Then Weaver remembered Brown telling him about Scott's GT, and he realized that at that very moment it no doubt was parked in some upscale, white neighborhood waiting for the cover of darkness when Scott could again go about his nefarious business.

"I know about the red GT," he said.

Years later, Weaver would still distinctly remember Scott's reaction. "It was like you had this flower and you poured boiling hot water on it. Scott just wilted."

Weaver realized that his key was within his grasp if only he looked in the right direction. "I knew the next question I asked would be the most important question in this interview, and maybe the most important question in the whole investigation, because it would let this guy know whether I was just fishing with the comment about the red GT, or whether I was really popping him with some stuff."

Weaver pretended to watch Scott squirm, saying nothing, allowing him time to respond. Meanwhile, he was frantically trying to frame his next question. Suddenly, his course presented itself.

"Let me ask you something, Wayne," he said. "How many people know about the red GT?"

"Well, I don't know," Scott answered quickly.

"But *I* know," Weaver said, pressing his index finger to his own chest. "What does that tell you?

"Somebody told on me," he said.

"There you go," Weaver said with a smile, sitting back down in front of Scott.

"I know about it and I know where it is, but those people out there don't know a thing about it," he said, pointing to the wall behind which were the offices of the Richmond Police Department detectives. Weaver stared into Scott's eyes.

"Wanna talk about Pernell?"

"I know him," Scott said.

The key had just turned, and now the door began to open. Over the next two hours, Scott talked his way through one tape and part of another. And when he had finished, Weaver knew that he had enough to charge Pernell Jefferson with murder. Now he had to find him.

24

A Visit from the Pope

At 2:30 on the afternoon of January 23, 1990, Jimmy Weaver swore out a warrant charging Pernell Jefferson with capital murder. When he called the Pricketts to tell them about it, Ben told him that the private investigator he'd hired had tracked Pernell to two places in Florida, Stuart and West Palm Beach, and that Pernell likely was still in one of those areas.

Weaver called the Florida Department of Law Enforcement and asked for help in finding Pernell. Special Agent Steve Emerson in the Miami office was assigned to the case. He made a records check and discovered that charges were pending in Palm Beach County against Pernell. He soon had traced Pernell to a cousin's house in Stuart.

On Saturday, February 3, 1990, while officers from the Stuart Police Department surrounded the house, Emerson climbed the short flight of stairs to the front porch and knocked at the door.

"I'm Special Agent Steve Emerson of the Florida Department of Law Enforcement," he told the man who answered. "I have a warrant here for the arrest of Pernell Jefferson. May I come in?"

"No, sir," the man responded. "This is a house of worship and I am a minister and you may not come in."

"And I'm the Pope and I've come to get Pernell Jefferson," Emerson said pushing past him with Stuart officers following. He found Pernell cowering in a closet.

Later, Pernell would say that he had known that the Florida Department of Law Enforcement was looking for him, because a cousin who worked for the Miami Police and a friend who worked for the Riviera Beach Police had told him. But he had not been on the run or hiding out, he said, and was not even aware of the extent of the charges against him.

"We've got your man," Emerson told Weaver by phone less than an hour later. "He's right here in the Martin County Jail."

"Fast work," a pleased Weaver said.

It was with even greater pleasure that Weaver dialed the Pricketts' number in Virginia Beach this time.

"We've got him," he told Carrie. "Pernell was just arrested in Florida. Your private investigator knew something."

"When will he be brought back?" she asked.

"We're not sure. We have to go through the extradition proceedings first, and he's got some charges pending against him down there. All that has to be worked out."

He and Terry would be going down to talk with him the next day, he said, and Carrie told him that they had friends who ran a motel in the Orlando area who would welcome them and offer a place to stay.

On Sunday, Weaver and Terry headed for Florida, planning to stop first in Benson to talk with Pernell's brother, Willie. That stop proved short, however. Willie declined to talk. After spending the night with the Pricketts' friends near Orlando, the officers drove on to Stuart, where they got their first look at Pernell when he seated himself across a table from them in an interview room at the jail on Monday afternoon.

"Do you know where Jeannie Butkowski's missing diamond ring is?" Terry asked him.

"I don't have it," Pernell answered.

"Has it been pawned?"

"I didn't do it," he said.

"Did you and Regina Butkowski care for each other?"

"We knew each other," Pernell, said, adding, "I don't think I want to talk to you gentlemen without an attorney."

"Well, you certainly don't have to talk to us," Weaver said, "but if this was a lovers' quarrel that just went bad, you ought to let me know."

"I told you, I'm not saying anything to you," Pernell said with a bite in his voice.

"I'm going to say just one thing to you, Mr. Jefferson," Weaver responded. "I won't be back and some day you'll wish you had talked to me. Let's get out of here, Wes."

The two men walked out, leaving Pernell with the guard who had brought him from his holding cell.

Years later, as Weaver looked back on his brief exchange with Pernell, he observed, "I probably wasn't disappointed he took the attitude he did. You know, *To hell with you, cop. Go ahead and prove it if you can.* When I left that room, I felt like I had a direct challenge. It made me want to work just that much harder."

Weaver knew that Pernell had repeatedly abused women and he was sure that he would keep doing it, no doubt killing again, unless somebody did something to stop him, and he was determined to be that somebody.

After leaving the jail, Weaver and Terry began trying to put together Pernell's life since he had left Richmond more than eight months earlier. They started by going with Agent Emerson and Stuart Detective James Egbers to talk with a beautiful young woman of Italian lineage who had dated Pernell after he arrived in Florida in June. Pernell had been introduced to Roseanne Lentini* by one of his cousins. Her father once had known his father, Pernell said later. Lentini, who was 24, told the detectives that when they met Pernell told her he was a private investigator who had been hired by the family of a former girlfriend to hunt down her murderer. Lentini had dated Pernell for only a couple of months before he had moved in with another woman in West Palm Beach. Pernell later claimed that although he had passionate feelings for Lentini, she was addicted to crack cocaine and he could not handle the stress of dealing with her addiction.

Terry showed Lentini a picture of the three-diamond engagement ring Jeannie and Tony had designed years before, one of the rings Jeannie had been wearing the night she was taken from her house in Chesapeake, and the young woman said she had seen the ring in photos Pernell had, but hadn't seen the ring itself.

"Ma'am, in the time you dated Pernell, did you ever notice anything suspicious about him?" Terry asked.

"Just one thing," she answered.

"And what was that?"

"I used to drive his little car, that gold Fiero, a lot. And I was driving it sometime last June or July and when I put on the brakes, this gun slid out from under the seat."

"What did the gun look like?"

"It was, like, a pistol, and it had sort of a dark color, like it was old or something."

"Do you know where it is now?" Terry asked.

"That's the only time I ever saw it."

The gun would never be found, but Weaver and Terry were convinced that was the gun that had been used to kill Jeannie.

To their surprise, Weaver and Terry also discovered that Pernell now was married. Soon after his arrival in Florida, Pernell had moved in with relatives in Stuart and landed a job tracking down delinquent accounts for a jewelry store in West Palm Beach, 40 miles away. Late in the summer, Pernell had stopped at an apartment in Riviera Beach to ask directions. The woman who answered the door, Cynthia Overman,* was older than he, in her mid-thirties, the daughter of Eastern European immigrants in Michigan, and a divorcee with a teen-aged daughter. Pernell struck up a conversation with her and she was very friendly. He began stopping to see her every time he was in her neighborhood, pouring on his relentless charm. Within a month, she had

179

invited him to move in with her, and Pernell, who had been driving an hour and a half back and forth to work from Stuart each day, accepted because it would put him much closer to his job. Within two months, they had married. Later, Pernell would not talk about the marriage, saying that he had promised to protect Cynthia's privacy. Cynthia, who divorced Pernell after his incarceration and later remarried and moved back to Michigan, could not be located to be questioned about her relationship with Pernell. Pernell claimed that he cared for her and never abused her, but at the time Weaver and Terry suspected otherwise. The charges against him that had led to his capture were the result of a blow-up with Cynthia but had not been lodged by her and indicated no abuse of her. Pernell would not discuss the incident that provoked the charges, except to call it minor.

On December 12, 1989, Pernell had been arrested by West Palm Beach police and charged with three counts: aggravated assault with a handgun, false imprisonment and grand theft of a firearm.

According to the police report, Pernell had learned that his new wife had moved out and was staying at the nearby apartment of a male acquaintance. Pernell had lured his wife's friend from his apartment by saying something was wrong with his car. Pernell and two accomplices then jumped the man, began beating him and took from him a revolver in a case, which the man had a permit to carry.

"Jefferson held the gun and told (the victim) to go back into the apt.," the police report stated. "While in the apt. Jefferson kept the gun and refused anyone permission to leave...while he tried to convince his wife to come home with him."

When police, summoned by security guards, arrived, Pernell dropped the gun into a garbage can, according to the report.

Later, Pernell claimed that the officer who arrested him asked, "Do I know you?" as he was taking him to the station.

"I said, 'I don't think so,'" Pernell recalled. "He wanted to know if I was an athlete, and I told him I'd played a little football. He asked me who I had played for. I told him the Browns. He said, 'Really? I'm from Cleveland and I think I remember you being with the Browns.'

"On the way, he called ahead and asked what my bond was going to be. They said $10,000. When we got there, he just said, 'Take care of Pernell.' They set my bond at $1,000 and I gave them the $100 cash and left."

Pernell reconciled with Cynthia, but it was his wife's daughter who gave police the information that led to his arrest.

After returning from Florida, Jimmy Weaver had extradition papers drawn but it would be months before Pernell was returned to Virginia because of the charges pending against him in Palm Beach County. His trial there had been scheduled for March 9, but it was twice postponed. After summer arrived and Pernell still hadn't been tried, a Florida judge, pressured by Virginia authorities, finally ordered that Pernell be extradited.

On July 10, two Amelia County deputies, Leonard Wiggins and Kenneth Lloyd flew to Florida to get him. Later, both would recall how personable Pernell had been.

"Under other circumstances," said Wiggins, "I would have been more than glad to invite him to my house for dinner or go to a movie with him.

It was hard to remember that he was being charged with murder. But Lloyd and I both knew that we had to remember that he was a potentially dangerous man while we were having easy conversations with him."

Pernell was placed in the Piedmont Correctional Center, a regional jail shared by five Virginia counties, at Farmville, 20 miles from Amelia, to await his trial, but that would be a long time coming.

Within days of Pernell's arrival at Farmville, Pernell's younger brother, Willie, called a friend in Richmond and asked for the names of the three best trial lawyers in the city. His friend called back with three names. The first was Steven D. Benjamin.

Willie called and got an appointment. He was as impressed with Benjamin's office in the gothic Old City Hall building near the capitol as he was with Benjamin himself. Benjamin, whose office once had been a judge's chamber and had 20-foot ceilings, was a young man, trim and athletic, with short-cropped, thinning brown hair, wire-rimmed glasses and a no-nonsense style. He wore suspenders with his fashionable suits and spoke softly, seldom smiling, occasionally looking over the top of his glasses.

Willie hired him, paid a $1,200 retainer and went home to borrow more money to pay for his brother's defense.

The key witness against Pernell, Wayne Scott, had agreed to plead guilty to charges of breaking and entering with intention to abduct Jeannie, and in August he appeared in court in Chesapeake where for the first time he made known publicly the events leading up to Jeannie's death. He was sentenced to 15 years, of which 10 years would be suspended if he testified against Pernell. He was sent to a prison in Roanoke to serve his sentence.

By the end of August, Commonwealth's Attorney Thomas Stark III had made a crucial decision about Pernell's case. Stark was 59. He had grown up in Amelia and had been the commonwealth's attorney of Amelia County for more than 30 years. A trim, gray-haired man of conservative dress and manner, he had tried many murder cases but never one in which it was uncertain even where the murder had occurred. After reviewing the evidence, Stark saw that the case against Pernell was totally circumstantial. Although Weaver and Terry had produced a great deal of scientific evidence, they had not found the murder weapon, nor had they been able to locate Jeannie's missing ring, physical evidence that might have been linked directly to Pernell.

Stark saw that he was going to have to depend on Wayne Scott and two other witnesses that Scott had led Weaver and Terry to, and although all three were in jail, two were soon to be released and might quickly disappear, making themselves unavailable to testify.

In Virginia, capital murder, with which Pernell had been charged, is a first degree felony, punishable upon conviction with only two sentences, death or life imprisonment. First degree murder is a second degree felony, punishable with a sentence of 20 years to life. A person convicted of first degree murder becomes eligible for parole in 12 years, but a person convicted of capital murder and given a life sentence does not become eligible for parole for 25 years.

Over the objections of Weaver, Terry and the Pricketts, Stark chose to try Pernell for capital murder but not to seek the death penalty. His reasons were two-fold. First, he thought the evidence was not strong enough to support the death penalty on appeal, and he did not want that to be the reason that a conviction got overturned, giving Pernell a chance, perhaps, to go free. Second, Pernell's lawyer, Steven Benjamin, had already requested a continuance. If it were granted, two of Stark's primary witnesses would be out of jail and likely out of his reach by the time the trial began, leaving him only with Wayne Scott to get a conviction—one questionable character's word against another. Stark knew that the judge who would be trying the case did not like to grant continuances, but if a person's life were at stake, he was apt to do so. By foregoing the death penalty, he knew the judge likely would deny the continuance and preserve his witnesses. Far better to have Pernell in jail for 25 years, he thought, than to try him for his life and run the risk of letting him be set free.

Still, the trial was months away, giving Pernell plenty of time to work his charms and schemes. Jimmy Weaver would soon become well aware of just how manipulative Pernell could be. Efforts to shift suspicion for Jeannie's murder to others began surfacing one after another, and every time Weaver saw Pernell's hand behind them. At one point an unsigned letter purporting to be from a former girlfriend of Wayne Scott's arrived, claiming that Scott and one of his "drug dealer friends" had killed Jeannie in her apartment. Weaver was never able to track down the letter writer, but he became convinced that

Pernell had persuaded someone to write it. Later, two inmates came forward to claim that they had heard that Scott was boasting of having killed Jeannie, but when Weaver explained the implications of involving themselves in a murder case, both recanted and said that Pernell had put them up to it.

Weaver never ceased to be amazed at Pernell's powers of persuasion. Before Pernell's trial, a female guard at the correctional institute where he was being held would be fired for having sex with him.

25

A Murder Trial in Walton Village

History hovers like a spectre over Amelia, Virginia, and at first glance it seems like a town lost in time.

It was at Amelia that General Robert E. Lee's retreating Confederate Army had expected to rendezvous with badly needed supplies near the end of the Civil War. Instead, the troops nearly starved at Amelia and Lee soon surrendered just down the road at Appomattox.

Since those dark days, little of note had occurred in the small farming town 40 miles south of Richmond. When Pernell Jefferson's trial began on March 28, 1991, nobody could even recall when the last capital murder trial had been held in the town's white-columned courthouse.

Few people attended the opening of the trial a day earlier, when the jury had been selected, but on the second day, with testimony scheduled to begin, the small courtroom was crowded. Two newspaper reporters and a television reporter, all from Richmond, sat together near the front of the spectator gallery. A dozen students on a field trip from a government class at Amelia County High School climbed with their teacher to the balcony, once reserved only for blacks.

Irene Demos, Susan's mother, had made the trip from Winston-Salem, and she took a seat across the aisle from Pernell's brother and sister, Willie and Blondie.

Ben and Sam took seats back of the table where Commonwealth's Attorney Thomas Stark was already seated, organizing notes and papers. Soon, Sheriff Weaver, who had become like a brother to Ben, was there, leaning close to whisper something.

"Behave yourself," he warned. Weaver had had long talks with Ben about his anger and his hatred for Pernell and he wanted no disruptive scenes.

"I will," Ben promised, but Weaver took a strategic seat halfway between Ben and Pernell nonetheless, and for a time, he watched no one but Ben.

Ben glowered at Pernell when sheriff's deputies led him into the courtroom, and he kept his eyes on him after he was seated. "I watched him sweat," Ben said years later, venom still in his voice.

Pernell seemed unaware of Ben's scrutiny.

Judge Thomas V. Warren, a tall, slender man with salt-and-pepper hair, entered the courtroom and took his seat at the bench. A man of great dignity, Warren was a native of nearby Fredericksburg and a graduate of Virginia Tech. At 51, he had served on the bench for nearly 14 years and had a reputation for being direct and tolerating no nonsense.

Pernell stood as the charges against him were read.

"How do you plead?" asked the clerk of court, R.E. Flippin.

"Not guilty, sir," Pernell said in a strong voice.

After the judge questioned Pernell to make certain that he understood the charges against him, the jury was brought in and empaneled. It included seven women and five men, nine white and three black. They had been chosen in quick order the day before from a pool of only 20 citizens of Amelia County. Years later, Weaver would remember them as "the perfect jury."

"No one in the county brought any baggage to the trial because no one in the county knew Jeannie and no one in the county knew Pernell," he said. "In the history of jury trials in this country, there probably has never been a more perfect jury for making an impartial decision."

Before testimony could begin, the jury was asked to leave the courtroom so that Benjamin could make the most important motion of the trial: to bar from evidence the tape mysteriously recorded by Jeannie's and Denise's answering machine.

"I have listened to the tape," Benjamin told Judge Warren. "The Commonwealth would proffer that there are two voices on that tape and, indeed, there are two voices. The Commonwealth will tell you that one voice is the voice of the deceased in this case. The other voice, the Commonwealth proffers, and I do not concede, is the voice of the defendant."

Benjamin paused to gather his thoughts and check his notes. "I represent that there is virtually nothing that the defendant, or the person alleged to be the defendant on that tape, says that is decipherable. Some of what the deceased says can be understood. Now, this is despite the best efforts of the FBI at enhancement.

"The voice that's supposed to be Mr. Jefferson's, although you can't tell what it is, it sounds calm. The voice which is the deceased's is...well, it will be argued that her voice sounds frightened, that she is at times sobbing, and that she makes statements to the effect of, 'Please leave me alone.'"

Benjamin emphasized that the incident on the tape took place in March, while the abduction that led to Jeannie's death happened in May.

His objections, Benjamin went on to point out, were several.

"Number one, hearsay. I obviously cannot cross examine the deceased as to what she meant when she made any of the statements on the tape. We're left to speculate. Was she, for example, sincerely frightened or was this part of some aspect of their relationship? Was it some form of play-acting? We don't know. We would have to speculate. We can't know and I can't ask her, 'Were you seriously saying, "Let go of me,"' 'Have you ever had this kind of conversation before?' 'Were you sincerely frightened or were you playing along?'

"I can't confront this witness and that's the basis for my objection.

"Number two, that this is evidence, no matter what we call it, and despite what theory of admissibility it will be cloaked in, it's evidence of, if the Commonwealth is believed, prior misconduct by this man.

"I am certain that the Commonwealth will tell you that there is a specific purpose for which it is being introduced which is proper under Virginia law, but I submit to you that if it has any probative value, and we say it does not, then that whatever probative value it has is so far outweighed by the extreme prejudice of this jury hearing this tape as to amount to a complete denial of Mr. Jefferson's right to a fair trial for what he's been accused of."

Benjamin said that if the tape recording were introduced into evidence, the jury "can't help but understand that this is a reflection on his character and the at least subconscious message for this jury, the danger we want to avoid, is that we're telling the jury, 'Look here, he did the same thing in March and that makes it more likely, doesn't it, that he did the thing in May?'

"Now, as logical as that might seem to us, the law says you're not allowed to prove guilt that way and that is really why that tape would be coming in....

"I think the court understands that the specific legal grounds would be that this would be in violation of his right to a fair trial, his right to confrontation of witnesses, his right to effective assistance of counsel, and his due process rights under the several U.S. amendments."

Stark was quick to defend the tape.

"There is, as Mr. Benjamin indicated, about seven minutes of extreme anguish on her part," he told the judge. "She calls his name. The question of identification is not going to be that tough. Moreover, his voice is recognizable.

"It is not the tape alone that the Commonwealth would offer in evidence so that the bare tape and the question of hearsay should not stand or should not be an appropriate objection because the tape is corroborated, number one, by the witness who lived in the same home who discovered the tape, who played the tape on the very night it was made, who received a phone call from the victim who was at that time in the custody of the defendant who made it known to the victim through this phone conversation that she had Jefferson on tape and that no harm had better come to Regina Butkowski.

"Regina Butkowski called back within a very short time and said, 'How do you mean on tape?' The witness explained and Regina Butkowski was returned home, not unharmed.

"There is further corrobotative evidence, pictures taken of her with abrasions, very substantial abrasions around her neck. A criminal complaint was filed with the Chesapeake Police Department. She did not follow through with the prosecution but this was no play-acting, as Mr. Benjamin would suggest."

Stark said he understood the limited use to which the tape could be used, but cited three earlier Commonwealth cases in making his point. The exceptions, Stark contended, were as well-established as the general rule itself.

"Those exceptions are, number one, to identify the accused," he said. "Number two, to show the relationship between the accused and the victim. Number three, to show motive. Number four, to show intent."

Now Benjamin addressed the court again.

"Judge, what happened in March is too remote from what happened in May, and what I think I'm hearing is that, well, this shows their relationship and it leads up to the offense.

"Well, it does not do that. It doesn't show anything. That's the first problem with it having no probative value....What does it prove? That just invites speculation...."

"Might I just make one comment, if Your Honor please?" Stark said, rising to be heard. "There was an ongoing boyfriend-girlfriend relationship between these parties that predated both the March and, obviously, the May incidents so I don't want the court to be misled that there was no relationship or prior relationship between these parties."

"And all of that will be in evidence including identification of the voices on the tape?" Judge Warren asked.

"Yes, sir," Stark responded.

"Well, clearly the evidence, if believed by the jury, would be prejudicial, just as much of the other Commonwealth's evidence will likely be prejudicial," Judge Warren said. "I don't think the hearsay objection would in any way stand when this is a conversation between a victim that was, and this will be the Commonwealth's theory, was murdered two months after this tape was taken, a tape of, if I'm understanding correctly, suggestive of rather violent behavior by the defendant toward the victim.

"I don't think March, two months before the incident, is remote when the relationship between the parties is continuing," the judge said.

"The Commonwealth's evidence will show, according to what I've heard, the identification, the relationship, a motive, a pattern, the intent, all of which is relevant for the jury to hear. It is evidence that is admissible and that the jury is entitled to weigh, so I would overrule the objection, and your exception is noted."

Benjamin and Pernell had suffered a major setback even before the first witness was called.

In his opening statement, Stark warned the jury that there would be some conflicting evidence before laying out the state's case against Pernell.

Pernell's lawyer told the jury that he might call no defense witnesses and warned that the state's witnesses would not be credible. "I can't promise that by Easter we're going to have any miracle and the true killer is going to leap from the stand or from the courtroom and say, 'I can't take it any more. I did it,'" he said. "There is no question I can ask that will prompt that disclosure, but I can tell you that by the end of this trial, we will be much closer to knowing, all of us, the truth about who killed her if not the identity of the actual assailant."

Testimony opened with Randy DuClau telling how he found Jeannie's skull. Deputy Leonard Wiggins and Virginia State Police Special Agent B.I. Robertson followed to tell how Jeannie's remains were recovered. Robertson said that Jeannie's bones had been scattered, probably by animals.

Carrie Prickett was the fourth witness. She was clearly nervous as she raised her hand to be sworn, and was suffering from a severe headache. She wore a beige and black button-up dress with elbow-length sleeves, and she was resentful about having to testify.

"It was like going through something that was not necessary, it seemed to me," she said in 1995. "Why do we have to prove things? We knew he did it."

Unlike her husband, she wouldn't allow herself to look at Pernell.

"Why would I?" she asked years later. "I had in mind that if I looked at him I would see nothing because I then considered him to be nothing."

Guided by Stark, Carrie told about her last conversation with Jeannie and Jeannie's failure to meet her as planned at the beauty shop. The memories clearly caused her deep distress.

When Stark asked her to identify a photograph of Jeannie, Benjamin spoke up. "I'll stipulate that that's her daughter if it would be easier," he said.

"Mrs. Prickett, did your daughter like jewelry?" Stark asked later.

"Yes, sir," she said in a voice so soft that the judge had to ask her to speak up and repeat her answer.

"Did she like to wear rings and bracelets and necklaces and that sort of thing?" Stark continued.

"Yes, sir."

Carrie's chore was becoming no easier. Now spread before her was the jewelry law enforcement officers had dug from the soil near Nibbs Creek. "Can you identify those objects, ma'am?" Stark asked.

"Yes, sir."

"And whose would they be?"

"They belonged to Regina," she said softly.

"Did she have another ring?"

"She had six rings on her fingers."

"Did she have one more prominent than the others?"

"Yes, sir. It was her wedding band."

Stark brought a photograph to the stand and asked her to identify it. It was a photo of the ring Jeannie and Tony had designed for her.

Later, Carrie would remember that as the hardest moment of her testimony.

"It was like looking at Jeannie," she remembered. "There it was, a picture of the ring on Jeannie's hand. It was like it was confirmation that Jeannie had lived, and now she was dead."

Denise had worn black for her testimony, a symbol of mourning for Jeannie. As soon as she took the stand, she fixed Pernell in her angry gaze and wouldn't let her eyes wander from his. If looks could kill, she later said, Pernell would have toppled over dead right there.

Stark led Denise through her last evening with Jeannie, May 5, 1989, and her discovery the following day that Jeannie was missing.

"I take it you have not seen Regina since."

"No, sir."

"Did she have any enemies that you know of?" Stark asked.

"Yes, there was someone who was harassing her," Denise answered. "I guess you would call that an enemy. I don't know if you'd call him an enemy or not, but she was harassed constantly by someone."

"And who would that be?"

"Pernell Jefferson," she said, glowering at Pernell.

"To the best of your knowledge," Stark continued, "had she received any recent threats of bodily harm from anyone?"

"Well, she had received bodily harm from him."

Benjamin rose to object that this was hearsay, but won only a partial concession. The judge agreed to strike Denise's last answer, but asked her a question himself. "You did see some evidence of physical abuse?"

"Yes, sir."

"Was Pernell Jefferson a friend of Regina's at one time?" Stark asked.

"Yes, sir, at one time he was."

"Did they date?"

"I don't know what the interpretation of 'dating' would be," she answered. "I would consider a date going out to dinner, to a movie, and I don't ever remember her doing that, but they did — they were in each other's company."

"Do you know how they happened to meet?"

"Yes, sir. They met at a gym in Virginia Beach. He was recommended to train her. He was a bodybuilder and he had the body to back it up and he was training her."

"And commencing some time in the spring of 1988, they saw each other from time to time?"

"They saw each other every day at the gym," she said.

"Did there come a time when Regina did not care to see Pernell any more?"

"Yes, there was."

"How do you know that?"

"Because, well, we talked about it."

Benjamin raised a hearsay objection and this time it was sustained. Stark continued.

"Can you describe the relationship between Pernell and Regina insofar as being peaceful, serene, turbulent, or how you might describe it?"

"Throughout the most part of the summer, she seemed like they were very peaceful...liked each other's company. And then towards the fall it started getting rocky. She wanted to pretty much go her own way. She told him that she would remain friends with him, that they could talk on the phone, just that he needed to get on with his life and her the same."

"Were there any specific instances of violence between the two of them?"

"Well, there was a time when he broke in my house in March...."

Benjamin rose quickly to object, but Warren ruled in the prosecution's favor.

Stark then led Denise to Jeannie's first abduction and her discovery of the tape recording of it on her answering machine. The moment Benjamin had hoped to avoid — the playing of the tape — had arrived. The tape had been enhanced for clarity by the Federal Bureau of Investigation, and the judge, jury, attorneys, Denise and Pernell were given earphones to listen to it. Before the tape began, Ben, Carrie and Sam rose and quietly left the courtroom.

Denise forced herself to continue staring at Pernell as the tape went on for more than seven minutes. The tape could be heard throughout the courtroom, and Pernell sat stone-faced as his voice resonated through it.

"You're going with me! Get in the car! Let's go. Let's go!"

190

"You've already ruined my life," the voice of Jeannie pleaded. "What else do you want? Leave me alone, Pernell. I'm not talking to you any more.

"Let go of me!" she screamed repeatedly on the tape.

"Do you want to die right here?" the man's voice asked.

As she listened, Denise dabbed at her eyes with a tissue.

After the earphones had been removed, Benjamin rose once again in objection. This time the ruling was deferred.

Denise and Pernell still sat glaring at each other.

"Do you recognize the voices on that tape?" Stark asked.

"Yes, sir," Denise answered.

"And they are?"

"Jeannie's and Pernell's." She still held Pernell's gaze.

"Do you know whether or not Regina was afraid of Pernell Jefferson?"

"Yes, she was."

Benjamin objected. "Judge, I mean, it's obviously hearsay and it puts me at a disadvantage."

"Not necessarily," Stark countered, then turned to Denise before the judge had a chance to rule and said, "How did she show it?"

"She had someone walk her from work to her car. She parked in a parking garage. From there she would go to her mother's or my mother's until I got home, until I called one of them and told her I was home. I would wait on the porch with the porch light on until she got in the house."

Judge Warren ruled on Benjamin's objection only with his silence.

"Did you receive an anonymous phone call from anyone after her disappearance?"

"Yes," Denise said, and described the telephone call in which a stranger told her that Jeannie was dead. She went on to tell how she had arranged for a subsequent phone conversation between the anonymous caller and a Chesapeake police detective before her testimony came to an end.

The prosecution now called Charles Zimmer. A tall young man who weighed more than 250 pounds, Zimmer had dark, curly hair and pale blue eyes.

When Stark asked his address, he replied, "I'm in the Chesterfield jail right now."

"And why are you in Chesterfield jail?"

"For grand larceny."

"Have you been convicted of more than one felony?"

"No."

"And have you been convicted of any misdemeanors involving lying, cheating, or stealing?"

"Yes. Stealing a can of tobacco one time."

"And how old were you then?"

"Eighteen...nineteen...."

Stark got him to admit that he had participated in a number of burglaries early in 1989 for which he had not been arrested, before questioning him about the the burglarly that had led to his arrest: a break-in at a home in Chesterfield County in which cash, jewelry and guns, including four handguns, had been stolen.

"Do you know what became of the handguns that were taken in the larceny?" Stark asked.

Zimmer replied that he had been told that the guns were given to Pernell Jefferson.

Stark now went to the heart of his reason for bringing this convicted felon to the stand.

"On the fifth of May of 1989, did you go to Tidewater with Mike Savin and Wayne Scott and Pernell Jefferson?"

"Yes."

"For what purpose?"

"To make some money, break and enter."

"Excuse me?"

"To break and enter a house and make some money," Zimmer repeated.

"Did you know whose house it was?"

"No, not specifically."

"Did you know anything about the person or person's home you were going to break into?"

"Yeah," Zimmer answered. "It was supposed to be a drug dealer that we were going to."

"Was this trip planned in advance?"

"Yeah. I knew about it maybe a week, three days to a week before."

"And whose plan was it? Whose idea was it?"

"Well, Pernell's, I believe. He was the one who approached Mike Savin and myself about it."

"Before leaving Richmond, did you make any stops?" Stark asked.

"Yeah, we stopped at Safeway on Jahnke Road...to pick up some gloves." Zimmer described them as yellow rubber dishwashing gloves.

"And who did that?"

"Myself and Wayne went inside to buy them. We all stopped."

"And with your money or whose money?"

"Pernell's," he said.

Zimmer went on to describe the trip to Chesapeake. When they arrived, he said, Pernell pointed out the house they were to break into and they drove to a nearby shopping center to call the house to find out if anyone was home.

"Who made the phone call?" Stark asked.

"I did."

"And who gave you the number?"

"Pernell."

"And did anyone answer the phone?"

"No."

Zimmer said that the four men then drove back to the neighborhood, this time parking about a block away, and made their way to the house on foot. As they drew near, he said, he, Pernell and Wayne Scott waited while Savin went on to the house to make a final check to determine if anyone was home.

"And then what happened?"

"Well, me and Mike went up to the door and Pernell and Wayne stayed on the side of the house looking around the corner, and we banged on the door and nobody answered, so Mike kicked the door in."

"And did that in effect splinter the door and knock it loose from its moorings?"

"Yeah, knocked it in."

"And did you go inside?"

Zimmer said that both he and Savin were about to enter the house, but Pernell and Scott burst past them and rushed inside.

"At that point," Stark asked, "did you see any guns?"

"Yes."

"Who had guns?"

"Pernell and Wayne."

The gun Pernell had looked like one of those he and Savin had stolen in the earlier burglary, he said, a .32 revolver.

"Had you all ever had a thirty-eight caliber among your inventory?" Stark asked.

"No."

"If I understand you correctly," Stark said, "Scott and Jefferson with guns at the ready go in ahead of you and Mike Savin. Was anyone in the house?"

"Yes."

"When did you discover that?"

"As soon as the door was kicked out."

"And what happened?"

"A girl walked around the corner and she yelled something."

"Do you recall what she said?"

"Yeah," Zimmer answered, "like, 'Oh my God!' Then, 'What are you doing?'"

"She was directing her remarks to you?"

"Towards me."

"And to Savin?"

"And Mike. Yeah."

"When Scott and Pernell came in, did she have anything else to say?"

"Yeah, she looked at him...at Pernell and said, 'What are you doing here?' She yelled it out. She said, 'Oh, my God, what are you doing here?'"

"And did Pernell answer her?"

"I believe he said, 'Shut up.' He said something gruff," Zimmer continued. "I couldn't make out what it was."

"What did Pernell do at that time?" Stark asked.

"He grabbed her and threw her on the floor and put his knee on her."

"Threw her down on the floor?" Stark continued.

"Uh-huh."

"And did he have the pistol in his hand all this time?"

"Yes."

"And then what happened?"

"Wayne went in the back rooms and checked to see if anybody else was there. And then Pernell turned around and looked at me and Mike and said, 'Y'all can go.' And we took off."

The man whose home had been burglarized by Zimmer and Savin, James deKrafft, came to the stand next to describe the four handguns that had been stolen: a .22 Reuger, a .32 Smith & Wesson with a two-inch blue-steel barrel, and a .32 chrome-plated Smith & Wesson, all revolvers. As he had waited to be called, deKrafft had told Sheriff Weaver that the blue-steel .32, the gun believed to have been used to kill Jeannie, a gun authorities had never found, had been purchased at a hardware store in Amelia.

"It was one of the unexpected ironies of the whole thing," Weaver later recalled. "Jeannie wasn't from here. Pernell wasn't from here. But the gun was."

When his name was called at mid-afternoon, Wayne Scott entered the courtroom. He had huge, rounded shoulders, close-cropped hair, and he was dressed in prison clothes. He seemed nervous. Pernell kept a close eye on him, but Scott hardly glanced at him.

"You are presently pulling time for what offense, Mr. Scott?" Stark asked.

"For breaking and entering to abduct."

"And where did that offense occur?"

"In Chesapeake, Virginia, sir."

"Is that the breaking and entering of Regina Butkowski's home and her abduction?" Stark asked. "Is that the offense?"

"Yes, sir."

"Let me direct your attention, please, to May fifth, 1989, the day on which you and Mister Jefferson and Mr. Savin and Mr. Zimmer took a trip to Tidewater. Are you with me?"

"Yes, sir."

"What was the purpose of going to Tidewater?"

"The purpose of going to Tidewater was to get one Butkowski to leave Pernell alone," Scott said. "He claims she was causing him financial problems and legal problems."

"And who decided that you needed more than just the two of you to go along?"

"Pernell."

"All right. And were there any firearms involved in this trip, in this caper?"

"Yes, sir."

"Who had what?"

"Pernell had a thirty-two and I had a twenty-five."

"Where did you get the twenty-five from?"

"I got the twenty-five from my brother, sir."

"Pernell, he had a what?"

"A thirty-two, sir."

"Can you describe its appearance?"

"Yes, sir. A six-inch barrel, tumbler, kind of darkish color."

"Darkish color?"

"Yes, brownish."

"Brownish color. Not chrome?"

"No, sir."

"Where did he get the gun from?"

"He got the gun from Mike and Chuck," he said, referring to Savin and Zimmer.

"Okay. When did he get the gun? When did Pernell get the gun from Mike and Chuck?"

"That night."

"The very night you left?"

"Yes, sir."

"Okay. Who gave it to him?"

"Mike."

"Have you testified concerning this matter before?"

"Yes, sir."

"Preliminary hearing?"

"Yes, sir."

"And on the preliminary hearing, what did you have to say about the gun?"

"I said it was a thirty-eight. You corrected me at the end and said it was a thirty-two."

"Well, do you know which it was?"

"I'm no expert, sir," Scott responded. "I can answer that truthfully."

"You've got to be wrong, I would think, one time or the other."

"Yes, sir."

"Was it a thirty-two or was it a thirty-eight?"

"Thirty-eight — two, sir," Scott stammered.

"A thirty-eight two?"

Scott laughed uneasily. "No, a thirty-two, sir."

"All right," Stark continued. "On preliminary hearing, you were asked about seeing some cartridges and being able to identify those cartridges...."

"Yes, sir."

"How did you identify them?"

"I held them in my hand and looked at them. I did not read the back of them."

"You held them in your hand and you looked at them?"

"Yes, sir."

"And you gauged it by size and shape?"

"Yes, sir."

"Not by writing?"

"No, sir."

"Okay, I believe you told Mr. Benjamin in response to his question that you read the back of the shells. Am I correct or not?"

"I looked at the back of the shells."

"But you didn't read the number?"

"No, sir."

Stark moved on to the trip to Chesapeake, and Scott testified that the four men stopped enroute only for beer and gas.

"Did you buy any gloves?"

"No, sir. Gloves were already in the car. I had a pair and Pernell had his pair."

Once the four reached Chesapeake and found the house, he said, he saw a car parked in the driveway.

"Saw what car?" Stark asked.

"The Three-hundred ZX."

"Can you describe it for me generally?"

"Sun roof, two-door sports car, kind of grayish. It looked like it was kind of grayish."

"Was it a dark color?"

"Yes, sir."

"OK. Do you remember anything about its license plate?"

"TIGRE Z."

Under further questioning, Scott described the events leading up to Jeannie's abduction.

"Mike and Chuck went up to the house, kicked the door in," he said. "Pernell told me to come along with him. I was behind Pernell. We entered the house. I went and checked the other rooms, came back, told him it was clear. At that time, Mike and Chuck left."

"Now, did you see anybody in the house?"

"A young lady," Scott said. "She would have been about five-six, about a hundred and thirty-five pounds, Caucasian, reddish hair."

"Reddish hair, all right. How was she taking all of this?"

"She asked Pernell what he was doing here, what did he want."

"Did she seem very calm, cool and collected?"

"No, sir."

"Was she excited and upset?"

"Frightened is more the word," Scott said.

"All right. And do you recall anything that she had to say?"

"Only, 'What are you doing here?' And "What do you want?'"

"And she directed those remarks to who?"

"Pernell."

"She appeared to know him?"

"Yes, sir."

"Did Pernell say anything to her?"

"'Get dressed.'"

"Pernell — did he have his pistol in his hand?"

"Yes, sir."

"You both came in with your pistols at the ready?"

"Yes, sir."

Scott testified that when Pernell told Zimmer and Savin they could leave, they quickly complied.

"That just left the three of you there?"

"Yes, sir."

"Then what happened?"

"Then Pernell and the young lady left together. Got in the Three-hundred ZX."

"Did she go with him willingly and cheerfully?"

"Pernell had her by the arm pulling her out the door."

"And how did they leave?"

"In the Three-hundred ZX. Pernell was driving."

"And what did you do."

"I left behind him and went and stayed at some friends' house that night."

Scott said that he next saw Pernell the following morning as he arrived for work at a business called Prime Time, next door to the rental store where Pernell worked.

"What did he have to say?" Stark asked.

"He told me that he took the car and that he had shot the young girl." Scott said that Pernell told him he needed to dispose of the car and Scott told him he had a friend who could get rid of it for him. On Sunday night, Scott said, he sold the car at Midlothian Village to Alphonso Brown. "The deal was for five-hundred dollars. He didn't have any at the time, so he gave me twenty-five dollars worth of coke and told me that he would give the rest of the money to me later."

"Well, now, did he give the money to you exclusively, or to Pernell, or how was the money divvied up, if at all?"

"The money never was divvied up because he never paid," Scott said.

"Alphonso never paid. You did get the quarter of coke, did you not?"

"Yes, sir."

"And who got that?"

"I asked Pernell did he want some and he said no."

"Did Pernell indicate to you that he wanted any part of the proceeds?"

"No, he said he didn't want none of it."

"All right. Were you ever inside of the Three-hundred ZX?"

"Yes, sir."

"When did you get in it?"

"When I was showing it to Alphonso."

"Were you wearing gloves on that occasion?"

"No, sir."

"How about Pernell, was he wearing gloves?"

"Yes, sir. He had gloves and a Windex bottle."

"Excuse me?"

"A Windex bottle."

"He had gloves and what?"

"A Windex bottle."

"What was he doing with that?"

"I do not know, sir."

Scott testified that he did not see Pernell again until "a couple of days later" when Pernell told him he needed to move Jeannie's body.

"Why you?" Stark asked.

"Because I was the one that gentlemanly went down there with him to Chesapeake," Scott answered. "I was scared but he told me once I did this, I would no longer be involved, my name would never be brought up in it."

"So, you figured if you went and moved the body, that that would somehow clear you of any involvement?"

"Yes, sir."

"Did you go?"

"Yes, sir."

"Who went? Just you and Pernell?"

"No, sir. It was Pernell, Mike and myself."

"Mike Savin?"

"Yes, sir."

Scott testified that it was dark when the three arrived at the site in a car Pernell had borrowed from a fellow employee at Remco, and he and Pernell got out of the car. "He told Mike to turn the car around, come back in a few seconds. At that time, I followed Pernell into a wooded area. We came upon a body that had a camouflage net over top of it with lime thrown on top of it."

"Did you have anything to put the body in?"

"Yes, sir. Pernell took a sheet from the car when we got out."

"Tell us exactly what took place then."

"We spread the sheet on the ground, body in the sheet, carried the body back to the car. Mike had just pulled up. Put the body into the trunk and then we drove out to Amelia County."

Scott went on to say that Pernell was driving and he got lost one time on the macabre journey.

"Where did you ultimately stop and where did you dispose of the body?" Stark asked.

"Some place in Amelia," Scott answered. "It was slightly like a ditch. It had a brook running across it. That's where we left the body."

"All right," Stark said, "the body's in the trunk of the car. You get it out. Do you recall whether you left the body right alongside the road, or did you go away from the road or just exactly what did you do?"

"Pernell and myself and Mike got out of the car. Pernell took a gallon jug with him. Gasoline was in the jug. He proceeded to carry the body back into the wooded area. Just as..."

"Back from the road?" Stark interrupted. "Away from the road?"

"Yes, sir. We crossed the stream, set the body down, Pernell poured gasoline on it, lit it, and then we left."

The Pricketts showed no emotion when Scott described burning Jeannie's body. They had heard it before when he had testified in his own trial in Chesapeake. Then Carrie had fled the courtroom in tears.

*   *   *

In cross examination, Benjamin skillfully solicited answers from Scott that would fit neatly into his closing arguments.

"When you went to help move the body, you discovered that it was stiff?" he asked.

"Yes, sir."

"You told the police that each time they interviewed you?"

"Yes, sir."

"And it was so stiff that it gave Jefferson trouble getting it into the trunk of the car?"

"Yes, sir."

"In fact, you heard the body crack at one point?"

"Yes, sir."

After questioning Scott about how he had found his way out of Jeannie's neighborhood after the abduction, Benjamin asked him to identify the friends he had stayed with in Norfolk that night.

"Their names," Scott said, pausing for a moment. "Perrys."

"Perrys?"

"Yes, sir."

"Their address?"

"I do not know their address, sir."

"Are they here today?"

"No, sir."

"And have you ever told any law enforcement officers how to get hold of the Perrys?" Benjamin continued.

"Yes, sir," Scott answered.

"Do you know if they did?"

"Yes, sir."

Benjamin then moved on to a matter that might affect Scott's credibility: the type of weapon Pernell had carried to abduct Jeannie. He knew that the bullet found in Jeannie's skull had been a .32.

"At the preliminary hearing, you said many times that Pernell had a thirty-eight caliber that night. Correct?" he said to Scott.

"Yes, sir."

"You were asked, weren't you, 'Do you know it was a thirty-eight?', and you said, 'Yes'?"

"Yes, sir."

"You were asked, 'How do you know it was a thirty-eight?' Do you remember that?"

"Yes, sir."

"You said, 'Because of the shells.' Right?"

"Yes, sir."

"And you said that you saw that they were thirty-eight-caliber shells?"

"Yes, sir, because I looked at them in my hand and they looked like thirty-eights."

"Had you ever had a thirty-eight before?"

"No, sir."

"Had you ever had thirty-eight ammunition before?"

"No, sir."

"Had you, to your knowledge, ever held thirty-eight ammunition before?"

"No, sir."

"You looked at the back of the cartridges, right?"

"Yes, sir."

"But you're telling us today that you didn't read the back of the cartridges?"

"No, sir."

"Do you agree, sir, that when we talked about whether or not it was a thirty-eight or a thirty-two at the last hearing that you told us that you read thirty-eight on the back?" Benjamin pressed. "That was your testimony, wasn't it?"

"No, sir. I said I looked at the back of the shells. I said they were thirty-eights."

"Let me see if you remember this question and this answer:" Benjamin said, reading from the transcript of the preliminary hearing. "Question — 'And those bullets all said thirty-eight, didn't they?' Answer — 'Yes, sir.' Wasn't that the question and the answer put to you?"

"Yes, sir."

"And that's how you answered, wasn't it?"

"Yes, sir."

"You were under oath at that hearing, weren't you?"

"Yes, sir."

"Jefferson never asked for a gun, did he?"

"I do not remember," Scott answered.

"Do you recall being asked whether or not Jefferson asked for a gun that night?"

"Yes, sir."

"Your answer was, 'Not to my knowledge.' Right?"

"No, sir."

Scott went on to tell Benjamin that he carried a gun in case "the gentleman" was home. The only male living in the same house as Jeannie, Denise and her daughter was Jerome, the construction worker, who was away visiting relatives for the weekend.

"So the gun was for the gentleman?" Benjamin said.

"No, sir."

"Well, why did you bring the gun then? Protection from who?"

"To make sure there was no trouble with the gentleman," Scott answered.

"You were going to point the gun at the gentleman?"

"If need be, yes, sir."

"And if need be, you were going to pull the trigger on the gentleman?"

"No, sir."

"You weren't going to shoot him?"

"No, sir."

"Your gun wasn't loaded, was it?"

"Yes, sir."

"Why was it loaded?"

"It always was loaded, sir."

"Just as a precaution?"

"Yes, sir."

"Just in case you really did need to pull the trigger?"

"Maybe, sir."

"Maybe so," Benjamin said sarcastically. "Maybe at him, the gentleman?"

"Maybe if he was there, sir."

"Now, at the preliminary hearing, you told us, didn't you, that you never took the gun out of your pocket, you never pulled it out and went in with it. Wasn't that your testimony before?"

"Yes, sir."

"You were lying, weren't you?"

"Yes, sir."

"Under oath?"

"Yes, sir."

"In the courtroom right next to this one?"

"Yes, sir."

Benjamin now had the point he wanted to make on record. Scott was a liar, and it had come from his own mouth.

26

"If I Can't Have Her..."

Thursday, the first day of testimony, had been mild for the season and clear, but Friday dawned overcast and chilly, casting a darker and gloomier air over the courtroom.

Michael Savin was the first witness called. Short and stocky, Savin, who once had shared an apartment in Richmond with Charles Zimmer, had been convicted of four felonies, all burglaries. He confirmed that he had given Pernell a .32 Smith & Wesson revolver and a .22 Reuger to sell for him before the trip to Chesapeake. He said the .32 Smith & Wesson Pernell had the night Jeannie was abducted was the same gun he had given him.

Savin confirmed Zimmer's testimony that the two thought they were going to Chesapeake to break into the house of a drug dealer. He described the trip and told how he, Scott and Zimmer waited in the darkness while Pernell went alone to the house. He said that Pernell soon returned and announced that no one was home.

"And then what happened?" Stark asked.

"Then Wayne and Pernell stayed on the side of the house and Chuck and I went to the front and broke down the door," Savin said.

As Pernell rushed past him, he said, he saw that he was holding the .32 Smith & Wesson he had given him to sell a few days earlier. After describing how Pernell had subdued the woman who had appeared unexpectedly, Savin said that Pernell turned to him and said, "You guys can go."

"And did you leave?" Stark asked.

"Yes, sir," Savin answered quickly.

"Where did you go?"

"We went to Virginia Beach and stayed in a Triton Towers motel."

"How long did you stay there?"

"For the weekend."

"When was the next time that you heard from Jefferson?"

"I guess about the middle of the week when we got back. Almost a week after that night."

"Did he call you or did you see him in person?"

"He called me on the phone," Savin said.

"What did he have to say?"

"He asked if I'd heard anything on the news or anything about what had happened."

"Did he tell you anything about what had happened to the girl?"

"He told me that the problem was over, that everything was taken care of."

Savin went on to tell that he had agreed to help Pernell move Jeannie's body to Amelia County where, Savin said, "Pernell took gasoline and poured the gasoline on it and lit a match."

"Did you willingly volunteer to come on this trip?" Stark asked.

"Yes."

"You weren't threatened at all?"

"Not threatened. I felt threatened," he said. "I wasn't, you know, physically shown a gun or anything like that. I was just threatened."

"Any threatening words said to you?"

"No," Savin answered. "I could just tell through the tone of voice when he asked if I would go."

"This was whose tone of voice?"

"Pernell's."

"The tone of voice, how would you describe it?"

"The tone of voice was that I'd better go and if not, you know, something could happen to me, possibly the same as what happened to her."

"Would you describe it as menacing?"

"Yes."

On cross examination, Benjamin questioned Savin about what he and Zimmer had done after the abduction.

"Stayed in the motel room," Savin said.

"Tell me more."

"That's it."

"Did you sit there?"

"Yes, sir."

"You and Chuck?"

"Yes, sir."

"Could you tell us any single thing you did after you got there besides sit there in your hotel room?" Benjamin pressed.

"We sat in the hotel room and thought about things," Savin answered.

"And that's it?"

"And that's it."

"All you can tell us about Saturday night and what you did?"

"That's it."

"Why not go back to Richmond?" Benjamin asked.

"Scared to go back to Richmond," Savin responded.

"Why?"

"We were afraid Pernell would be there looking for us."

"Why?"

"We were just afraid."

"Why?"

There was silence in the courtroom while Savin waited to answer. Finally he said, "Because he had gone in there and thrown the girl on the ground and had a gun drawn on her. That's enough to be afraid about, I think."

"What did you do Sunday morning?"

"Sunday morning we stayed at the motel until check-out and then came back to Richmond."

"Can you tell us anything you did Sunday morning other than that? Before you checked out, what did you do?"

"That's it," Savin answered yet again.

"Did you order room service?"

"No, sir. We didn't have any money."

The only food he and Zimmer ate during the two-day stay at Triton Towers was a free pizza given to them by one of Zimmer's friends who worked at the motel, Savin said. They drank only water from the bathroom tap.

"Did you have to get gas on the way back?"

"Yes, sir."

"Where did you stop to do that?"

"I'm not certain. Somewhere off of Sixty-four."

"Who paid for it?"

"I did," Savin said.

"How much did the gas cost?"

"Five dollars."

"That was money you had?"

"That was the only money I had."

Later, Benjamin questioned Savin closely about his drug taking on the trip, hoping to show that Savin was so heavily influenced by drugs that night that he couldn't reliably remember it.

"How do you take a hit of acid?" he asked.

"Swallow it," Savin responded.

"Well, what did the acid do to you?"

Savin laughed nervously. "About thirty or forty minutes later, it started chirping like, you know, like it's supposed to do."

"There are some of us who have not had LSD, an LSD trip before. Would you describe what that is like?"

"Hallucinations."

"What hallucinations did you have that night?"

Again Savin laughed nervously. "I don't remember. I've taken a lot of acid and I don't remember...the different, you know, kinds of hallucinations."

"Describe to us the different kinds of hallucinations that LSD causes for you."

"I would just see colors and things like that."

"Things like what?"

"Just basically colors and shapes. Look up in a corner of a room and see something moving and it just freaks you out."

"Like what?"

Again Savin laughed. "I don't know."

"I mean, does it have a recognizable form like spiders or elephants, or...."

"No."

"Just globs?"

"Yes."

"And they're moving?"

"Yeah."

"And they freak you out?"

"That's what you take it for, you know."

"What do you mean when you say that something freaks you out?"

"I mean I was high."

"It scares you when you're freaked out about something?"

"Not to the point where it scares me, no."

"The cocaine that you took, the eightball, before you went down to Chesapeake, what effect did that have on you?"

"Not too much. Cocaine doesn't last long in your system."

"Well, that depends on the person, doesn't it?"

"I don't know. I'm not a drug expert."

"You're not a drug expert?"

"No, I'm not."

"How much cocaine do you think you've taken in your short life?"

"It's hard to say," Savin said. "I don't like to think about it. It's behind me."

"All right," Benjamin said, speaking more loudly now, "but you've got to think about it. If we piled all the cocaine, all the eightballs you've taken in your short life, how far would it reach from the floor?"

"I don't know." Again, Savin laughed nervously.

206

"How big a pile of powder would it be?"

"I'm not sure."

"How many times have you taken cocaine?"

Savin did not respond.

"You don't know, do you?"

"No, I don't," Savin confessed.

"You've taken cocaine so many times you can't remember?"

"That's right."

"If we piled up each hit of acid, how big a pile would that make?"

"I don't know."

"You can't tell us," Benjamin said with a hint of disgust. "Would you agree that you have a little bit more experience in cocaine and acid than maybe the rest of us in the courtroom just by virtue of your experience?"

"I don't know what experience anybody else in this courtroom has with the drugs."

"What effect did the cocaine have on you that night?"

"By the time I got to Virginia Beach, there was no effects left from the cocaine."

"When did the LSD wear off, sir?"

"Sometime Saturday morning."

"That's when you stopped hallucinating?"

"I didn't hallucinate the whole time. It, basically, just keeps you awake and aware."

After Savin left the stand, Joey St. Augustine was called. He hesitated when he was asked to state his name and new address.

"I'd prefer not to give my address," he said.

"Would you tell these ladies and gentlemen of the jury why you would prefer not to do so?" Stark asked, but before St. Augustine could answer, Benjamin had stormed to his feet.

"Objection, judge. This is totally improper, inflammatory, irrelevant...."

"Well, if it has any basis..." Stark said, interrupting.

"Immaterial," cried Benjamin, raising his voice over Stark's.

"I think it is very material," Stark put in.

"Well, only if it has something that relates to the defendant," the judge said.

"If it does," Stark said, "then he might say so. And if it doesn't, then I assume he'll not say so."

"Well, you know, Mr. Stark," the judge said, "you've talked to him, and I just don't want something off the wall. I'm not requiring that he give his address and it's no big deal whether he gives his address or not. Now, if it's some sort of threat that's been directed to him from the defendant, then that's one thing. But if it's just some..."

"I make no..." Stark started to say.

"...feeling that he has..." the judge continued.

"I make no representation to the court that any threat has come to him direct from the defendant in person," Stark said, and the judge allowed St. Augustine to keep his address to himself.

"Do you know Mr. Jefferson?" Stark asked him.

"Yes, I do."

"How do you know him?"

"When I was working at a company called Remco, he came to work there."

"You and he worked together?"

"Yes."

"How long was that?"

"Approximately six months. Six, seven months."

"And how did you all get along?"

"For the first couple of months, we didn't get along. After that, the remaining four or five months, we got along pretty good."

"You all were good friends?"

"No. We were friends."

"Did he ever discuss with you girlfriends or girlfriend problems if there were any?"

"Yes, he did."

"Any in particular?"

"Yeah. There was a girl in the Virginia Beach area. He referred to her as Jeannie....She'd broken up with him and he just didn't like that. He was mad about that."

"Did he suggest to you or discuss with you taking any action against her?"

St. Augustine had appeared nervous from the beginning. Now he seemed to become even more uneasy. He paused before answering and seemed uncertain of what he was going to say.

"He did say that — when she broke the thing — broke it off, that, ah, if — that is — this is what he said to me — if he can't have her, nobody else can. And not in those exact words but...." His voice tailed off.

"Let me hear it again," Stark said.

More clearly now, St. Augustine said, "If he can't have her, no one else can."

"All right, did there come a time in March of 1989 that he broke into her home and abducted her?"

"Yes."

"Did he tell you about that?"

"Yes, he did. He said that he went down there and his main reason to go down there was to kill her. And when he'd told me about it, it was afterwards, after he'd gone down there. And he said that after he'd — after he'd broken into the house that at that point he just couldn't do it. They just — they talked and they drove around and talked. He took her back home and that was it."

"Now, did he discuss with you a later incident occurring in early May of 1989?"

"He did. He did ask me to be an alibi for a Friday night."

St. Augustine went on to testify that he had gotten a pre-dawn call from Pernell on Saturday morning, May 6, seeking help in hiding Jeannie's car, and that he later drove Pernell to Remco in time for work that Saturday.

"Did he tell you how he happened to be in possession of Jeannie's car?"

"Yeah. He told me that they'd went — he had went down to where she lived in the Virginia Beach area. They'd broken into her house — "

"Did he tell you who 'they' was?" Stark interrupted.

"No."

"He did not?"

"He did not."

"Okay. Go ahead."

"And he told me that they went down there and broke in and they got into her car and they were driving — "

Again Stark interrupted. "Who is 'they'?"

"Pernell and Jeannie."

"All right. Go ahead."

"And, well, he said they were driving back, they had a conversation. First they had started talking about Jeannie's financial problems, how she was in debt, and he'd said that Jeannie knew why he was there and what he was doing."

"And why — what was that?"

"The reason?" St. Augustine asked.

"Yes."

"She knew that he was there to kill her."

"How did that come out?" Stark asked.

"Well, he just — these aren't exact words, I'm not sure of the exact words, but he said she told him that she knew why they were there or why he'd come down and knew that Pernell was going to kill her at that time. And after that, she asked how he was going to do it. And Pernell said, 'With a gun,' And she asked to see it....He said that he had handed her the gun and she looked at it and handed it back....Then he said they were driving, he shot her."

"He shot her where?"

"He said he shot her in the head."

"How many times?"

"Ah, he never said how many. I was assuming once because he said after he shot her, he kind of described what happened, how she froze up and said blood came out of her mouth and — "

Once more, Stark interrupted. "Jefferson is telling you all of this?"

"Yes."

St. Augustine testified that he and Pernell worked together for part of the day on Saturday, May 6, 1989, and that evening Pernell appeared at his apartment.

"He came by and told me that I had to go with him to where he had dumped her body. He needed someone to drive because he didn't want his car to be parked off the side of the road."

"And did you do that?"

"Yes, I did."

"Did you have a shovel?"

"Yes, he had one."

"Where did he get that from, do you know?"

"He said he'd gotten it from one of Remco's customers."

"And so you went to this place in Chesterfield and then what?"

"He gave me directions. I was driving. And told me to stop. At first, we drove by, he threw the shovel out, and we turned around and came back and he got out. And he said to drive around about fifteen minutes and — "

Stark asked if he could remember what Pernell said when he returned to pick him up.

"He said he couldn't dig a hole because there were too many roots. Because it was in a kind of wooded area."

"Then what did you all do?"

"Went back to my apartment and I got out and he drove off."

"Do you recall seeing her purse at any point?"

"Ah, yes," St. Augustine said. "It was that same night, and we had driven to the apartment complex next to mine. It's called Newport Manor. And we went there and he got out in front of the trash can or dumpster and got the purse out from there. I think that was the same night."

"He gets the purse out of the dumpster and what does he do with it?"

"He hands it over to me and says I have to burn it, I have to get rid of it, and so that's what I do with it is burn it."

"What about the contents of the purse?"

"It had all her personal belongings, her wallet, driver's license, credit card — "

"Any cash?" Stark broke in.

" — business cards. Ah, yeah. It had some cash."

"What became of the cash?"

"He'd taken the cash out. He handed me twenty dollars and he kept the rest and that was it for the cash."

"Did you see a ring on that occasion?"

"He showed me a ring Saturday at work."

"Can you describe that ring for us?"

"I can't really describe it. I know it wasn't an ordinary looking ring."

"It was or was not?"

"It was not."

"Did it have any stones?"

"Ahh, if I remember, I think it had like about three diamonds in it."

Stark then placed Commonwealth exhibit number six, a picture of a ring, in front of St. Augustine and asked him if it resembled the ring Pernell had shown him that Saturday morning.

"Yes," he answered, "that was the ring."

"Did he say anything about the ring?"

"He said that it was a one-of-a-kind ring. He had it especially made for her."

Stark had finished his questions, and Judge Warren ordered a brief recess before cross examination began. During the recess, Stark realized that he had failed to ask some important questions, and when court reconvened Judge Warren allowed him to renew direct examination.

"Mr. St. Augustine," he began, "when you were told by Pernell on Saturday, the sixth of May, that he had killed Regina, did you tell anybody? Did you call anybody?"

"Saturday?"

"Well, I understand you were told on Saturday. I don't know whether you called on Saturday or some other day, but did you, in fact, tell anybody?"

"I called Jeannie's apartment that — I think it was a Wednesday."

"How did you happen to know her number?"

Pernell had once called Jeannie from his apartment, he said, and he searched back through old phone bills until he found the number.

"Who did you talk with, do you recall?"

"I think I talked to a detective. I don't really know who I talked to at first, but then I started talking to, I think, a detective."

"Did you identify yourself, give your name?"

"No, I didn't."

"Did you seek to make the call an anonymous call?"

"Yes, I did."

"What did you tell the people that you called and talked with?"

"I told them that Pernell had killed Jeannie."

"Did you tell them everything you knew?"

"No, I didn't."

"You did not? You held back?"

"Yes."

"Why was that?"

"At the time, I didn't want to be involved. I wanted to try to give enough to help the case but I did not want to be involved. I didn't want to do what I'm doing here now."

"Were you frightened?"

"Yes, I was."

In cross examination, Benjamin got St. Augustine to admit that he'd had a conversation with Stark before the trial about not revealing his new address.

"What instructions did he give you about testifying today?" Benjamin asked.

"Instructions?"

"Yeah. Did he tell you what to say, what not to say, what to emphasize, what not to emphasize?"

"No, he didn't tell me any of that."

"Did he tell you that you had to tell the truth?"

"Ahhh, yes."

"He did?"

"I think he did," St. Augustine said, speaking softly. "I don't know if it was today. I think it was probably around the preliminary hearings."

Judge Warren told St. Augustine he would have to talk louder.

"Okay," Benjamin continued, "around the last hearing, he told you to tell the truth?"

"You know, that I'd be under oath, yes," St. Augustine said, speaking louder.

"Why do you think he picked you out to tell you to tell the truth?"

"I didn't think that he'd picked me out."

"You hadn't been truthful up until that point, had you?"

"Up until what point?"

"Up until the hearing."

"Ahhh, no," St. Augustine said, now pausing as he spoke. "I told Chief Deputy Terry when I met with him — "

Benjamin interrupted. "Isn't it true, sir, that you told so many different versions of the events surrounding May fifth prior to your hearing next door that you can't remember what you did tell and what you didn't tell? Isn't that an accurate statement?"

Stark quickly objected, causing Benjamin to withdraw the question, but he continued pressing St. Augustine, his questions implying at one point that St. Augustine might have participated in moving Jeannie's body into Amelia County as early as Saturday night, May 6, the night after her murder.

"Had you ever before been asked to drive someone out to bury a body?" Benjamin asked.

"No, sir."

"Describe this shovel. Was it a long-handled shovel?"

"Yes, it was very long."

"And it's not the kind that's got a handle on top, it's one of those long-handled things, right?"

"Yes."

"With a pointed blade?"

"Ahh, I don't remember the blade."

"Okay, y'all took his car?"

"Yes."

"A Fiero?"

"Yes."

"A two-door Fiero?"

"Yes, it was."

"No back seat in the Fiero?"

"None."

"The back windshield is right up against the back of the two seats, right?"

"Yes, it is."

"And the trunk is very, very small on that, isn't it?"

"I think it is."

"Tell us where that long-handled shovel was in that Fiero."

"The blade part was on the floor and he had to have the window rolled down for it to stick out."

"So the blade is on the floor and he's got the handle coming across him and sticking out his driver's side window?"

"No. I was driving. He was in the passenger...." He demonstrated the positions.

"Why didn't you take your car?"

"Because I didn't want to take my car."

"Why not?"

"Because I didn't want it being seen."

"Because you knew you were going to go drop him off to bury a body?"

"Yeah."

"He told you that ahead of time?"

"He told me that then, yes."

Benjamin continued grilling St. Augustine, trying to show that he couldn't be believed, and by the time St. Augustine stepped down, the trial was effectively over.

Stark called only three more witnesses: Michael Thomas, who had been Pernell's and St. Augustine's boss at the Remco store in Richmond; and Detectives Michael Slezak of Chesapeake and Ray Williams of Richmond, who described their experiences with St. Augustine.

The state had taken less than two days to present its case, offering only 16 witnesses. Later, Stark would say that he didn't use half the evidence that had been accumulated, but he was confident of winning a conviction.

"We had the right man," he said.

The defense took even less time. Benjamin called only one witness, Dr. Marcella Fierro, the deputy chief medical examiner for the Central District of Virginia, who had written the autopsy report on Jeannie's remains.

Throughout her testimony, Fierro, who would later become the district's chief medical examiner, referred to her report.

"You did determine, did you not, that the cause of death was a gunshot wound to the left temple region?"

"Yes."

"And you retrieved that bullet and gave it to Ann Jones, a forensic ballistic examiner?"

"That's correct."

"You show on your page three diagram two holes in the skull which you have described as an entrance wound and an exit wound?"

"Yes."

"So that no one will wonder how there can be an exit and an entrance and yet the bullet be recovered inside the skull, could you give us an explanation?"

"Yes," Fierro answered. "When bullets go through the skull, they often make it through. In this case, it went through on the left side. It came out the bony part of the head on the right side but it didn't make it through the skin. It pushed a plug of bone out and then the skin sort of tented out and then came back in so that the bullet didn't exit. Under those circumstances, the bullet is pushed right back into the skull where it remains then until the brain decomposes or whatever. So it exited the skull but not the scalp."

"On page two of your report, you used the word 'articulated' when describing the condition of the spine. So that the jury reading the autopsy later understands, 'articulated' means what?"

214

"Still together," she answered. "When referring to the spine, when I say the spine is articulated, it means the vertebra are still together and held together by remnants of ligaments. If the body were completely decomposed for years, then those small ligaments would break down and the vertebra would separate. But if they're together, it's call 'articulated'."

"You also used the word 'perimortem.' That would mean what?"

"Perimortem means at or about the time of death."

"Rigor mortis — this is a stiffening of the body?"

"Yes."

"That condition begins after death?"

"That's correct."

"Let me ask you, does stress affect the onset of rigor mortis?"

"Sometimes."

"If it were a factor, would that cause rigor mortis to occur more quickly than other times?"

"Yes, the onset would be quicker."

"There is a classic example, I think, of a soldier in battle?" Benjamin continued.

"Yes."

"What is that example?"

"Well," she said, "the classical example that's used to describe what we call accelerated or more quickly than usual onset of rigor is the fellow who's actually pointing his gun at somebody and somebody shoots him right through the head and he stays right in that position. He's fixed."

"That is the stress factor?"

"Presumably," Fierro said. "This is all very anecdotal."

"A body that dies in May and is left above ground out of doors, would you estimate that would be stiff in twelve hours?"

"Under ordinary circumstances. It would depend partly on the weather."

"All right," Benjamin continued. "And it would be softer, ma'am, approximately how many hours after death?"

"We would expect rigor to pass in about forty-eight hours."

"All right. Now, at thirty-six hours, would there still be rigor present?"

"Yes, but it would be a little softer."

"And then your estimate of forty-eight hours, that's when the body would no longer be stiff?"

"Often it's not stiff. Sometimes it is. But I would expect that after forty-eight hours that I would be able to tell that rigor had passed, or was passing."

Though Benjamin never directly tied Fierro's explanation of how long rigor mortis remains viable, in earlier cross-examination he had questioned Scott about the condition of Jeannie's body when he, Pernell and Savin went to the church construction site to move it to Amelia County. In interviews with police, Scott had said the body had been moved on Thursday, almost six days, and perhaps as much as 130 hours, after Jeannie apparently was killed sometime early on Saturday morning, May 6. In cross-examination by Benjamin, Scott had confirmed his own preliminary hearing testimony that Jeannie's body was stiff so that it cracked when it was forced into the trunk of the car.

Although reporters speculated about whether Benjamin would allow Pernell to take the stand, Stark was not surprised that he didn't.

He thought the admission of the tape recording into evidence had eliminated that possibility. Benjamin, he was sure, did not want to expose Pernell to questions about what had happened on the night of March 7, 1989, when that tape had been mysteriously, perhaps miraculously, recorded.

Benjamin was still chafing about the admission of the tape, and after presenting his lone witness he moved for a mistrial, arguing that the tape had denied his client a fair trial.

"After hearing that tape, there is no way in the world that a jury could continue to presume Mr. Jefferson innocent or that they could intelligently, impartially and fairly weigh...the evidence...." Benjamin argued. "All the tape does is establish a propensity for violence or other bad character traits which were not in issue."

Judge Warren denied his request and adjourned court for the day, but not before setting an unusual Saturday session for closing arguments.

Outside, the clouds had opened up and rain was falling in torrents. Reporters had hurried from the courtroom to position themselves near the top of the stairs leading out of the courthouse, and when Carrie and Ben emerged, they began asking questions. Both days of testimony had been difficult for the Pricketts — hell, Ben called it — and they didn't want to talk about it.

"We've got nothing to say," Ben told them strongly. "Can't you just leave us alone?"

The Pricketts sought shelter in a witness room until the reporters and the rain had moved on.

27

The Missing Pieces

When Stark faced the jury to begin his closing remarks a few minutes after nine Saturday morning, he was well aware that his case rested on the testimony of some "unsavory characters," as he described his chief witnesses, and that there had been inconsistencies in their testimony.

Nobody had explained, for example, why officers hadn't been able to find Jeannie's body when St. Augustine led them to the church construction site more than five days after her death. Nobody had explained why the body had been stiff when Pernell had forced it into the trunk of a borrowed car. The contradictory testimony about rubber gloves and guns still hadn't been made clear. But none of that caused Stark great concern.

"I felt that none of those inconsistencies was sufficient to change the outcome of the trial," he said years later. "Almost any time you have more than one witness involved in relating the same action, you get inconsistencies. That's the difference in the way different people see the same events."

This was much the same message that Stark delivered to the jury.

"The people that were involved have different memories and different recollections of little matters, little details," he told them. "It is because either their memories have faded somewhat or their recall is faulty in some particular. And I ask each of you to put yourselves in the position of the several witnesses and think back to some event that you either witnessed or participated in the better part of two years ago and think can you remember exactly what color socks someone was wearing or shirt or exactly what time this or that happened. Most of us cannot.

"And I think that the witnesses that you heard testify these past two days could not either. But they were very clear and their recall was very good about the essential elements of what happened because, I submit to you, it was forever burned in their memory."

Stark told the jury that the four men who went to Chesapeake went for three different reasons, Savin and Zimmer to break into the home of a drug dealer, Scott to help Pernell scare his girlfriend, and Pernell for other purposes.

"It was Pernell who planned it all," Stark said. "It was Pernell who approached Savin and he, in turn, told Zimmer, 'We'll go down to Chesapeake and knock off this drug dealer.' He played the charade. Pernell knew that they weren't going to a drug dealer's house. Pernell knew that they were not going to simply scare Regina because it was his intention and his plan all the while to go and take her from her home and to kill her, and that's what he did."

Stark went on to detail Jeannie's death. "Regina knew that Jefferson was going to kill her," he said. "She had had earlier experiences with him. She had been abducted once before. He had threatened her life then and he'd been caught short because, miracle of miracles, there was a tape recording and he was made aware of it and he brought her back home. But this time, Regina knew that her luck had run out. She knew that she was going to be killed.... As they drove down the road, he turned and fired and shot her right in the head.

"Do you remember the testimony?" he asked, pausing for effect. "She froze and blood came out of her mouth. The medical examiner shows you where she was shot, right in the left side, right in the left temple. St. Augustine didn't know this." He waved the autopsy report. "He'd never seen this. All he knew was what Jefferson told him and Jefferson told him correctly — he shot her in the head while they were driving down the road."

Stark asked the jury to find Pernell guilty of capital murder.

"Now, what are the elements?" he asked rhetorically. "That the defendant killed Regina Marie Butkowski. I do not believe there can be any doubt in your minds that he did so. That the killing was willful, deliberate and premeditated. I do not see how there could be any doubt on that subject. It was cooly and calculatingly done. It was thoroughly planned. It was planned for a good while. As a matter of fact, there was an abortive attempt early on in March when he took her. You heard the tape. He intended to kill her then but he did not do so."

But in May, Stark said, "Regina knew that her luck had run out. She knew that she was going to be killed. They came to Amelia. And you know what occurred. They took the body out, dumped it near Nibbs Creek, poured gas on it, Jefferson did that, and he lit the fire."

In closing, Stark sought to deflect any confusion that might have been created by Wayne Scott's conflicting descriptions of the revolver Pernell had carried.

"Zimmer saw the pistol," he said. "He described it as black. Mr. deKrafft described it as blue steel. Savin saw the pistol. He described it as black. Brown saw the pistol. He described it as brownish.

"Nobody — nobody — saw a chrome-plated pistol.

"She was killed with a thirty-two. It was a thirty-two Smith & Wesson, as the Medical Examiner's report would indicate, and it was fired by Pernell Jefferson and nobody else.

"One final point, one final observation, if you will. Go back to the time when Regina and Pernell were having troubles. This was in March. And he goes down and takes her from the house, and you've heard the tape. He told Joey he intended to kill her but he didn't. He then told Joey when he came back, and this was before the May incident, 'If I can't have her, nobody will.'

"Think about it. A cold-blooded killing. Capital murder, ladies and gentlemen. Capital murder. Guilty. Capital murder. Life imprisonment. And that's what I ask you to do.

"Thank you."

After a ten-minute recess, Benjamin watched the jury file back into the courtroom. For a moment, he remained seated, a legal size notepad in front of him. For Benjamin, the case had too many missing pieces; too much police work had gone undone, he thought, and his client had been damaged by testimony from witnesses of doubtful credibility.

He didn't want to risk offending the jurors by casting aspersions on their law enforcement officers, however, and he began by praising Sheriff Jimmy Weaver and his chief deputy, Wes Terry.

"They did all that they could," he said. "It's important that you understand that, because your verdict is not a reflection on the Amelia authorities. Nothing I say or talk to you about today should in any way be taken as a reflection on them. They did their job.

"Let's also acknowledge something else and that is that the tape that you heard the first day was one of the most chilling things that I hope we're ever going to have to listen to. That tape froze our blood. That was the voice of a dead person calling back to us, and that was a horrible moment. That was horrible for all of us.

"We've got to deal with several things because of that tape. We've got to understand that that tape is admitted only for a very limited purpose. You can't listen to what occurred on that tape and think, well, you know, if Pernell is a bad person and he did this and caused this kind of grief, then that means it's likely that he did what he's accused of. You're not allowed to use the tape for that reason.

"You are not a mob. You are not just a crowd of people who've been assembled. You are here as a legal entity with a specific purpose and so it is important, very important, that you not give in to the rage, the anger, and the sorrow and the passion that that tape arouses in all of us. There isn't a one of us listening to that tape who doesn't want to somehow make it all right or somehow answer her plea. That's the human part of each one of us and there isn't a one of us, I don't think, who doesn't want to when we hear that tape join up with everybody and rise up and seek some vengeance. That's a natural feeling....We'll never know who killed Miss Butkowski....

"You understand that the only issue before you today is — it sounds a little odd, maybe, it's not guilt or innocence. You're not required to decide, yes, he's innocent, and when you come back and say not guilty, you're not saying he's innocent....The question is has the Commonwealth proven guilt beyond a reasonable doubt and if it has, you vote guilty. If it hasn't proven guilt, the only verdict you can return is not guilty. And all that's saying is we heard the evidence, it hasn't been proven, we have at least one reason to doubt your proof."

Benjamin then began to hammer at what he perceived to be weaknesses in the prosecution's case.

"Please understand that the case against Pernell Jefferson is only the testimony of Joey, Chuck, Mike and Wayne. That's it. They accuse him. There is no corroboration to what they say. Phone records — you've heard me talk about phone records. Now, phone records are not a case-breaker but they could provide corroboration. If Joey received a collect call early Saturday morning, that would be on his phone record. Denise Edwards said she called Pernell and she thought it might have been around eight-thirty Saturday night. Well, if it had been much later when she talked with Pernell, then that would have provided a very air-tight alibi. We would have known where Pernell was Saturday night for sure through Denise.

"That could be determined by phone records. But the phone records may have been thrown out. Well, if you're the Chesapeake Police, you need only go, don't you, to the C. & P. and say, 'We're with the police, we're investigating a murder, and we want the phone records of Denise Edwards, and we want the phone records of Joseph St. Augustine. A simple matter. Not provided to you.

"Triton Towers — for the same reason, Chuckie and Mike decided they needed an alibi for the rest of Friday night and, well, better do it for Saturday night, too. And so they rush off to Triton Towers. They say they signed in. Right? Chesapeake Police — Did you go down there? Surely, you did? Surely, you did? What did you find when you got down there? You asked, 'Let me see your books or your register sheet, your ledger.' Do we see those signatures? Do we see those names? Where is it? No corroboration for their alibi.

"The guy who delivered the pizza. Anything? Anything? Nothing for Triton Towers.

"The Perrys," he said, referring to the friends with whom Scott said he spent part of the night of Friday, May 5, after Pernell and Jeannie had left in her Nissan. "— Well, Wayne doesn't even — Wayne had to think a little bit to remember the Perrys' name. He didn't know where they lived. And, so, obviously, we don't have the Perrys here today.

"Now, the Chesapeake Police — Chesapeake indicted Wayne for the abduction, you understand that, and for the burglary. Now if we had — remember, Mrs. Perry said that she thought he got there at nine o'clock. Well, that would be a complete alibi for Wayne Scott, wouldn't it? Now, the Perrys aren't here but we went ahead and asked the Chesapeake fellow, 'Well, what did they say?' I could have objected and kept that out, but I wanted to hear. What did the Perrys have to say? Obviously, you have decided not to bring them here to say, 'Yes, Wayne Scott did show up at eleven-thirty or eleven-fifteen. He did come here.'

"If what Joey tells us is true, then why was Pernell not even questioned that week? Why did no one even go to his house and say, 'We have some questions to ask you'? He was at work each day. He was at home. Why not question him? Why not call him on the phone? Why wasn't he arrested? You know, Joey is saying, 'I told them that Pernell admitted murdering this girl.' Why not arrest him for abduction, for breaking and entering? For any of those? For murder? You don't need a body, not in this state.

"Then there's other little things. It'd be nice to see photographs of the door. Big deal, I know, but isn't that a reflection of what was not done in Chesapeake? No photographs of the door kicked in.

"How about a diagram of the house so when you talk about, 'He went into these rooms,' we could sketch it through the diagram so we could see on the diagram the driveway leading up to the garage, the driveway to the house, the corner where some of the witnesses say they stopped. Why not? Not much of a big deal except it kind of tells you something about what was and was not done by the Chesapeake folks and that means that you're deprived of information that you need to make your choice and your decision.

"There is nothing either associated with the scene where the remains were found or in the car or in any of the evidence or in the house where the abduction took place that points to Pernell. There is no physical evidence that says, 'Pernell did this.'

"There is no blood in that car. Now, according to the Commonwealth, she was shot in that car and she bled at least from the mouth. It doesn't take too much imagination to know that there would have been blood all over that seat, all over that car. You can't get blood out of upholstery. Try it.

"It all comes down to Wayne, Joey, Chuckie and Mike. Now, they're lying....

"Do they have a motive to lie? They have the best motive in the world, because what I told you from day one is that there was this trip to Chesapeake and that it ended with this young girl's death. Was it planned?

Was it intended? Did it just happen? We'll never know. We'll never know where it happened — inside the house, on the ground. We'll never know what else happened but it did happen and they were there.

"Murder is a motive for anyone to lie, so don't be fooled that there was no motive to lie."

Benjamin moved on to Stark's contention that the memories of the people involved in the abduction and the attempts to dispose of Jeannie's body had faded over the two years that had passed.

"Put yourself in the place of the two witnesses," Benjamin challenged the jurors. "Put yourself kicking into a house, abducting a young woman, finding out they say she's been murdered, burning her purse, picking up her body, which has lain on the ground for days, and taking her out to Amelia. Picture yourself pouring gasoline on her, setting her on fire.

"Oh, well, that's two years ago so you'd forget some details."

He paused for effect.

"You wouldn't forget that," he said, his voice rising. "Put yourself in their place, if you possibly can. Uh-uh. What happened that week is far, far different from anything else that happens to the rest of us two years ago."

To further stress the character of one of the principal witnesses, Benjamin dramatically tore open four containers of sweetener, emptying three of them and half of the fourth onto a paper and holding it for the jury to see.

"He said, 'I had me my eightball,'" Benjamin said of Savin's testimony, "an eightball of cocaine. I suspected that there may have been some of you who hadn't heard that term before so I asked him, 'What is an eightball? That would have been three and a half grams, wouldn't it there, sir?'

"He said, 'Yeah, that's right. Paid two-hundred and fifty dollars for it.' Old Mike, he fortifies himself before this field trip with three and a half grams.

"How does he take it? Well, he either smokes it or he puts it up his nose. You can do this at lunch. It's kind of interesting. One of the people upon whose word you have to make a decision took this substance, cocaine, and put it up their nose before they made the trip. Then halfway down — it's a two-hour trip, after all — the lad gets restless. Time to stop, take my oral hit of acid, LSD for this trip."

Moving on to St. Augustine, Benjamin called him "the Hannibal Lector type."

"Scratch beneath his surface," he said, "roll the log over, and you see what's inside of Joey. He's the dangerous one because he is so smooth."

It was on Wednesday when St. Augustine first talked to the police, Benjamin noted. "Tells them the body is off Belmont. He then goes and tells Wayne, 'The police are questioning me,' and Wayne says, 'What did you tell them?' 'I told them the body was off Belmont.'

"Okay, they agree then that if they're ever questioned, that it was Wednesday night that the body got moved to Amelia. See, that's when they're saying it happened, it happened Wednesday night, the same day Joey was questioned. They have to say Wednesday night because that's when Joey was questioned. He's not planning on getting caught in a lie. He's told the police the body is on Belmont. That's on Wednesday. And so they have to agree that if they're ever questioned, it was Wednesday night when they moved it to Amelia.

"How do you know they didn't move it that night? Because they didn't.

"Wayne had testified before and he knew what he was going to say. Wayne said, 'Yeah, when I went out there that Wednesday night to move the body, I helped Pernell, the body was stiff and when we put it in the trunk, why, I heard it crack.' He says it happened Wednesday night.

"Well, that's why we called Dr. Fierro and she told you about rigor mortis and she told you, 'Yes, a body will be stiff twelve hours after death. It might be sooner if there's extreme stress. And at thirty-six hours post mortem, after death, the body will be soft.'

"You know bodies decompose. Rigor mortis, you see, is a temporary state. That body was stiff on Saturday night. Wayne didn't know that. Now, he knows when he moved that body out to Amelia, it was stiff, so he stuck with that but we caught him. It didn't happen Wednesday. It couldn't have because he says it was stiff and he heard it crack. That body was moved Saturday night. It was moved to Amelia Saturday night. We know that because it was stiff and we know that because Joey lies about what he was doing Saturday night.

"We know that because the police went out on Wednesday after they talked with Joey and everyone agrees the body was supposed to be behind this church under construction on Belmont. The police went out there after they talked to Joey on Wednesday and they didn't just go out and say, 'No body,' for heaven's sake. They went out and searched behind that church and they didn't find it. Why? It had already been moved on Saturday night when it was still stiff.

"Now, that still doesn't tell you who killed Miss Butkowski. It still doesn't. It's a question you can never answer. But I will submit to you it was not Pernell. There is no proof that it was Pernell."

When Benjamin had finished his closing statement, Stark once more stood at the low railing surrounding the jury box. He swept into his hands the sweetner Benjamin had left there and offered it back to the defense attorney.

"Mr. Benjamin ought to be a mystery writer," Stark said, as though only to himself. "I have never heard such a vivid imagination in all my life."

The evidence was in, the arguments over, and by 11 Saturday morning, Judge Warren had completed his charge, instructing the jury that they could find Pernell guilty either of capital murder with a sentence of life imprisonment or first degree murder, or they could acquit him. The jurors filed out of the courtroom to begin deliberations.

The Pricketts and their friends went to the witness room to wait. Women from Amelia arrived with sandwiches, pizza and homemade pies, as they had done on the previous two days. No one talked about the trial.

For Denise, time dragged by. Since she had discovered the tape in her telephone answering machine, she felt that the case against Pernell was open and shut and nothing that had happened in two days of testimony had changed her mind. She just wanted it to be over and for Pernell to be sent to prison where he belonged.

Near noon, almost an hour into jury deliberations, Jimmy Weaver began to wonder what was taking so long. Irene Demos sat near Carrie as the wait stretched beyond an hour. Carrie only picked at her food. Ben also ate little. He did not feel well but he kept that to himself as he paced nervously, unable to relax.

Near one, a deputy appeared at the witness room door. Ben stopped pacing and looked at him expectantly.

"They've got a verdict," the deputy said.

Now Ben turned to Carrie. They stood looking at one another, saying nothing until Carrie took his arm to follow the deputy back to the courtroom.

Pernell watched intently as the jury entered. After the last juror was seated, the foreman passed a folded slip of paper to the bailiff, who handed it to the judge.

Judge Warren opened the paper, read the verdict silently and addressed the jury.

"All right, ladies and gentlemen, according to your foreman, you have reached a verdict. Your verdict is that you find the defendant guilty of capital murder as charged in the indictment and fix his punishment at life imprisonment. As I told you, your verdict must be unanimous and I'm going to ask each of you individually that question."

As the judge began querying the jurors, Ben turned to look into his wife's eyes. "It's over," he whispered, and she began to cry. Ben took a deep breath. Reporters later wrote that Pernell appeared stoic when the verdict was announced.

"What type of response can you have?" he asked later. "You've just gone through an ordeal. It has lasted for months and you get to the point that you want it to be over with. It's not that I didn't care. It's just that I was in such a state of shock, my mind just went blank."

Pernell would claim that he did not even hear the rest of Judge Warren's remarks or the polling of the jury.

The judge set sentencing for June 4 at 2 p.m. That would be only a formality for the punishment already had been determined.

After court was adjourned, Pernell whispered to his lawyer, turned and waved to Willie and Blondie, and was led away in handcuffs.

Ben and Carrie rose to leave, but now Ben was feeling so weak that he had to rely on Carrie for support. As they started out of the courthouse, his legs began to fold and he nearly collapsed. His friend Jim Irvin and his son Sam caught him and helped him back into the courthouse. They took him to the witness room while others called an ambulance. Paramedics arrived quickly and began to examine him as his worried family looked on.

"I felt like I was about to die," Ben later recalled. "I couldn't breathe. I couldn't talk. That was tough."

Ben's problem was diagnosed as an anxiety attack brought on by the pressures of the trial and his long history of bronchial and asthma problems. He was treated without having to be taken to a hospital.

"The thing is," Ben said, "you can keep things bottled up inside you for so long, but then it comes out, and when it did it came out in me as an anxiety attack."

When he felt strong enough to leave, he and Carrie went out to face the reporters. This time Carrie smiled at them.

"Yes, we're satisfied," she said. "No matter what they did to him, they could never bring Jeannie back to us."

Ben told reporters that the family was happy with the decision but would have preferred a stronger sentence.

"He took a life that was dear to us. He should have paid with his life. We knew what the sentence was going to be, but we hoped it would be without parole. We would have liked to see him be executed, but we have to go along with what the jury decided. The trial was conducted in a very proper manner, as was the investigation."

A reporter told Ben that Benjamin probably would appeal on the basis of the tape recording.

"Anything he wants to do," Ben said. If Pernell came again before a judge, he said, "We'll be there. I think he should be put in a dungeon with the door locked and they should throw away the key."

As townspeople accompanied the Pricketts and Denise to their cars, Pernell's brother, Willie, and his half-sister, Blondie, exited the courthouse. They had lingered to talk to Pernell before he was taken back to jail. Willie, who was carrying a Bible, was overcome with emotion, and at the top of the courthouse steps, he stopped and began shouting, "My brother got railroaded!"

Sheriff Weaver left the Pricketts and hurried to Willie, urging him to move on. Willie and Blondie walked slowly to their car, talking to reporter Overton McGehee of Richmond's *Times-Dispatch.*

"I don't think he got a fair trial in this little town," Willie said. "They didn't do anything to the other four guys." Later, Willie said that he thought race played a role in his brother's conviction. "There were three blacks on the jury. They were not going to vote opposite to what the white people voted. That's just the way it was."

Within thirty minutes, Pernell was back in his cell at Farmville. He lay down across his cot and fell asleep. He slept for three hours. The next day, he placed a collect telephone call to Susan Demos in Florida.

Susan had gotten daily reports of the trial from her mother. From the time in 1990 that she had learned that Pernell was being sought in Florida on a murder warrant, Susan had had more than a casual interest in the case.

"When I heard about Jeannie, I said to myself, 'Well, now, they'll see I was right,'" Susan remembered. "I had been telling people that Pernell was capable of terrible things. Jeannie had walked into something she couldn't even see coming. It was like walking into a lion's den, and that appalls me."

Still, she accepted Pernell's call.

"I lost," he told her.

"I know you did it," Susan told him calmly, "because Jeannie probably was trying to leave you and you couldn't let her do that. But it doesn't matter, Pernell, whether you did it or not because even if you didn't kill Jeannie, you've done enough in the past that you need to be in jail."

Later, recalling her reaction to Pernell's conviction, Susan remarked that she thought he would do fine in prison.

"He doesn't have to work," she said. "He's with the boys and he can kick back and talk about football and when he was with the Browns. The way Pernell looks at it is that he's there and it wasn't his fault. He's going to do great in prison. So let him stay there forever."

28

Where the Wild Flowers Grow

After Jeannie's body had been discovered, her brother Sam had felt drawn to the spot where she had been found. Sheriff Weaver had taken him there at the end of January 1990, less than four weeks after the discovery, but the experience had been so disturbing that he had stayed only a few minutes.

At the time, Jeannie's remains were still at the state medical examiner's office and would not be released until late in February. Just a few days before the remains were to be released, Sam's phone had rung in Richmond. His mother was calling.

"I need for you to do something for me," she said. "I want you to go to the place where Jeannie was and I want you to fill a shoe box full of dirt from there because I want to sprinkle that over her grave when she gets home."

Sam had not wanted to return to that place, but his bond with his mother had been special for all of his life, and he couldn't say no.

"It was probably the toughest thing I ever had to do," he said later. "I was surprised I was able to do it and the only reason I could do it is because mother wanted me to."

He went on the day before Jeannie's body was released to the funeral home. He went alone, carrying a shoe box and a small garden trowel. He found the crooked tree that marked the place where the wet-weather stream made its way to Nibbs Creek. There he knelt in the creek bed, pushed the trowel into the soft earth and deposited the first scoop of dirt into the box. With the next scoop, something caught his eye. He sifted through the dirt and felt a piece of cloth. He pulled it out and realized that he held the label from the blouse Jeannie had been wearing the night she died.

And he began to sob. "This is exactly where she lay," he told himself. "And I'm taking a little of her home. This is what Mama wanted. She wanted me to bring Jeannie home."

He finished filling the box and began to make his way back through the brush to his waiting car. Perhaps ten yards from the spot where he had been digging, Sam stopped and looked back at the lonely place. He knew that he would never see it again.

Yet only a few months later, when he was in Amelia on business, Sam had felt himself drawn irresistibly toward Nibbs Creek. He parked his car and made his way again to the dry creek. Only then did he realize why he had been drawn back.

"I just wanted to make my peace," he later recalled. "Jeannie was dead. That was a fact of life. And I was going to have to deal with it, and I thought the best place for me to deal with it was where she had been found."

He found himself remembering when she had been young and happy, and he began talking to her, speaking softly, telling her how much he missed her, how much he and their parents were hurting, how all of them were struggling to find some resolution to the madness that had taken her life and overwhelmed theirs.

Suddenly, he had a strong feeling that he was being watched. He let his eyes search quickly along the edge of the nearby woods. At the tree line no more than 40 yards away was a huge deer. Both stood looking at each other, neither moving.

"As we stood there, the deer and me, a calm came over me," Sam remembered. "I just had this feeling that Jeannie was helping me get things together, that everything was going to be all right and that I didn't have to come back any more."

But that would not be the case.

Pernell's sentencing was delayed twice, but it finally was held on August 6, 1991, the day after Jeannie would have turned 32. Sam and his parents were there, occupying the same row of benches on which they had sat through the trial.

Pernell's attorney, Steven Benjamin, rose to be heard before sentence was pronounced.

"Your Honor, I think that there is little to be decided today. The law imposes upon you but one sentence. I must say that the time that's passed since our trial in this courtroom has tempered not at all my shock that the jury accepted the word of these scoundrels, the witnesses who testified against Mr. Jefferson. The testimony and the evidence that we heard in this case, sir, raised many more questions than it answered. I have urged you in motions made at the time to set aside the verdict of the jury as being contrary to the law and the evidence. Obviously, I do not abandon that motion and wish you would take that action.

"Just as obviously, I wish that you would not impose the sentence returned by the jury. But the only reasons I can proffer to you for such action is that justice demands no other action. It is unfortunate that these scoundrels who, by their own admission, were so intimately involved with the disappearance and the murder of this young lady were able to avail themselves of the opportunity to testify against Mr. Jefferson to save their own hides and that the word of these people was accepted. I submit to you that the result in this case is not justice but we do understand the position of the court, given the jury's verdict, and I say to you now only that I am saddened. That's all."

Thomas Stark, the prosecuting attorney, was offended by Benjamin's remarks.

"Well, those comments can't go unaddressed, if Your Honor please, while I don't believe it has the slightest effect on the outcome. We're dealing here with a cold-blooded killer. We do not represent to the court nor did we ever represent to the court that the witnesses against him were Sunday School teachers; they were likewise criminals. But the evidence is clear and the jury found guilty."

Judge Warren asked Pernell if he had anything to say in his behalf. He declined, and the judge asked him to stand.

"The court enters the finding of guilty of murder in the commission of a robbery, capital murder, and imposes the sentence fixed by the jury, that of life imprisonment," Judge Warren said.

Under Virginia law, Pernell was facing a minimum of 25 years with time off for good behavior. He stood stoically. Since his arrest in Florida, Pernell already had spent more than 17 months behind bars in two states. Benjamin now asked to be named as a state-appointed attorney for Pernell's appeals, and the judge granted his request. For as long as he would represent Pernell, he would draw his fee from taxpayers. Pernell was led away as he had come, in handcuffs.

Now it truly was done.

The Pricketts lingered for a time talking with Sheriff Weaver and Chief Deputy Terry, with whom they had become close friends. Carrie hugged the two men; Ben and Sam exchanged warm handshakes with them. As they were leaving for home, Carrie suddenly turned to Ben.

"Let's go out there," she said.

"Out where?" Ben asked.

"I need to be where she was."

"But Mama..." Sam protested.

Carrie had not been able to bring herself to visit the spot before, although she had thought about it when she and Ben were in Amelia for the trial. She just hadn't been able to do it then.

"It'll be all right," she now assured her son.

Sam led the way in his car. Ben, Carrie and Denise followed. Ben could not bring himself to go to the site and remained alone in the car. Sam and Denise helped Carrie through the undergrowth until she stood on the bank of the dry creek bed where her daughter's body had lain.

"What an ugly place," Carrie said after a few minutes. "What a forsaken looking place. This place needs some flowers or something."

On the day after Christmas, 1991, Carrie returned to the lonely place where Jeannie had been found and there she spread 20 pounds of wild flower seeds, scattering them across the barren ground of the creek bed and into the nearby tree line.

She would return every Christmas thereafter to do the same thing.

"The place is something to see in the spring when everything comes alive again," Sheriff Weaver says. "There are flowers everywhere."

29

The Eyewitness Account

Craigsville is a dot on the map along Virginia Highway 42 halfway between Goshen and Buffalo Gap. It is two hours of hard driving northeast of Roanoke. The nearest metropolitan areas of any significant size are Lexington to the south and Staunton to the northeast, both nearly an hour away.

"When I first moved here over thirty years ago, we had five banks, five or six grocery stores, a dozen filling stations and a beer joint on every corner," says the woman who runs the town's only restaurant, which specializes in country cooking.

Craigsville survived then on the timber industry, which has since moved on. It also was the home of one of the region's most productive concrete plants, which now lies in ruin, its steel skeleton rusting away.

Now Craigsville is a quiet town with limited commerce of any kind. The homes, most of which predate World War II, are built of wood. Freight trains rumble through town three and four times a day, seldom slowing, never stopping. Had the Commonwealth of Virginia not chosen Craigsville as the site for a new prison more than a decade ago, Craigsville might have become a ghost town.

Augusta Correctional Center now provides sustenance for the town, as well as for much of the surrounding region. It is a dependable industry. There are no layoffs and it operates three shifts a day and never closes for weekends and holidays. Most of the working residents of Craigsville are employed in various capacities at the prison.

Flanked on the east by mountains where the Blue Ridge Parkway makes its way out of sight along the distant ridges, bounded on the west by rocky cliffs that once provided some of the best industrial limestone in the country, the prison with its high fences stacked with row upon row of razor wire seems incongruous to its beautiful setting. Here, a thousand of Virginia's toughest prisoners are locked away.

It was to Augusta that Pernell Jefferson was brought on May 8, 1992, after being held at Powhatan Receiving Center for several months. Although sentenced to a life term, he calculates that with good time, he will become eligible for parole after only 20 years, in the year 2,011. For every 30 days that he stays out of trouble, 10 days are deducted from his sentence.

By 1995, his case has been appealed two times and twice denied. Both appeals claimed the tape recording of Jeannie's earlier abduction should not have been permitted into evidence. Nevertheless, Pernell had not given up hope that his sentence yet would be overturned or reduced.

After arriving at Augusta, Pernell became a model prisoner, spending time in the library studying law, using computers to write dozens of letters to friends, attorneys and national experts on steroid abuse, which, he claims, lies at the root of his problem. He also created a large computer file on steroid abuse including extensive case studies involving athletes, particularly weightlifters. He volunteered to run the prison's athletic programs, became the commissioner of the flag football league and a referee at basketball games.

"They won't let me play football," he said during an interview, "and I'm glad. It's too rough for me. It's supposed to be flag football, but they take it to extremes sometimes."

He maintains his athletic build by spending hours each week in the prison weight room, and proudly claims to be the fifth strongest of all the inmates in any weight classification, a fete accomplished, he noted, without anabolic steroids which, he insists, transformed him from a "lovable, unselfish, well-mannered" person to a "monster with an aggressive nature."

"I'm not looking for excuses," he said. "I'm just trying to figure out what happened and do something positive. You know, you try to have a little pride. You try to say, 'Hey, this is me. This isn't TV stuff. This is real.'"

Yet, he adamantly denied killing Jeannie, pounding the table before him with his fist as he distinctly pronounced each word. "I was not the person to pull the trigger that killed Miss Butkowski. Let's talk logic. If you think I'm going to kill you and I give you the gun, no way are you going to give it back to me. In my mind, I never thought about killing or shooting her."

Until this interview, he said no one had ever asked him what had happened that night in May, 1989, including his defense attorney.

"This is the first time I've told this story to anyone," he said going on to give his version of what happened that night after Jeannie was taken from her home. He was driving Jeannie's car, he said. She was in the passenger seat. They were on I-64 headed for Richmond, where he had been sharing an apartment with his older sister, Blondie, for several months.

"Let's put it this way," he said. "I'm driving a five-speed car. I've already given the gun to her so she won't be afraid of me. I'm driving. She has the gun like this...." He held an imaginary revolver with his left hand beside his thigh.

232

"Next thing I know, I'm aware that she's brought the gun up...." He raised an imaginary weapon beside his head, the barrel pointing straight up. "I don't know if I reached out and grabbed the gun or what. But the next thing I know, there's a light of fire — a kind of flash — in the sun roof.

"When I saw that, I just stopped, almost in the middle of the road. I didn't see no blood, but it was night. I didn't see no blood. I shook her. Then I saw blood on her cheek. Just a little bit of blood.

"I was in shock. I just drove around for two or three hours. I kept thinking about what I should do. After I rode around, I knew I was in trouble."

As he drove, he said, Jeannie sat slumped beside him in the passenger seat.

Later, in a letter, Pernell offered a different version of events that night.

I told her I had to go home because I had to work the next morning at 7:00 a.m. So she agreed to let me drive myself to Richmond. We stopped off at Williamsburg to get a bite to eat. Then we continued to Richmond. On the way we talked about different things (concerning our relationships and their ups and downs). I talked about Susan and she talked about Tony. Her words were, and I quote —

My life is ruined because Tony found out you are black and I had been sleeping with you. He is never going to take me back ....

At that point she started crying. I was two blocks away from where I was staying in Belle Meade Apts. on Jefferson Davis Highway.

Jeannie asked was the gun real and I said, "I think so" because I was not familiar with guns. I gave her the gun and she opened the chamber and took out one bullet then put it back in. At that point I pulled up in the drive way in front of my sister's apt. Regina did not want me to leave her at that point. So we drove up and down Jefferson Davis Highway. We passed a police cruiser and he flashed his headlights because the headlights of Regina's car were not on. We were on the outskirts of the city limits and I pulled over on the side of the road to use the bathroom. I left the ignition on. She sat in the passenger seat with the gun in her hand. After I got back into the car to take off, Regina had the gun in the area of her head.

Simultaneously or a split second before, I grabbed the gun and it went off. At this point I'm in another world. I rode around for about 3 or 4 hours and went back past the same police cruiser. I did not know what to do.

During the interview, Pernell confirmed that he placed a call to Joe St. Augustine early on Saturday morning after the shooting.

"I said to him, 'Joe, something's happened.'

"He said. 'What?'

"I said, 'My ex-girlfriend is dead.' I never said I killed her. He came to get me and I told him that I've got to park her car and we went to an apartment complex he suggested. The situation about burying the victim came from that man. He lied to save his own hide. He carried me to a place they were building an apartment complex to get some concrete mix. He told me to throw that on her and put a tarp on her. He even showed me where the tarp was.

"Why wouldn't he say, 'I don't want anything to do with this'?

"The same guy told me to move the body. He suggested moving the body so he wouldn't get caught because he knew where the body was.

"And Pernell didn't buy no gas. Wayne Scott is the man who burned the victim's body and he got a plea out of all this and he's already out of the system.

"Later Joe came to me. He said, 'Pernell, they keep questioning me about this. They keep questioning me about that.'

"I said, 'Joe, I'm going to take my chances and go tell what happened.'

"He said, 'No, man, you've got to leave. They're not going to believe you. You broke up and that breaking and entering happened.' At that point, fear set in. He gave me his whole pay check — $180 — and said, 'Take this and go and I'll tell them you didn't do it.'"

Pernell said that on his birthday, June 4, almost a month after the shooting, he called from Florida to St. Augustine at 12:15 a.m. at a computer center where St. Augustine worked nights.

"I asked him, 'Did you tell the truth?' He told me to hold on while he went to another phone. Then he said, 'Naw, man. I told them you did the killing.'

"'Why?' I asked him.

"'To get them off by back,' he said. 'Now when they catch up with you, tell them I lied on you.'

"'Why don't you go to Spain?' he asked me. 'They'd never find you there.'

"'Right,' I said, and hung up the phone.

"I want people to see what I've been through. I'm not blaming nobody. There are some people out there who believe in me. They know something had to happen. And I hate every day that I let people down that stood by me.

"I think about her," he said of Jeannie. "But it's done. I know and she knows I didn't pull that trigger."

Epilogue

In the spring of 1994, Pernell taught a course for other inmates on how to control anger and aggression, and in June a Department of Corrections counselor placed a memo in Pernell's file in which he called Pernell "a role model for others."

He had indeed become a model prisoner, just as Susan predicted. He keeps out of trouble and remains an avid weightlifter. He religiously watches ESPN's "SportsCenter" on his personal, five-inch, black-and-white TV and has become captivated by the soap opera, "All My Children."

He corresponds regularly not only with national experts on the uses and abuses of anabolic steroids, but with several female pen pals whose pictures he keeps in a frame on the top of a small desk in the tiny cell he shares with another inmate. He still keeps in touch with his old college roommate Lamar, talking with him regularly by phone. They still talk a lot about football, especially Guilford College's 1984 victory over Elon. Lamar says they never speak of Jeannie's death.

Pernell's former coach, Tommy Saunders, still gets calls from Pernell as well and is impressed with how cheerful he usually sounds. "He still thinks that somehow and someway somebody's going to come down the pike and say this was all a mistake, and Pernell's going to be out," Saunders says.

After losing two appeals, Pernell is ready to make another based on his abuse of steroids, but Steven Benjamin is no longer his lawyer and no other attorney has yet agreed to take his case.

After his murder trial, Pernell still faced charges in Chesapeake of abducting Jeannie and breaking into Denise's house. He had been scheduled to go to trial on the abduction charges in July 1992, but his court-appointed lawyer in that case, Randolph D. Stowe, claimed the trial subjected Pernell to double jeopardy and the trial was postponed.

In June 1995, the Court of Appeals agreed with Stowe.

"The court ruled, interestingly, that the abduction began here," Chesapeake Commonwealth's Attorney Ann E. Poindexter said, "and continued up to the point of murder and therefore dismissed the abduction charges against him."

Left standing, however, were the burglary charges. Poindexter promised they would be pursued. "The problem we face in getting him to trial on burglary," she said, "is that the only people who can testify are those who were involved." Those involved were Scott, Zimmer and Savin, who have served their sentences. "And we had a hard enough time getting them to court the first time," she said. "The bottom line is that if we can't find the people involved, there's not much we can do." The problem solved itself early in December, 1995, when Pernell agreed to plead guilty to single charge of breaking and entering to abduct. He received a second life sentence to run concurrently with the first. A week later, he appealed the sentence.

For members of Pernell's family, the events of the last decade have taken their toll. His mother, now in failing health, keeps mostly to her small home in Benson where she raised her children. Willie says that Pernell's conviction "destroyed her."

"Mother has come to the conclusion he's done it," Willie said. "If he didn't do it, why's he locked up? That's the way she sees it."

Willie keeps busy working two jobs in Benson, including his own business as a carpet cleaner. But only once has he returned to South Johnston High School where both he and Pernell once were athletes of note.

"Lots of people around here know what happened to Pernell, but a few haven't heard," he said. "I'm afraid if I go over to the school somebody'll say, 'Aren't you Pernell's brother? Whatever happened to Pernell?' I've had people ask me that on the street. I just say he's working up north, and let it go at that."

No family members other than Willie have visited Pernell in prison. Willie went only once. He took Pernell's son, P.J., with him. Now a teenager, P.J. does well in school and is showing promise as an aspiring athlete. "But he still cries a lot," Willie reports.

In a letter dated March 31, 1995, addressed "to family, friends and my victims," Pernell offered apologies.

"I really think these are in order and certainly overdue," he wrote. "I do understand that any apology cannot and will not suffice for some individuals. But I do need to express my remorse and sorrow for my acts. Making it public will no doubt be a step in my continuous rehabilitation.

"I have asked forgiveness from God and once I have made my sincere apologies known to the people I have hurt then that part of my life can start to heal."

He then listed individual apologies:

Mama Jo: Thank you for rearing me with discipline, care and love. Please do not ever feel my problems stemmed from something you shorted me on because you gave me the best happiness and affection growing up. Love you!

Little P.J.: Champ, dad is very sorry not to be there in the most important years of your life. I need you to understand I love you more than any single thing in my life.

Prickett Family: Saying I am sorry does not amount to the pain and suffering you all have endured. I do have remorse for being a part of the total tragedy in which you lost a family member.

Susan: For the past eight years I have expressed my apologies to you through third parties. Maybe one day you will understand the whole scenario.

Family (Especially Linda H., Brick, Shirley, Linda Faye and Willie Jr.): I am sorry for my problems because they have taken away from our family unity. Thank you for still being supportive, both financially and spiritually.

Friends (Especially the Saunders, Herb Appenzeller, Lucylle and Nikki Nichols, Lamar and Glen): Through all this you have stood supportive in my corner. You have shown the true value of genuine friendship.

Sarah Wheeler: Please forgive me for leaving all the responsibilities of rearing our son on you. Thank you and your husband for allowing me to call little P.J. as often as I do.

Others: I am sorry to have caused you pain and heartbreak.

Susan Demos, who still works in professional soccer, remains haunted by her years with Pernell.

"There are still days I'd just love to kill Pernell Jefferson," she says. She remains bitter that law enforcement authorities in Miami didn't arrest him. "If someone had stopped him then," she says, "Jeannie wouldn't be dead."

Susan is still startled awake occasionally by a feeling that Pernell is somewhere in her apartment.

"When that happens," she says, "I have to get up, turn on every light in the apartment, look behind the drapes and in every closet before I can go back to sleep."

And in recent years, she has been troubled by a recurring dream.

"I see Pernell in the distance and I start running from him," she says, "and I'm running down this street lined with light poles. And I think I'm getting away from him, but every time I look up, he's sitting on the top of a light pole ahead of me.

"And finally I'm running into the dining hall at Quaker Lakes, a camp I used to attend as a little girl, and Pernell's behind me. There's nobody in the dining room, but there's this huge pot of stew simmering on the big camp stove. I look around and Pernell has turned into this huge lizard, like an iguana, and he's leaping at me and I'm trying to get away. Finally, he jumps onto this butcher block table and I get a big meat knife and — chop, chop, chop like Julia Child — I chop him up into little pieces. I look around and there's still nobody there. I put the little pieces of Pernell into the stew. 'No more Pernell,' I say to myself. It feels good."

In May 1994, almost exactly five years after Jeannie died, Susan's assistant at work took a message from someone calling for Susan. It read:

My name's Leon. Tell her I'm Pernell's cousin. Pernell will be at my house in 20 minutes and he wanted me to call Susan to tell her we're coming down for a visit.

Shaken, Susan quickly reported the incident to authorities, who assured her that Pernell was still locked up at Craigsville.

"He's still stalking me from prison," she says.

Susan's father has since died and her mother Irene regularly corresponds with the parole board in Virginia, hoping to ensure that Pernell remains in prison for as long as possible. She has become a close friend with Jeannie's mother, and they talk on the phone and correspond frequently.

Irene once sought unsuccessfully to have Pernell's name removed from the most prestigious athletic award presented to Guilford College athletes, the Nereus C. English Award. She did succeed, however, in persuading the English family to insist upon stricter guidelines in choosing annual winners.

Early in 1994, the Commonwealth of Virginia acquired a large parcel of land, including that where Jeannie's remains were found, and plans to turn it into a state-operated military cemetery.

"I guess it was always supposed to be a graveyard," Sheriff Jimmy Weaver said when he heard the news.

Mike Reardon, Jeannie's policeman friend who once was a Guilford College football teammate of Pernell's, has married. He has left the K-9 unit but remains an officer with the Norfolk Police Department, working the vice and narcotics beat. He still is bothered by Jeannie's death.

"I am sorry to say I was the one who introduced Jeannie to Pernell," he says, "and that's been hard to live with. I had to try for a long time to get that out of my head."

Tony Butkowski, Jeannie's former husband, is now married again and lives in New Jersey.

Denise has remarried and long ago moved away from the house in Chesapeake she shared with Jeannie. She still lives in the Tidewater area, but seldom sees Carrie and Ben any more.

"I'm not sure how they feel about me," she says, acknowledging that she still struggles with her own feelings of guilt about Jeannie's death. "The thing is, if I hadn't gone out that night, she might be alive today. The only way I can get by is by saying if Dawn and I had been there, maybe they would have gotten us too. Maybe we'd be dead."

Dawn, who was three and a half years old when Jeannie was murdered, remembers nothing of Pernell although she recalls that she once had an "Aunt Jeannie" and that her mother once spent a lot of time trying to find her.

Still, Dawn is affected by Denise's lingering fear. Her friends tease her because she is not permitted to go with them to a park two blocks from her home without her mother or adoptive father.

"She doesn't understand," Denise said. "I try to explain to Dawn that there is a very mean man who once did some very bad things that I will have to live with for the rest of my life. She doesn't understand that I can't bear to have her out of my sight. I hope some day she will understand."

Thomas Stark III, who successfully prosecuted the murder case against Pernell, lost in his bid to be re-elected Commonwealth's attorney for Amelia County. He now is in private practice in Amelia.

Sheriff Jimmy Weaver ran for another term and won by one of the largest popular vote margins in county history. Wes Terry remains his chief deputy. Weaver thinks that putting Pernell in prison will be one of the hallmarks of his career, and he isn't interested in hearing any excuses from Pernell.

"I see him as a person who had it made," he says. "He had God-given talent. He was more than just an athlete. He was handsome. He had a great personality. He was educated. He could have done wonders in corporate America. This guy was a very fortunate person, and he screwed it up."

In the months following Pernell's trial, Sam's marriage began to fall apart. Carrie sent some of Jeannie's jewelry to Sam and asked him to sell it. The proceeds were to go to a fund for victims of crimes in Virginia. Sam decided to keep one piece, however, the bear charm bracelet that had led to identifying Jeannie's remains. Sam married again in 1995 and has since become the father of a baby daughter. Sam still mourns for his sister, but he mourns as much for his parents.

"Not only did I lose a sister whom I loved very much," he said, "I also lost a mother and father. They will never again be the mother and father I used to know. That's what Pernell Jefferson took from me."

Carrie retired in 1991, Ben at the end of 1995. They never plan to leave Virginia Beach.

"This is where Jeannie is," Carrie says. "I will never leave my Jeannie."

She still drives to Rosewood Memorial Park every Tuesday to clip the grass and polish the bronze plaque that marks Jeannie's grave.

Never very talkative even in good times, Ben has become even more quiet and withdrawn. But he makes no secret of his hatred for Pernell.

"For as long as I live, the only safe place for Pernell Jefferson is in prison," he says. "If he ever gets out, I'll be an old man. I won't have a thing to lose. If I had my way, he'd already be dead."

Just before Jeannie's body was discovered, Carrie had become a member of a group called Families and Friends Against Crime Today, and after Pernell's trial, she joined Justice for Victims of Crimes, a group pushing, among other things, for anti-stalking laws in Virginia. Although Carrie always had trouble speaking in public, she appeared before a legislative committee in Richmond and held the legislators spellbound while she spoke for ten minutes from her heart.

"You can't do anything for me," she told them. "There's no way you can keep me from hurting. I have already lived your worst nightmare."

In March of 1992, Governor Thornton Wilder signed into law Virginia's first anti-stalking legislation.

Later, Carrie joined a third group, Virginians United Against Crime, and on June 15, 1994, she spoke at a town meeting called by Virginia's new governor, George Allen, to consider new laws that would deny parole to violent criminals. The legislature later eliminated the possibility of parole for those convicted of capital murder, but the law does not apply to Pernell who was convicted before its passage.

Carrie remains active in all three organizations, is an officer in two of them, and is now pushing for even stronger anti-stalking laws. Her car and Ben's pickup truck both bear bumper stickers that read: *Someone I Love Was Murdered.*

"They say when you lose a loved one by natural causes, it takes about a year of mourning, Carrie says. "When you lose a child, it takes longer. If you lose a child by violence, they say it takes about five years. But I'll never get over this.

"Not long ago, someone asked me how I feel about Pernell's mother. Pernell's mother can go to a prison and she can reach through the bars and touch her son. I can put flowers on a grave."